MW00477482

This Burd Street Press publication
was printed by
Beidel Printing House, Inc.
63 West Burd Street
Shippensburg, PA 17257-0152 USA

In respect for the scholarship contained herein, the acid-free paper used in this book meets the guidelines for permanence and durability of the Committee on Production Guidelines for Book Longevity of the Council on Library Resources.

For a complete list of available publications
please write
Burd Street Press
Division of White Mane Publishing Company, Inc.
P.O. Box 152
Shippensburg, PA 17257-0152 USA

Library of Congress Cataloging-in-Publication Data

Cornwell, Robert Thompson, 1835-1927.
      Libby Prison and beyond : a Union staff officer in the East,
   1862-1865 / [edited, with background information] by Thomas M. Boaz.
          p.   cm.
      Includes bibliographical references and index.
      ISBN 1-57249-123-X (alk. paper)
      1. Cornwell, Robert Thompson, 1835-1927--Correspondence.
   2. Cornwell, Robert Thompson, 1835-1927--Diaries. 3. Libby Prison.
   4. Prisoners of war--United States--Correspondence. 5. Prisoners of
   war--United States--Diaries. 6. United States--History--Civil War,
   1861-1865--Prisoners and prisons. 7. Soldiers--United States-
   -Biography. 8. Shenandoah Valley Campaign, 1864 (August-November)-
   -Personal narratives. 9. United States--History--Civil War,
   1861-1865--Personal narratives. 10. Chester County (Pa.)-
   -Biography. I. Boaz, Thomas, 1943-   .   II. Title.
   E612.L6C67   1999
   973.7'71'092--dc21   99-11789
                                                                    CIP

PRINTED IN THE UNITED STATES OF AMERICA

Contents

Illustrations

Acknowledgments

The scholarship in this book is due to a number of individuals who took an interest in the project and gave freely of their knowledge and resources. Foremost among these were Daniel Cornwell of Chester County, Pennsylvania, a great-grandson of Robert T. Cornwell, and his kinsman Richard Cornwell of Escondido, California. Both gentlemen were active participants in the preparation of this book, responding quickly to my frequent and sometimes lengthy requests for information about their ancestor.

Roger De Mik, lawyer and Civil War scholar, provided some useful research contacts. Professor James I. Robertson of Virginia Polytechnic University took time from the launch of his monumental biography of Stonewall Jackson to answer my inquiry and to introduce me to Sandra V. Parker. Sandy is one of the leading experts on Libby Prison and was unstinting with her advice to me on a number of occasions. Those wishing to know more about the military prison system in the Confederate capitol would do well to read her book, *Richmond's Civil War Prisons*.

John Craft and his expert staff at the Civil War Library and Museum in Philadelphia provided helpful advice and guided me through their collection of Libby Prison artifacts. As well, the research librarians at the Chester County Historical Society were of great help during the many hours I worked in their facility.

Historian Philip Katcher was, as usual, instrumental in helping me in a number of important ways with the research for this book. Stephanie Westerberg used her research skills to identify and locate some of the illustrations used in the text. Reverend Douglas Scott, the rector of my church, suggested the title for the book.

Russ A. Pritchard and George W. Juno of the American Ordnance Preservation Association, Ltd. of Bryn Mawr, Pennsylvania were kind enough to provide expert answers to my questions about the pistols owned by Robert T. Cornwell.

Mark Miller's monograph about the 67th Pennsylvania Infantry was helpful in understanding the early history of this relatively unstudied regiment.

The preparation of a work of historical fact is extremely time-consuming. I therefore deeply appreciate the patience of Barbara and Tory Boaz, my wife and daughter, during the time it took to research and write this book, and I dedicate it to both of them. I also wish to particularly acknowledge the editorial skills of my wife. She is knowledgeable about the Civil War in her own right, and her comments and ideas on my earlier drafts helped make the final product much better.

Introduction

The idea for this book occurred when Dan Cornwell placed a thick binder on my desk. Dan is a business associate of mine, and knowing of my interest in the Civil War said he thought I might enjoy reading some letters written during the war by his great-grandfather, an officer in a Pennsylvania regiment. I was delighted to receive them and looked forward to a pleasant evening of reading.

As I discovered, the binder contained typescript copies of letters as well as diary entries, and that Dan's great-grandfather, Robert T. Cornwell, had served as a captain in the 67th Pennsylvania Volunteer Infantry. The typescript was prepared a number of years ago by another member of the family named Jack Cornwell, now deceased. He painstakingly typed copies of every letter and diary entry on 8.5-by-11-inch sheets of paper. These were chronologically assembled, together with photocopies of the original letters and most of the diary entries. It was a labor of love, intended to serve as a record for future Cornwell generations of the service of their ancestor during the Civil War.

In all, there were some 262 separate letters and diary entries, spanning the period from August 29, 1862, to October 20, 1864. All the letters, and some of them were quite long, were written to Captain Cornwell's wife, Lydia (whom he called "Lillie"). The 1862, 1863, and about half the 1864 letters were written on plain paper, but many of the those after June 1864 were on printed letterhead reading "Headquarters Third Division, Sixth Corps, Office Assistant Adjutant General." Cornwell served as a staff officer in that division after his release from Libby Prison in May 1864, and used the official letterhead for personal use.

His pocket diaries, typical of those carried by many Civil War soldiers, are approximately 3 x 6 inches in size. A separate page was provided for each day, printed at the top with the name of the day of the week and the month, date and year. Cornwell's written entries usually fill most of a page for a given date, but some contain just a few words and others run two or more pages.

Letters written by Civil War officers often differ from those of enlisted men because of the perspectives involved. Although there are certainly exceptions, enlisted men tended to write heartfelt letters about how they or their immediate circle of friends were personally affected by events. Officers naturally included the same information in their letters, but often also discussed the significance and overall impact of the events in which they participated. On the other hand, officers' letters sometimes have a certain lack of emotion, and I was curious to learn what Captain Cornwell had to say.

Once I began reading the letter book it quickly became evident that his writings were far from ordinary. He had a college education and was a preparatory school teacher and college instructor before the war. There is a certain erudition to his writing, and he possessed a writer's instinct for describing the interesting and unusual aspects of a Union officer's life. As a result, his letters and diary entries are filled with the kind of rich detail that is often lacking in other contemporary accounts.

Moreover, Cornwell's writings chronicled a diverse military career. He began as an officer in a company of infantry he raised, but saw no action for months. He was captured at Winchester in June 1863 and then imprisoned for nine months in Libby Prison. Upon his release he joined the staff of Gen. James B. Ricketts as provost marshal of the Third Division of the Union army's veteran VI Corps. In that role he was an eyewitness participant in some of the important battles of the war.

At the beginning, Cornwell's writings show in great detail what it was like for a new officer to assemble, equip, and train an equally new company of infantry. He did not see any fighting for a number of months, and therefore filled his letters with details about what he wore, where he obtained his personal equipment and what it cost. He describes what he ate and how his wall tent was furnished, what the duties were of an Officer of the Day, and he complained about the time-consuming paperwork required of a company officer.

Although the new captain had no previous training in the military arts, it is evident that he had a natural ability to command. As a company-grade officer he was diligent in managing his men, whom he treated with an evenhandedness that earned their respect.

Later, while in Libby Prison, Cornwell paints an extraordinarily vivid picture of nine months of life in that converted warehouse. Although others have written of their experiences in Libby, many of those accounts were published months or years later. Some were embellished in an attempt to secure a pension or a book contract with a publisher. Cornwell's diary and letters, however, have the advantage of being a contemporaneous eyewitness account of conditions at Libby at the peak of its overcrowding. He shows the unflagging spirit of most of the captives; they make a Stars and Stripes flag out of scraps of cloth for a Fourth of July celebration, and there is great jubilation when 109 officers escape through a tunnel. But he also describes the struggles the prisoners endured on a daily basis, as well as the simple pleasures they created to while away their time.

The changing political currents regarding prisoner of war treatment directly affected Cornwell. He gained weight when he entered Libby, but was so short of food nine months later that others had to share their supplies with him. When he returned to duty as provost marshal, he did so just as Confederates under Jubal Early attacked and almost captured Washington. He participated in the battle of Monocacy and then in Sheridan's hard-fighting campaign to drive Early out of the Shenandoah Valley. Cornwell's story ends with his eyewitness account of the battle at Cedar Creek. There, Sheridan's galloping return to the battlefield inspired his men to turn a major rout of the Union army into a decisive victory. Cornwell's writings during this period combine both insightful personal comments as well as a staff officer's detailed and vivid account of these key events and personalities.

Suffice it to say that I thought Cornwell's writings offered a new and interesting perspective, further enhanced by the quality of his writing. In all, I found them to be a valuable and informative addition to the body of work regarding the nation's Civil War history. I am delighted my publisher agreed to put the letters and diaries in print.

On a personal level, I was intrigued by what seemed to be some parallels between Captain Cornwell and myself. Before the war, he moved to Pennsylvania to teach, and he married a local woman. He served in the Union army, and spent most of his time in Virginia. Afterward, he lived and worked in West Chester. I moved from Jacksonville, Florida, to work in Pennsylvania, and I also married a native Pennsylvanian. My people served in the Confederate army during the Civil War. Several of them, including one man who was an officer, fought with Early in the 1864 Valley campaign. More than 130 years later I now work in West Chester with Robert Cornwell's great-grandson. I leave it to the reader to decide if there is any meaning to this.

Their historical value aside, Cornwell's writings are also a poignant reminder that the Civil War was, for the most part, fought by young men. Officers and soldiers alike carried with them the normal passions of youth, and Cornwell was no exception. He was twenty-six years old when he volunteered in 1861, had been married for just two years and was the father of an infant son. His letters to Lillie reveal emotions ranging from tenderness to humor, and he was particularly demanding of her during the time he was in Libby Prison. On a number of occasions he asked her to obtain and ship substantial quantities of food to him there, and he pestered her to have her photograph taken. When she finally sent the photographs, he complained that he did not like the way she appeared in them.

With one exception, Lillie's letters are not known to have survived the passage of time. However, even though Cornwell's writings are a monologue it is evident from them just how much he depended upon her. Along with good wishes, love, and family photographs, she also sent clothing, food, writing materials, and a host of items not available to him in the field. That these packages were warmly received is clear from his letters to her, as he often wrote and told of his delight in receiving the items she sent. More importantly, the "boxes" she sent him while he was in Libby certainly made a terrible period in his life more bearable. The food and clothing she sent to the prison preserved his health, and it is very likely that the contents of the boxes saved his life.

Lillie lived with her family during most of the time Robert was in the army. Her father's farm was located near the town of West Chester, which since 1796 has been the county seat of Chester County, Pennsylvania. Located roughly thirty-five miles southwest of Philadelphia, West Chester traces its origin to four farms established at a crossroads junction in 1760. The town grew quickly, and by the beginning of the Civil War was the burgeoning commercial and legal center of a prosperous rural area. West Chester was fortunate in that as it grew it did so with beauty and grace. Eventually, West Chester contained so much Greek Revival architecture that it became known as the "Athens of Pennsylvania."

As with most families in the North, Lillie and her family were spared from direct contact with the horrors of war. They never endured any shortage of food, medicine or other commodities. Their money retained its buying power. No vengeful officer ordered the burning of her father's farm, or stole his livestock or destroyed his crops. She was not insulted by the soldiers of an invading army.

Nonetheless, we can appreciate the almost constant worry that must have been part of each of her days. To begin with, she did not want her husband to join the army. Her only surviving wartime letter, undated but believed to have been written in May 1861, was sent to her sister, Mary. In it she wrote:

> The time will not come, I hope, when R. will have to go away with his company-he is not strong enough to endure the fatigues of Camp Life, I am sure, much less that of the field. There are thousands of rugged, hale men waiting and anxious to join the Army, and while that is the case I feel as if he must not go; when it becomes necessary for all, or as many as go, then I will try and give him up: he is a *true patriot* and willing to sacrifice all for his Country; this doubtless you are well aware of.

As it turned out, life in the army seemed to do wonders for Cornwell's health. Despite several bouts of severe illness during his service, he lived to be more than ninety years old.

Of greater concern to Lillie should have been the fact that her husband was an officer. As such, he enjoyed far better conditions than the enlisted men, but he shared their dangers on the battlefield. More so, perhaps, because Civil War officers led from the front and were compelling targets to the enemy. If anything, Robert Cornwell was more vulnerable to being wounded or killed than were his men.

When he was captured in 1863, Lillie's fears for his safety may have been allayed at first; as a prisoner of war he was removed from the field of battle. Under the conditions of the parole and exchange system, she would have expected him to have been paroled within a few days and then be sent to a parole camp to await exchange. There, she could have visited him while he waited for notification of his exchange. Instead, however, growing political pressures on the exchange system eliminated any chance for Robert's release. He spent the next nine months in Libby Prison, one of the most infamous prisons in Civil War history.

Robert Thompson Cornwell was born January 29, 1835, in Thompsons
Ridge, Orange County, New York. He was the son of Daniel and Elizabeth Thompson Cornwell, both of whom were of Scotch-Irish descent.[1] The Cornwell
name existed in America since early days, and family tradition has it that at least
one of Robert's forebears served in the Revolutionary War.

The 1850 census of Sullivan County, New York, shows Daniel Cornwell,
"innkeeper," age forty-five, and his wife, Elizabeth, thirty-nine. Their children
are listed as Robert, fifteen; Mary, fourteen; Helen, three; and James, one. Each
member of the family was a native of New York.[2] Also included in the household
was Isaac Anderson, age twenty-seven, a native New Yorker who listed his occupation as "teacher." Possibly, Anderson was boarding at the inn while he taught
in the local school. One wonders whether his presence may have influenced
Robert to pursue a career as a teacher himself. The last member of the household
was Irish-born Catherine Daily, age twenty-one. She may have been the household servant, a common occupation in America at that time for single young
women living in the countryside.

Robert received his early education at the Monticello Academy in Sullivan
County, New York, then attended the University of Northern Pennsylvania located in Bethany, Wayne County, Pennsylvania. He taught mathematics and grammar at the university for a short time after his graduation. When the school was
sold he returned to Sullivan County to take a teaching position.[3]

In 1855 Robert was recommended for a teaching post at the Lancaster
County Normal Institute, a school located in rural Lancaster County, Pennsylvania, that offered additional training to teachers during the Summer months. The
institute became an immediate success, prompting the county in the same year to
establish a new full-time institution, the Lancaster County Normal School. This
was the first state teachers' school in Pennsylvania, and Cornwell accepted an
invitation to teach mathematics and grammar.[4] In 1858, he left Millersville and
with another teacher went to Indiana County, Pennsylvania, where they established the Indiana County Academy and Normal School. It grew quickly until the
increasing need for soldiers in the Union army ended its operations.[5]

On May 3, 1859, Cornwell married Lydia Ann "Lillie" Jackson. At age
twenty-five, she was the oldest daughter of Joseph T. and Mary Gray Jackson of
Chester County, Pennsylvania. Her father, a Virginian, was apparently a prosperous farmer; in 1860 he owned land in Westtown Township worth $11,900, a
considerable sum for the time.[6] Lillie's mother, Mary, was a native Pennsylvanian.

Robert and Lillie lived in Indiana County after their marriage. Their first
child, a son named Gibbons Gray Cornwell, was born there on August 18, 1861.
Named after his maternal great-grandfather, Gibbons Gray of West Chester, he
was the "Gibbie" so often mentioned in Cornwell's letters.

In April 1861, immediately following the outbreak of the war, Cornwell
organized a company of volunteers, which included a number of his students.
However, the company was not accepted into the service because the state of
Pennsylvania had already filled its quota.[7] He returned to teaching, but in August

such works as *U.S. Infantry Tactics* and Silas Casey's three-volume *Infantry Tactics, for the Instruction, Exercise, and Manouevres of the Soldier*. One of the most popular manuals, despite the fact that its author was now a general in the Confederate army, was William J. Hardee's *Rifle and Light-Infantry Tactics*.

Despite its serious purpose, the situation of green officers attempting to instruct their equally green men in the art of drilling was a staple of Civil War humor. One New Hampshire soldier said "the appearance of the line can be better imagined than described. Drill is aching funny. We are all green. Mistakes are corrected by making still worse mistakes. The men in the ranks grin, giggle and snicker, and now and then break out into a coarse, country hee-haw." Another New Hampshire recruit described the ordeal of his drill: "ambitious officers of the line, who had been cramming Casey for a fortnight, were in a vertebral cold-shiver temperature…That the men got into a snarl, a tangle, a double and twisted, inextricable tactical knot, is tame delineation."[6]

In addition to training his men, Cornwell was also the father figure of his company. He was responsible for their health and welfare and for maintaining discipline among them. In this he was aided by army regulations and the Articles of War. They provided an established system of reward and punishment, but it required careful application by an officer. Those who handled their men too strongly risked becoming a martinet; those who were too lenient often lost the respect of their men.

Moreover, officers had to wield their power judiciously in volunteer units, where many of the men hailed from the same geographic area and were often related. Cornwell quickly realized his diverse role as a company commander, saying in one early letter "If he [an officer] has charge of a Company of men, he must be master of it.…I devote my whole time to them [his men].…[I am] their friend in everything, but if they don't come up to scratch, I come down on them."

From his letters, it appears that he ran his company with a firm but fair hand. The punishments mentioned seem to fit the occasions, and discipline is counterbalanced by promotions for those who earned them. Perhaps the most telling thing is the fact that he was proud of his men and thought his was the best company in the regiment.

Cornwell commanded a company, the basic infantry component of the army. Under ideal conditions, which did not often exist in the field, a full-strength company officially consisted of about one hundred men. These included three officers, one first sergeant, four sergeants, eight corporals, a wagoner, drummer and fifer; and at least sixty-four but not more than eighty-two privates. However, battle casualties, illness, and desertion often reduced the effective size of a company to 50 percent or less of its authorized strength.

The commissioned officers of a company were a captain, who commanded it, as well as one first lieutenant and one second lieutenant. If the company was subdivided into two platoons, the captain commanded one platoon, the first lieutenant the other.

The next highest component was the regiment, which in volunteer units was made up of ten companies commanded overall by a colonel. Thus, at full strength, Cornwell's 67th Regiment would have had some 1,000 officers and men. If fewer than ten companies were available, the combined unit was known as a battalion. It was usually commanded by a major or lieutenant colonel. Next was the brigade, consisting of three to six regiments commanded by a brigadier general but often by a colonel. Then came the division, three or four brigades commanded by a major general. Above this was the corps of two or four divisions also under the command of a major general. The largest command was the army, composed of corps located within the same geographic area, and usually named after a river in the army's area of operation, such as the Army of the Potomac.

The term "dinner," much used by Cornwell, had a different meaning in the nineteenth century. In those days, dinner was the noontime, and usually the largest, meal of the day. Officers from more than middling backgrounds might also have had an afternoon tea in camp. That repast, however, was often quite plain compared to civilian tables, and merely took the edge off hunger. "Supper" was the evening meal and usually consisted of lighter fare. It was well after the Civil War, particularly in the North, when the word "lunch" replaced dinner, and dinner became the evening, and for most people the largest, meal of the day. However, the old terms and their meanings continue to this day in the South and in England.

Cornwell's first surviving letter describes his frustration at paperwork, the bane of officers since the invention of writing. The Civil War was the beginning of modern warfare in terms of the weapons employed, and it was equally the beginning of the modern period of military paperwork. Officers of both armies faced a vast array of highly detailed government forms that had to filled in, often in triplicate, according to regulations and returned within a proscribed time. Virtually every soldier and every piece of equipment from a cartridge to a battery of artillery had to be periodically accounted for on the proper government forms.

On December 9, after Cornwell took command of his own company, he complained to Lillie that his predecessor in command left the company's records in a "complete jumble and wreck." The absence of those reports was more than a minor annoyance, however, as the information contained in them showed the fighting strength and readiness of a company.

The self-descriptive "Quarterly Return of Clothing, Camp & Garrison Equippage" that he mentions was highly important. On a more frequent basis, the "Morning Reports," taken immediately after reveille each morning, listed each man in a company and whether or not he was present and fit for duty. The "Special Requisition for Ordnance and Ordnance Stores" showed the number of arms on hand as well as the number needed. According to August Kautz, then a captain in the Union army, the latter report was of critical importance, because a company "once completely armed and equipped cannot be resupplied until the arms and equipment already issued to them have been inspected and condemned or ordered to be turned in."[7]

So burdensome was the task of properly entering information on this and a myriad of other official forms that same Captain Kautz (1828–1895), a German-born

West Point graduate, wrote a 142-page manual expressly for the purpose of showing company officers and clerks how to properly fill in the forms. He called it *The Company Clerk: Showing How And When To Make All The Returns, Reports, Rolls, And Other Papers, And What To Do With Them.*

The manual became something of a military bestseller, for as Kautz said in his preface, the problems officers had with the forms were "caused more by the difficulty of finding out *how* to do what is required, than from any innate carelessness or intent to neglect their duty" A copy of an original Clothing, Camp and Garrison Equippage form, similar to the one mentioned by Cornwell, is reproduced in Appendix A.

The detail-oriented Kautz finished the war as an experienced, if not particularly successful, brigadier general. In 1865 he was one of the members of the military commission that tried the conspirators in the Lincoln assassination.[8]

In his September 24 letter Cornwell, by now a commissioned officer, described in some detail his "military suit" and accessories as well as the cost of each item. He did so because he had to pay for them out of his own pocket. Unlike the enlisted men, Civil War officers on both sides generally did not receive uniforms or equipment from quartermaster's stores. Instead, they were expected to purchase their uniforms and equipment privately. It was a considerable expense for a new officer to outfit himself, and he was not reimbursed by his government for the expenditures.

However, one advantage of the private-purchase system was that an officer's uniform was usually of far better fit and quality than that the government issued to his men. The term "shoddy" came into use during the Civil War because unscrupulous Union army contractors made uniforms out of that product. Shoddy was a material that combined new and old wool. It looked good at first, but quickly fell apart, especially after being wet. Moreover, officers were limited only by the thickness of their wallets regarding the great range of military and personal accessories from which they could choose. As a new officer located well away from direct combat, Cornwell seems to have acquired virtually every item thought to be necessary.

The military suit, although tailor made for him, was most likely the standard uniform pattern specified for company-grade officers in the Union army: a dark blue, single-breasted frock coat having one row of nine regimental buttons, and sky-blue trousers.

Swords were carried by officers both as a badge of rank and as a personal weapon. Officially, company-grade officers were to carry the Model 1850 foot officers' sword, although there was some variation in actual practice. The belt he mentioned was the sword belt, to which the sword was attached on the wearer's left side by straps. A hook on the left side of the belt allowed the sword to hang easily at the side, the hilt reversed, without interfering with the wearer's legs.

The sash was a carryover from seventeenth- and eighteenth-century officers' uniforms, and served no purpose other than as another badge of officer status. As an infantry officer, Cornwell's sash would have been made of crimson silk, some six to seven feet in length. It was worn around the waist on the outside of the coat under the sword belt and tied on the left side with the loose ends hanging down the leg above the knee. Except for ceremonial occasions or when serving as Officer of the Day, sashes were not worn much in the field where their bright color made the wearer an inviting target for the enemy.

Cornwell's gloves may have been leather gauntlets, a fashionable component of the uniform but not widely used in the field by experienced officers. The gum blanket, however, was very useful. Made of rubberized canvas, it provided protection when sleeping on wet ground, and when slit in the center it could be worn over the shoulders as a waterproof poncho.

The sword knot was another relic of the past. Originally, the leather knot was designed to prevent a man from accidentally losing his sword in combat. One end attached to the guard or hilt of the sword and the other end, a loop, fastened over the wearer's wrist. However, by the time of the Civil War sword knots were ceremonial items made of heavily gilded material. Like the sash, they were impractical for use in the field.

Cornwell's first letter is interesting in its own right although, as previously noted, he was evidently separated from the service soon after writing it.

January 4, 1862
Camp 67th P. V. [Pennsylvania Volunteers]
Annapolis, Md.
DEAREST LILLIE,

I have put off writing much longer than I meant to. But you will excuse it, I trust. I have told you before that the Camp is a poor place for writing. And lately, I have had all the writing to do that I could attend to and it is not all done yet. The 31st day of December was the end of a Quarter. And every Captain at such time must make out Quarterly Returns of Clothing, Camp, and Garrison Equippage, Clothing Receipt Rolls, for the whole Company, and an Ordnance return. It was also Muster day and we had to make out Muster Rolls, four in number, for the whole Company. Also our Monthly Return. These things must be all be made out in triplicates and necessitates a great amount of writing. I used to think that school reports were a great deal of trouble but they are not a circumstance.

Mary Young[9] arrived here night before last and I think will remain as long as the regiment lies here. Her father has closed up his house and I think he will come [unclear] before long. James Young is attending school at Eldersridge. So there is no one to remain at home except the old man.

I do wish I could bring you down now with Gibbie[10] but I have no money nor will get any till pay-day which we are constantly expecting. I would have sent you my photograph before but for the same reason. I do not say this in the way of begging for if I wanted you send me money I would ask you for it. I can get along very well here without money. Scarcely an officer in the Regiment has a cent to flip himself with. The Regiment has not been paid for over six months.

I do wish you would send Gibbie's picture to me and your own with it. Tell Sallie[11] she will get my photograph after pay day [for] sure. Harry White is at Harrisburg to attend the Senate. He has leave of absence during the session from the War Department.[12]

You have, I presume, seen some malicious attacks on our Colonel (Staunton) in the [Philadelphia] *Inquirer*. Some consummate scoundrels, among whom is our Lieut. Colonel, are trying to overthrow him but they will not succeed. Col. Staunton is now under arrest, but I am confident will be released in a few days. He is a better man, a better soldier, and knows more military than all his enemies put together. How is Aunt Massey?

Give my love to all our friends and relatives

Truly your own

Robert

Cornwell arrived at Camp Curtin, near Harrisburg, on August 29, 1862, the same day the battle of Second Manassas (Bull Run) commenced. It ended the next day, with the Confederates under Lee, Jackson, and Longstreet victorious and in good position, and the battered Union army in disarray outside Washington. By September 2, Union Major General John Pope's Army of Virginia was entrenched around the capitol, awaiting what was expected to be an imminent attack on the city by Robert E. Lee's Army of Northern Virginia.

In the first days of September Cornwell, still an uncommissioned volunteer, and the rest of the men at Camp Curtin were sent to join the 67th Regiment, which was stationed at Annapolis. The main body of the regiment had been sent to Maryland five months earlier to relieve the 11th Pennsylvania. They spent the next several months guarding rail lines and on provost duty in Annapolis, Baltimore, and in the other parts of Maryland that fell within the jurisdiction of the Federal Middle Department.[13] On September 4, the Army of Northern Virginia abandoned their positions outside Washington and began assembling in Frederick, Maryland. This caused much worry in the North that Lee's next move might be an attack on Baltimore or towns in southeastern Pennsylvania. In the meantime, Cornwell and his unit were diverted from Annapolis and sent to join the defenses around Washington.

Pressure on the capitol eased as Lee moved into Maryland, and Cornwell was able to proceed to Harrisburg on September 15 to obtain his commission. He found the city a scene of feverish activity as a result of Governor Curtin's call for 50,000 volunteers to defend the state against a possible attack by Lee. That same day 28,000 Union soldiers engaged some 18,000 Confederates at South Mountain, Maryland, in an attempt to head off a Confederate advance upon Harpers Ferry. As Cornwell noted in his letter, the Confederate army was engaged very heavily on its flanks. After severe fighting, it withdrew late in the evening. The next day, however, other Confederates under Stonewall Jackson captured Harpers Ferry and took 12,000 Union prisoners.

Cornwell returned to duty at Annapolis, where much of his time for the next few months was occupied with the affairs of guarding "Camp Parole." This was a camp built to house "parole prisoners," who were Union soldiers captured and then released or "paroled" by the Confederate army. Under terms agreed to by both sides at that time, military prisoners were paroled by their captors within ten days of capture and sent back to their own lines. Once returned, they were prohibited from bearing arms or participating in military activities until officially exchanged. Parole prisoners were a burden to their own side because separate camps had to be built for them and they had to be guarded by their own men. Capt. Lynford Trock (or Troch) of Co. "H," 67th Pennsylvania Regiment, was the provost marshal of Camp Parole at this time.[14] The system of parole and exchange is examined in fuller detail in a subsequent chapter.

August 29, 1862
Harrisburg, Pa.
MY DEAR LILLIE,

We arrived here Wednesday morning about day break, safe and sound, though considerably fatigued with an all night ride. The men had their breakfast from a table set in the railroad depot especially prepared for such arrivals, after which we marched to Camp Curtain [sic],[15] about two miles from the depot. Barracks were assigned the men, and as soon as they were somewhat rested they were marched to the head quarters of the Camp, from whence they were sent to the examining Surgeon's office where they were stripped of their clothing and subjected to a very close examination. Four of our men were rejected on account of apprehended physical ability. It is surprising that men should dislike so much to be rejected. I saw one squad examined just before our own, and invariably when they found that they would not "pass" they cried and begged most pitifully to be allowed to go; but it was of no use—the decree was irrevocable.

All of our squad except the rejected ones were then marched [to] the quarter Master's department where they received their new clothes [uniforms]. This took up the greater part of the day. On the next afternoon they were marched to Captain Dodge's office in the city where they were "mustered in" and received their bounty.[16] Today more than half of them have been doing guard duty and the remainder I have drilled both forenoon and afternoon in the school of the soldier.[17] There are now between 7[00] and a thousand men encamped here.

There are some things of course that are unpleasant. First, the Camp is the meanest and unpleasantest place I have ever attempted to remain in long at a time. It is so dry that the ground is covered with a thick cloud of dust which the wind drives and whirls about in clouds perfectly blinding and choking; added to all this the sun pours down with burning effect and its heat is unrelieved by a single shade tree in or about the whole camp. Again the Government has detailed a few Lieutenants, and a mass of Sargents and Corporals to oversee and execute the orders of the Camp. These, judging by the air of importance which they put on, one would be likely to mistake for *Major Generals*. They seem to regard it as their chief business to swear at [and] drive the men about. A Lieutenant came swilling around our barracks today, and when I asked him a civil question about whether he wanted our men on dress parade at that time or not, he answered me in a very arbitrary and over bearing style and ordered me to fall into the ranks.

I told him I would do no such thing, but went immediately to headquarters and asked Capt. Hunt if he had any right to make such an order. Hunt asked me if I had reported myself there for duty, and I told him I had not, when he said the Lieutenant had no right to make such an order, so I walked around there after that unmolested by Mr. Lieu's [Lieutenant's] orders.

Otherwise I am quite satisfied. My whole time is occupied with the men, drilling, then helping them in packing up their old clothes, sending their money home, etc., etc. My health is good. I am boarding at the United States Hotel in town and walk back and forward to camp three times a day over a distance of about two miles [and] with other necessary labor generally [it] makes me pretty tired by night. The men are all in good health with the exception of two or three who have slight attacks of diarhea [*sic*]. They are all anxious to go on to the Regiment which we will do next Monday.

I am anxious to hear from you, but can not expect to receive a letter from you until you have received one from me from the Regiment, as you would not know how to address it. When you write, tell me all about Gibbie, the school, etc. etc. Give my regards to Mr. and Mrs. Westlake[18] and Mr. Hoffman and family.

Affectionately Yours,

Robert

September 5, 1862.
Camp Opposite Washington, D.C.
DEAREST LILLIE,

You would have received this long ago had it been possible for me to mail it. But for a few days all communications between this place and Washington or any other post office has been entirely cut off.[19] We arrived at Baltimore Monday [September 1] night about 8 o'clock, it raining heavily at the time. We went to what is called the "Soldier's Retreat" where thousands of troops are fed daily. After waiting for some time our turn to eat dry bread and salt pork and drink a cup of coffee came, and we were satisfied. But the sleeping accommodations were already crowded with soldiers and we were obliged to sleep on the depot platform.

At four o'clock in the morning we roused up, partook of a breakfast precisely similar to the supper, took the cars[20] and went to Washington, as the officer said it would be necessary for us to go to the latter place to report. Arriving at the city we were immediately sent to the river, took boat and sent to Alexandria [Virginia] about 8 miles distant. William McClaran who came with us to obtain a position in the Regiment remained at the Capitol, and I have not seen him since. Arriving at Alexandria we marched to Fort Ellsworth[21] about two miles from where the boat landed. Failing here to obtain a waggon [sic] to take my trunk, and fearing to remain behind the men lest I should not find them again, our men kindly assisted me in carrying it all the way to the fort.

Here we expected to get something to eat and be sent to our regiment. But the officers sent from Camp Curtain [sic] here left us in charge of the Col. Commanding the post who told us that owing to the position and rather critical condition of affairs Gen. McClelland [sic][22] had issued an order that morning [September 2] that all squads without reference to the regiments to which they belong should organized into temporary Companies and the companies into regiments and sent forward to do service. We all acquiesced willingly to the necessities of the case. Every thing was excitement. The roads were crowded with the trains of wagons as far as the eye could reach, rebel prisoners in large and small squads were marching strongly guarded towards the river. Riders, and officers of all kinds were galloping to and fro along the road and indeed the whole scene can be better imagined than described.

September 8, 1862 [Continued in the preceding letter.—T.M.B.]
Opposite Washington, D. C.

Having filled the other sheet just at the hour for drill, I could not conveniently get to writing again until this forenoon.

To proceed with the narrative [the letter of September 5 was not mailed] of our experience where I left off. We sat down about fifteen minutes at Fort Ellsworth when the order came to "fall in" and we were marched about one and a half miles to what is called the Round House where I was directed to detail men to prepare tents and draw rations for the men. This was about 5 o'clock P. M. on Tuesday and we had not had a bite to eat since before daylight in the morning at Baltimore.

Having worked about half an hour hard preparing tents, I went down to the Round House and drew rations. We got some very hard crackers that had been brought back from Harrison's Landing, as appeared from the mark on the box in which they were packed, [and] some salt pork and coffee. I had no sooner had the rations carried over to the tents than we were ordered into ranks, marched down to the Round House, armed, provided with 40 rounds of ammunition each, and with about 4 thousand more men started on a march, the destination of which none of us knew.

Our men went from want of food and the load under which they were marching and being entirely new men in the service soon became very much fatigued. Indeed four of them after marching about two miles fell out of the ranks along the road and up to this time we have not seen them. Another became so exhausted that he could not carry his knap sack farther and threw it down. I knew that he would nearly freeze when we encamped without his blanket and over coat, so I picked it up, shouldered it and carried it to the end of the march.[23]

After marching about 10 miles we were halted and ordered about 11 1/2 o'clock at night to stack arms. We were glad to do so. And after nibbling a few hard crackers and coffee (for the pork and coffee was uncooked and of course not eatable) we laid down in an open field without tents or any roof except the star spangled canopy of heaven. The dew was very heavy and the night became so cold that some time before day I became so cold that I could not lie longer, but jumped up, built a fire and walked about. About day light each made a cup of coffee and roasted a piece of pork on a stick over the fire, all of which tasted very good. We are lying between Fort Albany and the Arlington House, somewhat above but nearly opposite Washington.

We laid here four days and nights without tents, but yesterday the Col.[24] gave us five tents and I detailed some men to put them up. Last night was the first night that I have slept warm since leaving Harrisburg.[25] The Col. has given me charge of the whole camp and I detail men on duty, draw rations, for all the squads and stragglers in it. So you see I am, although a civilian in every sense of the word (uncommissioned and in civilian dress) a very important man and they call me "Captain."

I did not tell you that I saw the boys of Co. "B" 11th Reg. Pa. [unclear]. The day after we arrived here they arrived here from the famous Saturday and Monday fight[26] and encamped within a quarter mile of us. I had a long talk with Captain Porter and his command. They have seen very hard service, and the day they arrived here was the 15th day of continuous hard marching and fighting. Of course, they looked hard and worn out. I went up to their Camp and found nearly all asleep in the middle of the afternoon. They had nothing with them but their oil cloth blankets and arms. Henderson Howard was killed in Saturday's fight. Capt. Porter ran a very narrow escape. A minnie [sic] ball struck his canteen, went through one side and nearly the other. The canteen probably saved him from a dangerous wound.

I do not have time to write more just at present. I do not know when I shall be able to mail this letter for all communication between us and Washington is cut off.

Affectionately Yours,

Robert

September 11, 1862
Annapolis, Md.
MY DEAR,

Our Lieu. Col.[27] In charge, who would not allow us to leave because he was not certain as to the whereabouts of our Reg.[iment] now released us and that evening [September 8] we crossed the long bridge to Washington. Secured transportation to this place, staid [sic] over night at the Soldier's Retreat, took the Annapolis train the next morning, and arrived here at 10 o'clock A. M. We met with a warm reception, and all feel at home. Adjutant Young, Lieut. Carpenter, and Dr. Barr[28] are very kind, and their hospitality is invaluable to me. I shall soon be on duty here. The Col. Says it is his intention to make me Captain. I will soon purchase the necessaries that I need in the way of clothing, etc.

Dearest, I am very sorry that I have been compelled to keep you waiting for a letter so long. I will write now frequently and hope very soon to hear from you. I have not had a sick hour, and indeed the boys think I am improving on it. How is our dear Gibbie. Oh! how I would like to see him. Tell me all about him and yourself.

Affectionately Yours,

R.T. Cornwell

P.S. Address your letters for

Capt. R.T. Cornwell
67th Reg. Pa. Vol.
Annapolis, Md.

September 15, 1862.

Harrisburg, Pa.[29]

DEAR LILLIE,

I arrived this place at 3 o'clock this morning from Annapolis. Major White[30] is with me. I came here to obtain a Captain's Commission and to be mustered into the service.[31] Have not yet applied for these things but will write to you soon again giving results. Return to the Regiment soon. Will probably go by way of Philadelphia and will probably call at West Chester. Suppose you have been somewhat alarmed concerning the safety of your friends in Chester County recently? What glorious news we had last night. The rebels under Gen. Lee have been completely whipped on the left, right and center. I am only fearful that they will get back to Virginia too soon.

Gen. McClellan is the man with the Army. You can't find a soldier that wouldn't die for him. Oh! I feel that these are the most promising times we have yet had.

What an uprising is here manifested. It is indeed gratifying in the highest degree to see such a display of loyalty on the part of the people. I see acquaintances here from almost every quarter of the State. Harrisburg is literally thronged with volunteers and Militia and they are constantly leaving for Chambersburg and other points while as many or more are arriving. Write me soon and often at the Regiment [at] Annapolis.

I enclose many warm kisses for yourself and dear little Gibbie.

Give my regards to the lucky teachers and also tender them my hearty acknowledgments for the flattering testimonial that fell on my eye in the columns of the *True American.*

Affectionately your own,

Robert

September 24, 1862
Annapolis, Md.
MY DEAR LILLIE,

Well, I was duly commissioned[32] and sworn into the service of the United States as captain of Company B of the 67th Reg. P. V. [Pennsylvania Volunteers]. I went to West Chester immediately after but did not arrive there until Wednesday evening of last week [September 17]. Of course they were all surprised to see me arriving without any previous warning about 10 1/2 o'clock at night on the evening of the above mentioned day. I left the railroad at Oakland about 9 1/2 o'clock at night and walked over. When I rang the bell, [your] mother came into the hall and called out "Who's there?" 'What would you give to know' said I. She knew my voice and enquired if it was Robert. I 'asked' [*sic*] her 'yes mam' and she let me in." Of course we had a good time [and] a social chit chat, and I had some supper. It was late before I retired, but I tell you, I hadn't slept on the ground so long that that nice feather bed in the front room didn't feel a great deal better. I called at Aunt Massey's and Cheyney's[33] the next morning and then went to Philadelphia. Came back to West Chester that night and returned to Philadelphia next morning where I remained until Sunday morning [September 21] when I again went to West Chester (which latter place I rather made "head quarters"). Stayed at West Chester until Monday morning when I started for this place by way of Phil.[adelphia], arriving here on that evening.

My friends in West Chester were very kind. They made me two shirts (flannel). Aunt Massey made one and Mother and Sallie the other Mother and Sallie made me some towels. Gave me a needle book, buttons, thread, pins, and needles all complete besides presenting me with a very good blanket.[34] Aunt Massey presented me with two bottles of raspberry syrup and two glasses of very nice jelly. With the syrup I have treated my friends and they all pronounce it magnificent. God bless my West Chester friends! Well, I called on Benjamin Passmore and drew the $50 spoken of. But I could not pay the full bill for a military suit. The man who measured me and made them while I was there, on the introduction of Major White would have waited until pay day for the bill. But I paid him $15 down. The suit cost $38. There were a great many other things to buy. I paid $14 for a sword, $3 for a belt, $9 for a sash, $1 for gloves, $3 1/2 for a gum blanket, 50 cts for a sword knot, $7 for a traveling bag, besides buying shirting material, drawers, under shirts, collars, scissors, comb, brush, whisk, handkerchiefs, stockings (woolen and cotton), etc. To the above was added my traveling expenses for I paid full fare every where I went.

I will pay the balance due on my clothing when pay day arrives. You ask if I need anything that you can furnish. I think not, my dear, I am very well supplied and I think of nothing that you can do for me that you have not already done. What a shame it is that I lost all those nice things that you fixed for me. I am sure they were worth more to me than they can be to anybody else, simply because you prepared them. My military suit fits elegantly. The finest fit my friends say that they have seen.

Grandfather, I suppose, has made you a visit and you have had a fine time. He said he started on Thursday [and] he said that he might arrive at Indiana [County] on Friday and be with you on Saturday and Sunday. You must tell me what he said about Gibbie.

Since I have returned I have been unable to fit up a tent for myself and have been living in Major White's. I want to tell you that I think a very great deal about John Young. He has as large a soul in him as any man I know of. I never knew him while I was in Indiana [County]. How is Mary Young? You will call on her if she is still sick, frequently, will you not?

I ordered a cheap fatigue suit while in Phil.[adelphia] costing $12 [so] that I might save my better dress for special occasions. I received the fatigue suit today and find it just the thing.[35]

I received a very fine, long letter from Mr. Westlake, but have not answered it because I heard he had gone out with the militia and [I] did not know where to address him. If he is at home, give him my warmest regards and say that I will soon write to him. Say also that I am too busy now to write for the paper. For every minute that I am off duty, I have to study Tactics and army regulations to avoid making worthless mistakes in Company and Battalion drill. Kiss dear little Gibbie for me. Remember me to Mrs. Westlake and the lady teachers. Tell the latter that I often think of our pleasant associations and how different is my present from my old association.

Fondly your own,

Robert

October 6, 1862
Annapolis, Md.
DEAR LILLIE,

I wrote you about one week since and have not received an answer. Perhaps you did not receive it. John Young has sent several letters home recently that his folks never received. Where the fault is, I cannot tell. One thing I forgot when replying to your last. It did not occur to me when writing. You ask if you had not better sell our furniture[36] if you can do so.

Well, my dear I hardly know what to say. Are there not a great many things that you would not wish to part with any way, and which would either have to stowed away in some room in Indiana [Pennsylvania] or boxed up and taken along? My books and book case, guns, your fancy table, pitcher, tumblers, the bed (I mean mattress) and bedding, all the pictures and all the drawers contain, for example. If you have to store away the most of these things would it not be as well to treat the bedstead, lounge, and chairs in the same way? Especially since we can hardly hope to sell them except at a sacrifice. We could hardly get what the carpet is worth and it suits our purpose exactly.

However if you think otherwise, and especially if you have an opportunity to sell the last mentioned articles for a fair price I am entirely satisfied. If we conclude to store them away could not our sleeping room be obtained from Mrs. Hoffman for that purpose? I am very sorry to hear that Mrs. Hoffman conducts herself in such a manner as to worry you or render you in any measure unhappy, for I know that you have enough to perplex and trouble you without any harassing interference. Mid your troubles my dear keep up a serene stout heart. You have the love of Heaven, the consciousness of right, and the assurance of a heart full of love here to support you.

I am well, *very well*, better than I have been for years. Were it not for being separated from my family, I should be entirely satisfied. How is Gibbie? How I should like to see him! Wonder if he would know me?

We are getting a large number (about 5000) parole prisoners here. There have been as high as 20,000.[37] The 10,000 taken at Harpers Ferry at the time Col. Miles was killed were here but have been sent West to fight the Indians.[38] These paroles are very troublesome. They lay waste the whole country about here, burning fences and stealing everything they can lay their hands on, Lieut. Col. George Smith who used to be Sallie's beau, and Albert Shirts who used to attend school at Millersville are among them.[39] They were both considerably surprised to find that I am in the service. The parole camp is about two miles from ours and is terribly filthy. In short it is one large *privy*. Their officers are down in town here all the time or off at home and the men are only restrained by our guard which is of course insufficient to guard so many men if they are illy [sic] disposed. One of our own men had to shoot one of them the other day and it had a very salutary effect on the remainder. The 131st New York regiment has been sent here to assist us. To be a paroled prisoner is any thing but an honor any longer. Too many are purposely taken in order to lay back for a year or so with nothing to do as a parole.

Brig. Gen. Emory[40] was here yesterday and ours and the New York Regiment were reviewed before him. We did some fine marching and were highly complimented. We will probably [be] sent away from here as soon as these parole prisoners are exchanged.

Annapolis is any thing else than a pleasant town. The Navy yard and Navy school buildings constitute all the attractions it possesses. Two thirds of the inhabitants are blacks, and the whites are nearly all secessionists. The streets are dirty and the whole town stinks. It is laid out from two circles (the State house and Church) from these two circles all the streets radiate. You can imagine what an awkward arrangement it must be.

Affectionately your own,

Robert

October 26, 1862
Annapolis, Md.
MY DEAR LILLIE,

I am almost frightened when I think how long it is since I have written to you [the last letter was 20 days previously]. I could have done it sooner and should have done so but have procrastinated. My time is very much cut up during the day with duties of different kinds and I never know when I am to have ten minutes of leisure, not that I regard the duties as hard but quite continuous. Besides it has been so cold nights and evenings recently as to be uncomfortable to sit down and write in my tent or rather marquee.[41]

This day is exceedingly stormy, raining hard and continuously. Very unpleasant for sentinels and officers on duty, but I rather like to be out in the worst of weather, feeling well and strong to endure most anything for all of which I strive to feel thankful. I have been Officer of the Day twice during the past week.[42] Presume you are not acquainted with the duties of such an officer. Well, Captains of Companies take their regular turn as Officer of the day. When acting in such a capacity we are not allowed to sleep or take off any part of our uniform for twenty four hours or during the day and night. You can readily distinguish an Officer of the Day by his wearing his sash over his right shoulder as well as around his waist. He is during that day next in Command to the Col.[onel]. He must see that the Camp is kept perfectly clean. He has control of the guard, puts on the *parole* and *countersign*, must visit the sentinels frequently during the day and night at their different posts and once at least after midnight making "Grand Rounds" to see that they challenge correctly.[43] The prospect is that this will be a hard night for the Officer of the Day.

I am very much delighted with your representations of our dear little Gibbie. How much I would like to see him. He would be apt to shrink from his own Papa now, not remembering him. By the way, my dear, it is very doubtful, indeed very improbable that I will not be able to go home at the time your school closes.[44] You cannot appreciate how difficult it is to get away; not that the duties are so imperative as to keep us here, but there has been a general order issued against granting passes. Many officers have been trying for months to get passes or furloughs but cannot do it. I will come if possible.

You may wonder that Major White can go to and from home so frequently and none of the rest of us, but he is on recruiting service and any two Commissioned officers are allowed to leave the regiment on such service at one time. Major has been here since you wrote last but when he left Harrisburg did not expect to come so far as Annapolis and therefore left the package you sent with him at Harrisburg. He has not been here since and therefore I have not yet received it.

You ask when I sleep, etc, etc. The officers all sleep in Camp. I drew two blankets from the Quarter Master and have enough to make a comfortable bed. We eat at present in town at a hotel, but are taking measures to establish a mess in Camp. The only difficulty we have is in obtaining a good cook. I have boarded at a hotel ever since I have been here and have good food, paying $3 1/2 per week. Some, boarding at other hotels, pay as high as $5.

You must not imagine my dear that I am undergoing hardships here. Quite the reverse. True we have to be out sometimes in very bad weather but that does us good and we have drill enough, (though it makes us a little sore sometimes) for a healthy amount of exercise.

The men are well cared for. They have large Sibley tents with stoves in them and floors. Their food is very good. Bread fresh from the oven. Fresh beef. Corn ground coarse, dried peas, beans, rice, sugar, molasses, coffee, etc.

I wish if I cannot go home when school is out and we remain here to have you come and see me. Nearly all the officers who are married have had their wives here and it makes me very anxious to see mine. You can be well accommodated at a hotel or if you prefer at a very nice private house.

Fondly your own,

Robert

P.S. Thank you for both bunches of stamps.

October 31, 1862
Annapolis, Md.
DEAR LILLIE,

This is a great day among us. All the troops have today been inspected and mustered preparatory to pay, but when the money will come it's hard to tell. They have had no pay in this Regiment since the 30th of June. I do not expect to get any thing on pay day for they say the government always keeps two months behind.

I am very well, indeed. And the health of the Regiment is generally better than it has been recently. Still, the major does not arrive and of course I have not received the package. How strange that he stays so! The officers are becoming dissatisfied, thinking that he is using his recruiting privileges for political purposes. Do not let this be circulated, however.

About two weeks ago I was finally assigned to a Company. When I came here I and the other recruits who came with me expected to go into Co.[mpany] "B" and I was mustered into that Company. But after I returned from Harrisburg Mr. Greer[45] from Westmoreland County arrived with forty-five recruits. The Col. thought he would not make a good captain, and as Greer was satisfied with a 1st Lieutenancy he concluded to promote Lieut. Tucker (the former 1st Lieut. Of Co. B)[46] to the Captaincy, make Greer 1st Lieut. and put me and my men in Co. "I" which has accordingly been done. I have spent a great deal of time and labor this week in making out the Muster and Pay Rolls of Co. "I." I have now a maximum Company, and, with the exception of three or four pretty hard characters, a very good one. I have yet much to do in making out their clothing and other accounts and receipting for the property of the Company. A Captain who attends to the affairs of a Company, as they should be attended to has his hands full.

[This letter was continued on Nov. 7.—T.M.B.]. One week ago yesterday I wrote the preceding page of this letter, and from that time to this I have failed to get myself in a writing attitude. I am well, with the exception of an almost unnatural appetite. Having no stove in my tent, I have to fill my natural stove very full of fuel on these cool days and nights. Perhaps you think that we are so far South that it is not cold here, but when I tell you that on Friday last there fell 10 inches of *snow* here in less than 10 hours, and on last night and the night before ice froze an inch in thickness, you can form some idea of the temperature.

The wind blows so here that we think our muslin houses are going to be carried into the bay. A night or two ago I got up and packed up my things, thinking surely I would soon be left houseless. On the night before the large hospital tents blew over and in a cold and drenching rain storm we turned out at 11 o'clock at night and carried the sick into a board [ing] house not far distant.

I received your last [letter] this morning, and it as very acceptable, indeed. You ask about Clawson. He is in my Company and is now nearly well. He did not have the fever but the jaundice; not sick enough to go to the hospital.

I have had bad luck with two of my men. One by name John DeHavens shot his thumb off above the first joint while on guard. It was a cold morning and he was dancing around to keep warm, struck the cock of his gun against something when it went off and carried away one thumb. His hand will soon be well again. Another by name Clark Rowland, while writhing under a severe attack of Camp Colic, ruptured himself. He will probably soon be discharged.

The affair to which you alluded concerning Capt. Tucker was a most disgraceful one, as well as most touching. Captain Tucker was a married man. His wife lives in Philadelphia and is a beautiful, intelligent loving little woman from Bucks County. Captain Tucker, intemperate and licentious though he was, had many good qualities. Meanness, in the common acception [*sic*] of the term, he could not be guilty of. He was as brave as a lion; magnanimous and ardently attached to his friends. These qualities with his high degree of intelligence and experience as a soldier and officer made him popular with his Company and indeed with the whole Regiment. He was, moreover, quite fine looking and there is no doubt but that his wife loved him with a passionate ardor. She did not know that he ever drank or was unfaithful to his marriage ties. He used to say himself, and those officers here who were well acquainted with him and his family say, that she never knew that he drank or engaged in licentious practices. That when he got on a spree he went from home and never returned until he was entirely over it.

Dr. Goodman, a druggist here, has an amorous and enticing looking daughter about 18 years of age whose *tail* troubles her very much. In short, though she does not live at a house of ill-fame is never the less a *whore*. A Lieutenant in this Regiment, a young man from Philadelphia, has more than once had criminal connection with her in her bed-chamber and in the very room in which Captain Tucker was shot. This fact is *potent*.

She used to come out into Camp at dress parade and wait for him to go into town with her, and he has a perfect stack of letters that he has received from her. Captain Tucker had the faculty of becoming acquainted with girls of this character, and a week ago last Tuesday she made an arrangement with him to meet in her bed that night. Dr. Goodman got an inkling of what was going on and very coolly exchanged beds with his daughter. About 12 o'clock at night Captain Tucker climbed on a fence back of the house, and from that he ascended to a kitchen roof which rested immediately under the window of her room. He raised the window cautiously, climbed in but hearing a footstep crouched under it on the floor.

Dr. G. hearing the window, raised took his pistol and silently advancing in the dark to the window saw the top of Tucker's head and bringing the pistol within a few inches of his face, shot. His wife rose and lit the candle and Dr. G. went down to the front door and called one of the Provost Guard.[47] I was Officer of the Day that night and was sitting in the Guard House when a messenger coming up was challenged by the sentinel and in reply was answered "I am after the Doctor,—Captain Tucker is shot." After learning where the event took place I went down there and up to the room.

Col. Staunton and several line officers were already there, and in one corner under the window laid Capt. Tucker, a most horrid spectacle. I had no idea that a pistol shot wound would bleed so copiously. His clothes were saturated with his own gore and a large pool was under him on the floor. He moaned and gurgled frightfully as he breathed. Dr. Barr soon arrived but said at once that nothing could be done for him. The brain protruded from the hole. The ball entered in the middle of his forehead just below the hair and as a post-mortem examination afterwards showed, wedged against the inside of the skull low down in the back part of his head.

When I went into the room, Mrs. Goodman sat holding a little child in her lap and in tears. Dr. G. sat by her side, with a very rigid expression or countenance. The daughter was not to be seen. A stretcher was sent for and we placed the captain on it and carried him to the General Hospital. Strange to say he lived five days after receiving that terrible wound. His wife was telegraphed to, and on Thursday she arrived here. She did not know when she arrived here that he had been shot. Tucker had been sick some time before and they merely telegraphed that he was worse. She said Oh! That he had received it [the wound] on the battle-field.

The officers all evaded the truth and pleaded ignorance when she asked them concerning the circumstances. But the hospital Steward upon her urgent solicitation made all known to her.[48] That lovely woman was crazy when he died and until she left here, since which time I have heard from her. He became entirely blind a few days before death, whether it was the ball or the powder which sprinkled his whole forehead and eyes, so close was the pistol to his when discharged, I cannot tell.

I can hardly hope, my dear, to get home when you go East, and I will have to leave everything to your own management. My books and bookcase I would like Mr. Westlake to take if it would not be too much trouble to him. Do you think he has any place to put it? Major White is making an effort to get the drafted men from Indiana County into the Regiment. I will consult with you at another time about bringing Gibbie with you when you come to see me. I would dearly like to see him. You will excuse the appearance of this letter, for the wind shakes my muslin house so that I can with difficulty write at all.

Remember me to Mrs. Brown. Kiss Gibbie for his Papa.

Ever your own,

Robert

November 24, 1862
Annapolis, Md.
MY DEAR LILLIE,

I have been waiting with considerable anxiety to hear from you at West Chester for I presume that unless something unlooked [*sic*] for has occurred, you are with your friends again. I hardly know whether to direct this to West Chester or not, but will do so at a venture. I can imagine the rapture of your meeting with mother, grandfather, Sallie and all. And there is Gibbie, too. He will feel that he has arrived among strangers, and will scarcely recognize the place of his birth. Kiss the dear little fellow for me. I will not venture to bring you down here until pay-day arrives. We are looking for paymaster Johnston daily but he does not yet arrive. I do not expect to receive any more than pay from the day of *muster* (September 17) until the 31st of October, the day the regiment was last "mustered for pay." At the rate of about $130 per month.[49]

I have no news in particular to give. I have a stove and live quite comfortably. My health is good, and as cool weather comes on that of the whole regiment improves. My Company came down off of the Rail Road last Monday. Heretofore it has been guarding the Annapolis and Elkridge Rail Road between this point and the road between Baltimore and Washington. I have two sick men—one of the old members and one of the new recruits. We are going to build barracks here soon in place of our tents. Our tents have become very old and the Government has no new ones with which to supply us. Hence the barracks built of boards. Major White has not arrived yet and I have almost ceased to expect him. We have now four Companies guarding Parole Camp. They have moved out there Officers, tents and all.

Two Companies are on the Rail Road so that we have but four Companies in Camp. Of these two, one Captain is sick and another (Company "B") has no Captain, so that but two Captains are on duty here at Camp. And I am Officer of the Day every other twenty-four hours.

When you write, tell me all about how you disposed of our things at Indiana. How Gibbie is and all the friends at West Chester.

Give love to Mother Sallie and the rest of the family. Also to Aunt Massey and George and Tommy Cheyney's family's.

Ever Your own fond,

Robert

December 9, 1862

Annapolis, Md.

DEAREST LILLIE,

Your last was duly and joyfully received. Your safe arrival [at West Chester], your warm reception by kind friends and relatives as well as your proud and glowing recital of our dear Gibbie's cute and endearing ways were all subjects of profound interest. Major White has at length arrived, and with him the package in a box so long on the road. The school yard bouquet was of course withered to crumbling. The grapes were much shriveled and dried, but eatible [*sic*]. But the stockings were as good as ever. They came in good time. I had only two pairs that I purchased in West Chester when there. They were poor things and lasted only by repeated mending till the arrival of those sent by you. I shall enjoy them much during such weather as this. The weather has been piercing cold for several days past. I gave my old stockings, nicely mended till they were holeless, to some of my men who had none.

I have a fine Company. The finest looking one in the Regiment. Some of the men are unruly and require a tight rein held on them. The discipline of the Company was very much injured by bad management before it came into our hands. They had been for seven months on the railroad about 10 miles from here, where they did just about as they chose, drinking and [unclear] almost without restraint. I determined that when I came in command they should soon find out who was boss. I put one man in the Guard house the first day. Since which time I have put in that domicile about twenty, on one occasion six at one time for absence without leave. We are beginning to understand one another pretty well now, and I have less trouble. It is no use, if an officer has charge of a Company of men he must be master of it. If he is not, he might a great deal better be at home. I devote my whole time to them. Contributing to their comfort in every way possible. Their friend in every thing, but if they don't come up to the scratch I come down on them "like a thousand of brick."

When I took hold of the Company all its affairs were a complete jumble and wreck. The Clothing book, Descriptive book, Order Book, all without head or tail. The Adjutant says that before I took charge there never was even a morning report properly made out, and two thirds of the time none at all. There never before me has been made out a Quarterly Return of Clothing, Camp & Garrison Equippage or Ordnance and Ordnance Stores. The result of this will probably be that Lieut. Simpson,[50] my predecessor in Command, will be hauled over the coals and made to pay for missing property.

You ask me about my Lieutenants. Lieut. Simpson, my first Lieut., is a poor stick and drinks hard. I can place very little reliance upon him. Eugene K. Weeks, my second Lieut., is a first rate fellow and attends to his business well. He is a brother of the Weeks who went to the Normal School from Safe Harbor when you and I were there.

Give my love to all our friends. Kiss dear little Gibbie for me and always remember me as affectionately your own,

Robert

———————

January 11, 1863
Annapolis, Md.
DEAREST LILLIE,

Your kind and loving letter with all its promises of goodies is just received. It is now 10 o'clock at night and the rain pours down heavily. I am Officer of the Day and so have to be up to arrest whiskey drinkers and put them in the Guard house, as well as to visit all the Sentinels through the rain after 12 o'clock tonight. But that is nothing; I have water proof boots and a thick felt overcoat. I pity the Sentinels such nights. However, they have good shoes and overcoats and most of them *gum blankets*.

I wish you were here to see my cozy little canvas house. It is about 11 ft. square, is perfectly water proof, and closes up tightly in front. In the left hand corner next to the door is a good coal stove with a fixture on the top to keep hot water in. A coal box sits along side. The remainder of that side is occupied with a long table with a shelf underneath, on which are stored my company books and little boxes as well as other little necessaries. Across the end I have a fixture to hang my clothes, sword, etc. on. Along the other side I have a good bed with a good husk mattress, for which I paid $3.50. Under the bed, I have not a [unclear], but my Company clothing box, made to order, by one of my men who is a carpenter. These, with my traveling bag, a pail, washbasin, and tin cup for water, broom and two camp chairs, constitute my furniture. I can sleep here as comfortably as I ever slept in my life [unclear] before I was married [unclear].

I am entitled to this tent alone, and another small tent for a servant, but I have given the small tent to our Cooks and have taken my orderly Sergeant in with me. I have told you I think he is acknowledged to be the best orderly in the Regiment, and that is saying a great deal. If I expected to stay in the Army for my whole life, such a man would be worth his weight in gold to me. His name is Edward W. Gay and he is from Phoenixville, Chester Co. [unty]. He keeps my tent as neat as a pin and every thing in good order.

When you come down here I suppose we will be out of tents and into barracks. We are busy building them now. And they look quite well.

It makes my mouth water to think of all the good things I shall find in the box, and it makes my heart swell with gratitude and love for my many kind hearted friends. I feel proud of them. Give them my love, and thanks. Tell Aunt Massy in particular that I appreciate her kindness and well wishes. What a dear woman she is! It fills my heart with no ordinary sadness to think that there is a prospect of our soon losing her from among our earthly friends.

And Sallie sends the wristers, does she? Well, I will kiss them when they come. It is the best I can do, you know. Tell Mother that I will warm the pies before cutting them, for I have just the stove to do it. And [I] will think of her when I cut them.

And now dear Lillie how I wish I could see you. Won't your picture be among the photographs [?]. And Gibbie's. I wonder how the dear little fellow will look. When you come down here I shall take you to Mrs. Green's, a private family and a very pleasant one. Mary Young[51] is now there. Mary's health seems to be improving. She comes out to see our dress parades every pleasant evening, and we officers who are acquainted go and have a chat with her. It is something rich to see a female acquaintance here, and we make the best of the opportunity. It will be a great day for me when you come. Mary and John Young are very anxious to have you come now. But I would prefer to have some money about me when that time comes.

Our Lieut. Col. is H.B. Burnham[52] from Mauch Chunk—a kind of natural fool, puffed up with vanity. Very disrespectful, if not insubordinate, language that, but it is a private truth. This is the second time he has been engaged in an attempt, a malicious, selfish underhanded plot to overthrow

Col. Staunton, that he might step into command. And thank God this is the second time he has failed, for Col. S. [taunton] is reinstated again. The officers and men despise Burnham, and the Regiment would break to pieces if he should ever be placed permanently in command.

There is no immediate prospect of our moving from here. Still, we do not expect to receive much warning.

There is no possibility of my getting home to you that I know of without resigning [his commission]. There are men here who have begged for months and even prayed, have written to friends in Washington to intercede with the war Department, have written to Governor Curtin for his influence for a furlough for a short time, but all to no purpose. We are tied fast.

I must close this long scrawl and go out. The night is very dark and muddy. I will take a thorough wash, change my clothes and take a good snuze [*sic*] tomorrow.

Good night my dearest

Sleep sweetly for I am well

and my heart is with you.

Robert

2

The Nearing Conflict
January 13, 1863–August 7, 1863

The box Cornwell expected from Lillie arrived on January 13. Among the items was a pocket diary for the year 1863. Many soldiers in both armies carried these small diaries in which they wrote the highlights of each day. Cornwell began his on the day it arrived, and was diligent in making concise entries about the significant events and people he encountered almost every day. Hereinafter, diary entries are so indicated following the date of each entry.

Cornwell, whose regiment was still in Annapolis, was looking forward to an anticipated two-week visit from Lillie during the first week in February. His letter of January 24 provided her with precise traveling directions, and Lillie's sense of adventure must be admired. The trip, which required taking four different trains, probably required about ten hours. Moreover, although Maryland did not secede from the Union, there was strong support for the Confederacy throughout much of the state. Many of her men would go on to serve in the Confederate army. Despite a strong Union army presence in Maryland, Lillie was to a degree traveling through occupied territory.

The trip was not to be, however. On February 3 the 67th Regiment, then numbering about nine hundred men, was relieved by a unit of loyal Maryland militia and entrained for Harpers Ferry, Virginia.[1]

Harpers Ferry, located on a peninsula at the confluence of the Potomac and Shenandoah Rivers, was of some strategic importance to both sides. The largest Federal weapons factory and armory in the South were located there. The Baltimore & Ohio Railroad and the Chesapeake and Ohio Canal passed through the town. The rail line, the largest in the country, crossed the Potomac River at Harpers Ferry on a massive 900-foot roofed bridge. Both the railroad and the canal were major commercial routes to the West. Control of the rail line by the South would have allowed the Confederate army to outflank Washington. Control by the North would have provided the Union army with a direct invasion route into the Shenandoah Valley of Virginia.

Harpers Ferry suffered greatly before and during the war as a result of its military importance. On October 16, 1859, John Brown and eighteen of his followers captured the arsenal in an attempt to seize some 100,000 weapons stored there. They intended to turn them over to an army of slaves who were to rise up and fight for the abolitionist cause. Instead, two days later Brown and his men were themselves captured by a detachment of Marines commanded by Lt. Col. Robert E. Lee, an army officer. Fifteen men died in the incident, including four residents of the town. No slaves revolted against their owners.

In April 1861 a Confederate force captured the town from a small Union garrison. Five thousand finished arms were seized, as well as the highly important weapons machinery. The equipment used to manufacture the army's Model 1841 rifle and Model 1855 rifle-musket was sent to factories in the South. In the process, the factory buildings were burned and much of the town sustained damage.

More actions occurred at Harpers Ferry later, and the town became second only to Winchester, Virginia, as the scene of so much fighting. As Cornwell described, the town was very badly damaged and by the time he arrived many residents had fled to safer areas. Bolivar Heights, the location of the Union camp, was on high ground about one and one-half miles northwest of the town.

By April 23 Cornwell's regiment had moved to Berryville, a farming village located about ten miles east of Winchester in the northern end of the Shenandoah Valley. As with Harpers Ferry, the area was of strategic importance to both sides, for Winchester was the gateway to the Valley. It was also an important transportation center from which an invasion, either to the North or to the South, could be launched.

The preceding May, Maj. Gen. Thomas J. "Stonewall" Jackson (1824–1863), commenced a four-day series of running attacks on Union forces in the northern part of the Valley. Ignoring his religious scruples, Jackson and his "foot cavalry" attacked on Sunday, May 25. They defeated Union troops commanded by Maj. Gen. Nathaniel P. Banks (1816–1894). The battle became known as "First Winchester," and Jackson's losses were small, only about four hundred men. Banks, however, lost more than 3,000 as well as a wagon train of supplies that stretched unbroken for more than six miles. The contents of the wagons were joyfully received by Confederate soldiers, who dubbed the hapless general "Commissary" Banks in honor of his unintended largesse.

Cornwell "saw the elephant" for the first time on May 6, 1863, when part of his regiment had its first engagement with the enemy near Upperville in a botched attempt to capture Maj. John S. Mosby's partisan rangers. Cornwell acquitted himself well, but noted with dismay that during the confusion of fighting some inexperienced Union soldiers fired on their own cavalry. One man was killed and four others, including an infantryman of the 67th Regiment, were wounded.

Near the end of the month Cornwell became severely ill with typhoid fever, a not-uncommon ailment among soldiers. He spent most of the month of June in bed, writing little and unable to participate in any of the fighting. While he was recovering in Berryville, Robert E. Lee's 75,000-man Army of Northern

Virginia began a fighting movement westward from Fredericksburg on June 3. It was the beginning of the Gettysburg campaign.

There was a skirmish at Berryville on June 6, followed by a major cavalry battle June 9 at Brandy Station. The vanguard of Lee's army was under the command of Lt. Gen. Richard S. Ewell (1817–1872), a Virginian who served as a division commander under Jackson during the 1862 campaign in the Valley. Ewell entered the Valley on June 12, heading toward Winchester. There was some skirmishing along the way, and on the 13th, as Cornwell notes, Ewell "came into Berryville."

Cornwell and the other men in hospital at Berryville were taken prisoner. Most of the able-bodied Union soldiers retreated to Winchester, where they joined Maj. Gen. Robert H. Milroy's (1816–1890) command, the VIII Corp's Second Division, garrisoned in Winchester.

Milroy was told by his superiors that his position was a threat to Lee's advance and that his 6,900 men were badly outnumbered. He was warned, and possibly ordered, to withdraw his force to safety at Harpers Ferry, about thirty miles away. Milroy ignored the warning and was attacked on June 14. He was forced to abandon the town the next day, but got only about four miles away when he was attacked again and badly defeated by Ewell. Milroy himself escaped but almost 4,000 of his men were captured in this "Second Winchester."

Ewell's division entered Berryville on June 13. Cornwell was in the town, but was so seriously ill that he could not escape to Winchester with the rest of his men. He was taken prisoner by the Confederates, but immediately paroled. A week later, somewhat recovered, he and the rest of the paroled prisoners started on their way to Harpers Ferry. Confederate officers ordered him and some others to go back to Winchester, where he spent the next week recovering his health. Ten days later he was in Staunton, where he and other officers from his regiment remained for a few days. On August 5 they were put on a train for Richmond. He entered Libby Prison the next day.

January 13, 1863
Annapolis, Md.
DEAR LILLIE,

This sheet of paper tells the story. My box is here. It arrived this evening just as I was going out to supper. I couldn't wait until after my meal before opening it, but proceeded to explore it immediately. Good Heavens, how it was packed. Why, after getting the things out I couldn't get them half in again. The Diary is just what I have been wanting but never obtained till I got yours. It is very nice. I will commence writing in it this very night. The photograph of Gibbie is most admirable. I will never get through looking at [it]. He stands up like a brave little soldier, and looks so intelligent. It is a most admirable picture. I never saw a better one. It would take a small fortune to buy it from me. Your picture is good, but not so good as darling's. Ar'nt [*sic*] you getting thin! Ar'nt [*sic*] your dresses getting too large for you? I think you will have to *wean* that big boy before long. Have you been entirely well? You have never complained of ill health any. Have you no cause to? Come now, I don't want you to conceal anything. I value your picture highly. What nice wristers.[2] You must kiss Sallie for me. The Handkerchief is a splendid one. The Col. saw me have it in my hand, and wanted to know where I got that. He thought that never grew in Maryland. The Drawers, Shirts, and Stockings, though not pressingly needed will be useful. Sergeant Gay and myself have tried the pies and both conclude they are "not *hard* to *take*." What nice peaches, plums, jelly, raspberry syrup, raspberry vinegar, cakes, apples, chestnuts, shellbarks, etc. I wonder what I will do with all my stone jugs, bottles, etc. after the contents is [*sic*] consumed. We can't eat it very rapidly just at present, but the things will keep and shortly we will have a "mess" here in Camp and then they will come in very good.

They came very good, nothing broke, nothing spilt. I think I shall enjoy the pickles very much. Again I return my thanks to all my kind donors.

Things move on here old style. Nothing new. Mens barracks are nearly completed.

P.S. Did you get more than one photograph of Gibbie? I hope you had quite a number taken. Do send one to Mother, Mrs. Elizabeth Cornwell, Chemung Co. She will be tickled wonderfully with it. Do send one.

Robert

———

January 13, 1863 (Diary)
Annapolis, Md.

Cloudy. No rain. Reported Corp. William W. Branson to the Col. with a request that he be reduced to the ranks for drunkenness. The Adjutant and myself wrote a petition to Gov. Austin for the removal of Lieut. Col. H. B. Burnham. Signed a request for Lieut. Col. to resign.

———

January 14, 1863 (Diary)
Annapolis, Md.

Weather as on yesterday. Corp. Branson was reduced to the ranks for Order No. 4, read on Dress Parade. In the evening at 8 o'clock attended the wedding ceremony of Lieut. McCabe at the Catholic Church, followed by a grand entertainment at St. John's College.

———

January 15, 1863 (Diary)
Annapolis, Md.

    Officer of the Day. Cloudy all day. Commenced raining about midnight. Went with Col. Staunton the Adj't & Lieut. Borchers[3] to Dunker's Metropolitan Hotel at night and feasted on steamed oysters.

January 16, 1863 (Diary)
Annapolis, Md.

    Clear and cold. Very windy in the afternoon and evening. Major White and Mr. Huston arrived here from Harrisburg.

January 17, 1863 (Diary)
Annapolis, Md.

    Clear, windy and cold. Major White and Mr. Huston took the morning train on their return to Harrisburg. Sergeant Gay on leave of absence. Paid a visit to his old Quarter on the A & E R.R.

January 18, 1863 (Diary)
Annapolis, Md.

    Cool and windy. Lieut. Weeks from Parole Camp paid me a visit. Spent most of the time reading "What will he do with it" by Edward Bullware [*sic*] Lytton.[4]

January 19, 1863 (Diary)
Annapolis, Md.

    Cloudy and windy. Occupied my spare time in making out vouchers for Ordnance and Ordnance Stores to Lieut. George W. Simpson.

January 20, 1863 (Diary)
Annapolis, Md.

    Cloudy. Commenced raining about 9 o'clock. P. M. Was Officer of the Day. Drew my Quarter's clothing and issued a portion of it.

January 21, 1863 (Diary)

Annapolis, Md.

Rainy all day, with much heavy wind. Blew many of the tents over. Weather so bad could not issue clothing. Read "What will he do with it." An excellent work.

January 24, 1863

Annapolis, Md.

DEAREST LILLIE:–

Our Regiment was paid yesterday up to October 31st. I enclose herewith a $50 note, with a request that you come down here next week. Write to me the day before you start, stating the day you leave West Chester [so] that I may know when to expect you. Will meet you at Annapolis Junction if I find it possible to leave here. Come prepared to stay at least two weeks. I scarcely know what to say about bringing Gibbie. Should most ardently enjoy seeing him. He will be quite a burden to you in traveling, and there is some diphtheria here. I do not know whether the maternal relations between you and him would enable you to leave him or not. *Do as you think best.*

I advise you to leave West Chester in the *morning* for Philadelphia. The Thirteenth Street cars will take you to the Baltimore Depot. Buy a ticket for Baltimore and take the train leaving between 11 & 12 o'clock A. M. Before reaching B.[altimore] an agent will take your check and deliver your baggage at the Baltimore & Washington depot for 25 cts. Arriving at Baltimore, you remain in the cars and they will be drawn through the city to the other depot by horses,—for which city ride you must pay 25 cts. more. Arriving at the depot, buy a ticket for Annapolis.

Change cars at Annapolis Junction—about 19 miles from Baltimore. Here I will meet you if possible. If I am not there, you will take the Annapolis train standing in readiness for you and arrive here about dark.

Robert

January 28, 1863 (Diary)

Annapolis, Md.

Snow and rain all day. Worked nearly all night at my Quarterly returns of Clothing, Camp & Garrison Equippage.

January 29, 1863 (Diary)

Annapolis, Md.

Snow and wind all day. Parole Guard relieved. Sent by Lieut. Dutton[5] $35 to Epstein, Philadelphia.[6]

January 30, 1863 (Diary)

Annapolis, Md.

Muddy but not stormy. Received a letter from Lillie stating her intention to start for this place on Monday [three days hence]. Telegraphed her not to come. Sent her a letter & $50. [Letter not in collection.—T.M.B.]. Officer of the day.

January 31, 1863 (Diary)

Annapolis, Md.

Muddy but clear. Review and Inspection. A very long line. Wrote a letter to sister Isabella.[7] Bought a Haversack and Skeleton Knapsack for $5. Sold Company savings to amt. $17.15.

February 1, 1863 (Diary)

Annapolis, Md.

Cold and windy. Packed my clothing boxes preparatory to leaving.

February 2, 1863 (Diary)

Annapolis, Md.

Colder, some snow. Battalion drill. Finished packing my effects. Paid Dunker $4 in full for board.

February 3, 1863 (Diary)

Annapolis, Md.

Very cold and windy. Transportation for our Reg't. arrived. Loaded my effects on the cars. Reg't. Marched to the cars about 6 P. M. Train started about 8 o'clock. Arrived at the Junction about midnight. Ride very tedious.

February 4, 1863 (Diary)

Bolivar, Va.

Arrived Harpers Ferry about 2 P. M. Marched to Bolivar Heights, crossing the Potomac on a pontoon bridge. Marched back to the town of Bolivar and quartered our companies in vacated buildings. Procured entertainment for myself at Mr. Fossett's (Union).

February 5, 1863 (Diary)

Bolivar, Va.

Snow. Men bucked [cut] wood for their quarters. Slept on a feather bed in a house for the first time since leaving West Chester. Mrs. Fossett gave me a graphic description of the occurrences in their village since the breaking out of the war.

February 6, 1863 (Diary)

Bolivar, Va.

Sloppy. Still quartered with my two Lieutenants at Mrs. Fossett's. Wrote to Lillie.

February 6, 1863

Bolivar Heights near Harpers Ferry, Va.

DEAR LILLIE,

You see we have left Annapolis. Contrary to expectation, we did not get off until Tuesday evening [February 3]. On Monday evening I went to the Depot to see if you had come, for I did not know but I almost hoped that my telegraphic dispatch had not reached you. I did want to see you so much, even though it was but for a few hours. I suppose you did not receive my letter containing the $50 and apprising you of our departure before Monday afternoon.

Tuesday was a bitter cold day and the night was still colder. We had a tedious ride to this place, not arriving here until Wednesday at 2 o'clock P. M. Our Regiment made a splendid show, and when marching through Harpers Ferry with our band at the head elicited much praise and applause. Arriving here the weather was intensely cold, and Gen. Kelly [*sic*][8] had no inclination of our coming, so that no preparations were made for our accommodation. We marched to Bolivar Heights and then back to the town of Bolivar, where they stowed our troops away in buildings that had been vacated by the owners. Two doors below where my Company is quartered I found a private family (apparently *Union*) who agreed to accommodate myself and two Lieutenants. Here I am still awaiting orders. We have to send the men out two miles to the mountains, snow two feet deep, to buck wood for their fires. Our Company property I have unloaded from the cars and stowed away in a ware house down at the Ferry. What will be done with our Regiment I can not tell. Some talk of sending us on to Winchester [Virginia]. So undecided is the matter that I dare not ask you to come here for the present.

Mary Young and her father are here. The father came on to Annapolis the day we left and brought her over on the passenger train. She is not well, and I cannot think that she will live long.

Harpers Ferry, as well as Bolivar, is a very dilapidated town. There has been so much fighting here that most of the inhabitants have left for either the North or South and every house so left, and some of them very fine ones, have been torn till there is no wood about them, nothing but the bare brick walls. Many of the buildings have been shot through and through with shell or shot.

The mountain scenery is magnificent. The way of access here is easy. You can come all the way by rail.

My love to all,

Your own,

Robert

February 7, 1863 (Diary)

Bolivar, Va.

Muddy. Dress Parade for the first time since arriving at Bolivar. Long line in Bolivar Heights. Hill strewn with dead horses.

February 8, 1863 (Diary)

Bolivar, Va.

Still very muddy. Still dress parade, on dead horse hill! Promoted Corp. Schofield and Corp. Gilbert to Sergeants and James Davidson, John Adams, Saml. Irwin and Saml. Clawson to Corporals.

February 9, 1863 (Diary)

Bolivar, Va.

Muddy. Visited Jefferson's Rock. Found it literally covered with names. Did not inscribe my own. Scenery magnificent from that point.

February 10, 1863 (Diary)

Bolivar, Va.

Very muddy. No Dress Parade.

February 11, 1863 (Diary)

Bolivar, Va.

Very muddy. Some snow. No Dress Parade.

February 12, 1863 (Diary)

Bolivar, Va.

Muddy. Very. Officer of the Day. Ball at the Ferry in the evening. Did not attend. Went to bed at 5 1/2 A. M. on the following day. No Dress Parade.

February 13, 1863 (Diary)

Bolivar, Va.

Extremely muddy. Had my boots half-soled by a Dutchman up town. Price $1.00. Dress Parade. Received a letter from Lillie.

[There are no further letters from Cornwell until April 23 and no diary entries until June 3. This may be due to the fact, as the April 23 letter suggests, that Lillie came to visit Robert in camp at Bolivar for awhile during this time.—T.M.B.]

April 23, 1863

Berryville, Va.

DEAREST LILLIE,

I have almost forgotten when I wrote you last and whether I have received a letter from you since or not. This however matters little. I am tired of writing on "Clothing Receipt Rolls," so I will divert my mind with a scribble to you.

Allow me to commence with a question. What has become of the two letters I left with you the evening I was so hurried away from Harpers Ferry and you to go to Winchester? I have succeeded in bringing him back to the Company and he wants the letters, asserting that there was $5 in one of them.[9] Did you take them home with you? If so, send them to me. If you have lost them it matters very little, for under the circumstances I am not responsible for them.

I sent three hundred dollars with adjutant Young to Philadelphia yesterday, to be forewarded [*sic*] from there to you by Adams Express.[10] We were paid last Monday and I sent with the adjutant from our Company to Pennsylvania over three thousand dollars. Some was sent in other ways. The Adjutant left here for the "Keystone"[11] with about twenty-five thousand dollars to be delivered to the friends of the soldiers. Will you send $60 to Oliver Young, Port Jervis, Orange County, N.[ew] York.[12] Present my regrets that I was unable to return the money before, and thank him for the indulgence he has extended to me. I will send about $25 to Mr. Westlake from here.

The health of my Company does not improve. I have nine men down with Typhoid fever. Samuel D. Peterson from Indiana County, a fine fellow, very low. I think he cannot get well. John Ferrier, James Davidson, the college graduate, William Graham, Robert Adams, James R. Adams and Isaac Walker, all from Indiana County, very low. I almost despair for the lives of most of them. The rest are not so bad. Two gentlemen friends of Wm. J. Robb from Pa. are here after his body. I think I told you about his death. My own health is good. We have a great deal of wet weather here which renders the tents damp and cold all the time. I hope that when the weather settles, the health of the camp will improve.

A part of a Company from our Brigade crossed the river two nights ago and captured Capt. Leopold and seven of his men. They were brought here and put in the guard house and sent this morning to Winchester. They are not soldiers, but a set of *highway robbers* and ought to be hung without scruple or sympathy. They favor the secessionists but disclaim belonging to either army. Upon being asked where they obtained provisions, Capt. Leopold answered, "We draw rations neither from the North or South. We commute [obtain] our own rations." When asked what kind of game they shot he answered, "We shoot no game smaller than Yankees." Capt. L. is from Baltimore and says he was part of a mob that attacked the Massachusetts 6th on the 19th of April 2 years ago.[13] He says he seceded before Virginia did. Most of his men are from Baltimore. They inhabit the mountains of this region as the barbarous hordes used to infest Italy. Capt. L. says it was his party that killed and wounded the pickets I told you about in my last. He says it was his party that attacked our pickets at Halltown[14] and that they were then on their way to Sheppardstown in Maryland, a secession hole. Where they go to have a good time with their friends and to get all the news from the North and take it South. They put on a great deal of bravado. They have taken prisoners he says three or four times and been paroled again, when they return and begin to shoot pickets. He says they never attack infantry but always Cavalry, to get the horses. I do trust they will now be hung and not released again. If they are, I am decidedly in favor of shooting them down next time and not making prisoners of them.

Hope you are all well. Would like very much to visit you. How is Gibbie, Grandfather, Mother and Sallie? Give them my love. I am not messing in Camp. Tell Mother she ought to see us sit down to our meals spread on a big clothing box. We live very well and have detailed a pretty good cook from the Company.

I think of you much. You are cherished much by your own fond,

Robert

P.S. The letters referred to were directed to Theophilus Carr, Co. "J" 67 P.V.

P.S. No. 2. Please send me some postage stamps for I can't get any here.

R.T.C.

═══════════

May 10, 1863
Camp 67th Pa. Vols.
Berryville, Va.
DEAREST LILLIE,

Your sweet letter is at hand, arrived this afternoon. Am satisfied to know that you are all well. Gibbie's accident was startling because it might have been so much worse. I hope he will not be disfigured by it. His welfare like our own is in the hands of Providence, and truly He has been merciful to us.

The weather is much more pleasant then heretofore and the ground is becoming settled. Not so much so here however, the Adjutant says, as with you. James Davidson, that most estimable young man I was telling you of, is dead. He died on the evening of the 30th ult.[Ultimo, i.e., date]. I miss him much. The rest of our sick are getting much better except Elias Sides from Indiana Co.[unty], who I do not think can live much longer. We could not send Davidson's body home because decomposition set in too rapidly. The body could not have been taken out of the coffin after carting it over a rough road to Harpers Ferry, and then waiting there till a metallic coffin could have been obtained from Baltimore.

Last Wednesday [May 6] evening Col. Staunton in command of five Companies (450 men) from our own Regiment, 2 Companies of New York Cavalry from the New York 1st [regiment] and one section[15] of Artillery, crossed the Shenandoah River and made an effort to capture Major Moseby's [sic] Cavalry which was infesting the country down in Loudoun County near Upperville, about 21 miles from here.

We started from camp about 9 o'clock at night. It was then raining smartly and had been raining heavily for nearly twenty-four hours before. The roads were very bad, in some places we had to wade through the water over boot top. We marched to Snicker's Ferry—six miles, the Cavalry and artillery ahead. Arriving we found but one flat boat, which had to be poled over and the current was so strong and the river so high from recent rains that the boat would drift down stream about a quarter of a mile every time we crossed. I had command of the first Company on the right of our Battalion, composed of 45 of my own men and 45 of Company "A."

I crossed first with 50 men, but so slow and fatiguing was the process, the night so dark, and the weather so unpleasant, that all the Infantry did not get over until after daylight. The Artillery did not go with us any further but remained at the ferry to cover our retreat should a retreat be necessary. We left one Company of Infantry in the Gap of the mountains on the other side of the river, to guard the boat and prevent our being surprised by an ambuscade.

The Cavalry had not yet crossed and we went on without them and reached Snickersville, about 4 miles from the ferry, by 8 o'clock in the morning. Here we stopped to rest and ate some breakfast from our haversacks. We then started on and after marching about two miles came suddenly on a squad of about 6 cavalry men who were at the time dismounted. A few of them succeeded in reaching their horses and making their escape. I sent out one section[16] of my Company as skirmishers in pursuit of the rest, and so hotly did they pursue and sharp did they fire on them that two of the rebels threw up their hats, handed over their arms, and gave themselves up as prisoners. I then stationed pickets over the eminences with a part of my Company, and placed a chain on sentinels around a house and barn in the vicinity and instituted a thorough search of the whole premises, but could find no more [Confederate soldiers].

The rest of the Battalion remained in line, as there we had no use for more than one Company. We then started for Bloomfield, about 3 miles distant. Just as we were starting for that place, sixteen of our Cavalry came up with us, stating that it was so slow a process to get them over the river that Col. McReynolds had concluded not to wait to send any more. The 16 Cavalry went on ahead of us, scouring the country. We reached Bloomfield about 1 o'clock P. M. Here we ate dinner from our haversacks, fed the horses, and started on for Upperville. We then had about 6 miles to go. The Cavalry was ahead of us and my Company [was] at the head of our Column, for we were marching by the right flank. When within about 2 1/2 miles of Upperville I suddenly heard sharp firing ahead and almost at the same moment saw our cavalry retreating back to us at the top of their speed, closely pursued by the rebels [unclear] Moseby.

The Col. was by my side at the head of the Column at the moment we saw our cavalry coming about 400 yds. ahead. We were between two fences, woods on one side and a small field on the other. The Col. ordered me to throw down the fence on our right and turn the head of the Column into the field. I did so immediately, moved off into the field until he ordered me to halt, then I fronted and dressed[17] my Company. Our own Cavalry were then galloping down the road near us at the top of their speed. It was difficult to tell the rebel Cavalry from our own, for two of them [Confederates] had blue coats on like our own. Nor could I tell certainly until the rebels saw our line and turned to flee.

The Col. then told me to fire on them and my Company immediately did so, killing one of the three who were in advance and wounding another. The remainder of the rebels we could not hit, for they were considerable distance off and could only be indistinctly seen through the woods. Unfortunately, at this juncture the left of the battalion which was not yet in line and were in a state of momentary confusion, taking our own Cavalry for the enemy and killing one and wounding three others slightly. Also wounding in the face quite seriously a man in Company "E" who was just crossing the fence at the time. This event is very much deplored by the Regiment and will doubtless injure us. It made me feel sick at the time to think of it. Where the blame is mainly chargeable, I will not attempt to say. The matter will probably be investigated.

We then proceeded to Upperville, on all sides of which place on top of the hills we could see rebels. We threw out pickets, and wet and weary we availed ourselves of such accommodations as the village would afford. That night we were called out in line of battle twice in consequence of alarms. The next morning three men under Lieut. Hubble[18] from our Regt.

shot another rebel. We then started back to Snickers Ferry, capturing on the way 21 horses and one prisoner. We did not reach the ferry until after dark and slept on the ground, it raining on us all night. The next morning we crossed the river and reached our Camp about 1 o'clock P. M. I do not think that the Scout has injured my health or that of the men materially. I did not even catch cold.

Lieut. Weeks of my Company is now sick with Typhoid Fever, though not seriously ill as yet.

Neither of my Lieut.'s was with me on the Scout. Lieut. Simpson being on picket at the time and Lieut. Weeks sick.

Give my love to all our friends and may God protect you.

Fondly your own,

Robert

May 19th, 1863

Berryville, Va.

DEAREST LILLIE

Yours of the 13th inst. has just been received and welcomely. In it you state that you have not heard from me for some time. You could not at the time of writing have received mine of the 10th inst., in which I gave you an account of our Scout into Loudoun and Fauquier Counties. I returned last evening from another similar trip, starting the previous day from hereabout noon and marching about 42 miles.

Took five prisoners but had no engagement. The rebel cavalry avoid the infantry and will not fight them if they can avoid it. On the night of the 17th inst. the rebel cavalry took a company of Union Cavalry stationed at Charles Town prisoners. A detachment of the New York 1st [cavalry] from this place pursued them across the river and after a chase of about 30 miles overtook them, took back our prisoners, killed several of the enemy, and took ten prisoners of the enemy.

Elias Sides of my Company from Indiana County died of Typhoid fever since I last wrote you. I am glad to say that I have no others that are now considered dangerous.

I am very glad to know that you are all well.

Lovingly your own

Robert

June 3, 1863 (Diary)
Berryville, Va.
> Detailed on Court Martial. Harry White Tresselant. Not well.

June 4, 1863 (Diary)
Berryville, Va.
> Obliged to leave Court Martial and went to Mrs. Sheppard's and went to bed with Typhoid Fever.

June 5, 1863 (Diary)
Berryville, Va.
> Sick a [*sic*] bed.
> ["Sick" is the only entry for each of the next eight days.—T.M.B.]

June 5th/63
Berryville, Va.
DEAREST LILLIE,
> I have been sick for about two weeks with fever & ague. The doctor has now succeeded in breaking the chills and I am much better. I am living at a private house with as fine a family as lives anywhere. My every want is anticipated. Do not harass your mind.
> Truly your own fond
> Robert

June 13, 1863 (Diary)
Berryville, Va.
> Sick. Ewel's [*sic*] division came into Berryville. Our men retreated to Winchester, harassed all the way by the enemy. I was taken prisoner and paroled together with all those in the hospital.

June 14, 1863 (Diary)
Berryville, Va.
> Heard heavy firing at Winchester. Milroy would not surrender though he had but 7,000 against 37,000.

June 15, 1863 (Diary)
Berryville, Va.

Fighting still continues at Winchester. Col. S.[taunton] leaves the field. Lt. Col. B.[19] led the reg't and was killed. Capt. Arndt,[20] Capt. Truck[21] and Dr. Barr killed. Dr. Corson wounded. Maj. White led the Reg't nobly but was obliged to surrender it.

June 16, 1863 (Diary)
Berryville, Va.

Sick at Berryville. Heard all sorts of stories about the fight. None reliable.

June 17, 1863 (Diary)
Berryville, Va.

Sick at B—.

June 18, 1863 (Diary)
Berryville, Va.

Sick at B—but begin to get better.

June 19, 1863 (Diary)
Berryville, Va.

Still improving, but slowly.

June 20, 1863 (Diary)
Berryville, Va.

Started with the boys and women from our regiment with our parole and a flag of truce for Harpers Ferry. I had hired a carriage. Proceeded about 5 m.[iles] and was sent back by some Confederate officers who took us to Winchester. Was placed in Taylor's Hospital with about 250 wounded and sick of Typhoid fever and small Pox. Found Dr. Enler [sp.] 1st ass't. surg. 67 [first assistant surgeon of the 67th Regiment] and James Imes there with about 50 wounded from our Reg't but none from my Company.

June 21, 1863 (Diary)

Winchester, Va.

   About 5 die daily. Fed on half rations of bread and coffee and tea.

June 22, 1863 (Diary)

Winchester, Va.

   Not allowed to go on the street. A family with whom I was acquainted in town sent me nice victuals. Several union ladies, like Angels of Mercy, brought in a great many nice things for our boys to eat.

June 23, 1863 (Diary)

Winchester, Va.

   Some of the guards wanted to stop the ladies from bringing food to our boys and asked them why they didn't take it to Confederate wounded. One of the ladies answered, ["] I am a Union lady, let the numerous Secession ladies in this place attend them ["].

June 24, 1863 (Diary)

Winchester, Va.

   Feel considerably better. Our nurse left for Richmond. Took his place as nurse in our room. Sent a letter to Lillie by way of Richmond. Unsealed.

June 25, 1863 (Diary)

Winchester, Va.

   Still improving. Troubled considerably with diaraeah [*sic*]. James Mckennon badly wounded in our room. Belonged to 110 Ohio [110th Ohio Regiment].

June 26, 1863 (Diary)

Winchester, Va.

   Nothing new except numerous reports of fighting in the [Shenandoah] valley. No dependence to be placed in them.[22]

[There are no letters or diary entries for the period June 27 to July 29, or for July 31, August 2, and August 4.—T.M.B.]

July 30, 1863 (Diary)
Staunton, Va.

Arrived at Staunton and encamped on a hill above the town.

August 1, 1863 (Diary)
Staunton, Va. ?

Took our money from us.

August 3, 1863 (Diary)
Staunton, Va.

Adjutant M'Guire, Maj. Cornell & Adjutant Lee took a French
["French Leave, "i.e., unauthorized leave] with two of the Doctors
starting in the evening.

August 5, 1863 (Diary)
Staunton, Va.

Took box cars about 10 A. M. and started for Richmond.

August 6, 1863 (Diary)
Richmond, Va.

Arrived in Richmond about 5 o'clock A. M. About 8 A. M. marched
to Libby Prison. Took away our Canteens and Haversacks and searched us
very closely for money. Then sent us to our rooms.

August 7, 1863 (Diary)
Libby Prison, Richmond, Va.

Wrote to Lillie. [Letter not in the collection.—T.M.B.]

3

Libby Prison: A Fresh Fish
August 31, 1863–January 31, 1864

Following his capture at Winchester, Robert Cornwell spent the next nine months as a prisoner of war at Libby Prison in Richmond. Libby earned the notoriety of being one of the worst of the one hundred fifty various Civil War prisons, and Cornwell was there at the height of its overcrowding.

Libby, probably more than any other Southern prison, was well known in the North during the war. There were two reasons for this: the prisoners were officers and the prison was located in the enemy's capitol city. This made it a perfect subject for Northern newspapers and magazines, and Libby coverage was frequent, if not always accurate. In fact, as bad as conditions were in Libby, the prisoners there lived under relatively far better conditions than those prevailing at many other Civil War prisons in either section of the country.

To this day there is a continuing bias regarding Civil War military prisons. It is generally assumed that conditions at prison camps in the North were tolerable, and that Confederate prisoners were supplied with adequate shelter and basic necessities. After all, the North had unlimited land in secure areas to locate prison camps and unlimited resources and transportation to provide for Confederate prisoners. By contrast, the reputation of military prisons in the South is that they were all Andersonvilles.

Camp Sumter, the proper name for Andersonville, was indeed a horrific prison; 13,000 Union prisoners died in the fourteen months of the prison's existence. Since the Civil War, its deservedly bad reputation has been the ongoing subject of a number of scholarly and popular books and even a recent television film. Less, however, has been said about prison camps in the North, even though condition in those camps was no better. For example, during the one year of its existence, the camp at Elmira, New York, 25 percent or more of the 12,123 Confederate prisoners died. That is an average of more than eight prisoner deaths each day.[1] Conditions throughout Elmira were terrible, not the least of which was the diet. John Brusnan, a Confederate soldier described the food ration: "For breakfast I get one-third of a pound of bread and a small piece of meat; for supper the same quantity of bread and not any meat, but a small plate of warm water called soup."[2]

With certain exceptions, determined principally by the abilities and conscientiousness of the commandants, there was not a great deal of difference between the conditions in Northern or Southern prison camps. The stories related by hapless prisoners in either army had virtually identical themes: extreme hunger, lack of clothing and shelter, untreated illness and brutal guards. Richard H. Dibbrell, a Richmond merchant and member of the "Ambulance Committee," made this observation about Confederate prisoners released from the Union prison at Savannah. "They were so enfeebled and emaciated that we lifted them like little children....The clothing of the privates was in a wretched state of tatters and filth."[3]

Indeed, most soldiers who were in any prisoner of war camp endured a vile existence. If they were fortunate, they survived the experience, although often broken in health. Had they the opportunity to discuss the subject, Union and Confederate prisoners would have found much in common with their experiences in the prison camps.

To appreciate Cornwell's account of prison life it will be helpful to have a general understanding of Civil War prisons. According to an informed postwar estimate, 193,743 Union and about 214,865 Confederate soldiers were imprisoned during the Civil War. Of these, about 12 percent of Confederate prisoners died in Northern prisons and 15.5 percent of Union prisoners died in Southern prisons.[4] Almost all the deaths were due to non-battle-related disease or complications from disease. The figures appear high, but are not substantially greater than the typical rates of death from disease in either army.

One of the sad facts about mortality in Civil War armies is that more men died of disease than from battlefield wounds. The diseases resulting in the highest mortality were typhoid fever, typhus, malaria, pneumonia, smallpox, measles, and consumption. In the Union army, 110,100 men died from battlefield wounds, but there were 126,180 deaths from disease.[5] In Cornwell's own regiment almost twice as many men (158) died from disease as from deaths and mortal wounds (79) on the battlefield.[6] There are no accurate figures for the Confederate army, but one authoritative estimate states that for every Southern soldier who died from battle injuries, three or more died from disease.[7] Given the abundance of food, medical supplies and all the other resources in the North, and the lack of same in the South, the similarity of prisoner of war death rates is surprising.

Some of the poor reputation of the prisons can be blamed upon a combination of self-serving books written by former prisoners, as well as the propaganda efforts of both sides to portray the enemy as inhumane. This was particularly so in the North,[8] where exchanged prisoners found a ready market for their tales. Horror stories abounded, featuring the worst examples of mistreatment, lack of food, and the like. Rarely were good conditions or humane treatment mentioned.

Part of the problem stemmed from the fact that at the beginning of the war military prisons and prison administration systems were rudimentary in the North and nonexistent in the South. Both sides initially thought it would be a short war followed by a speedy cessation of hostilities. Neither, therefore, was much concerned with the possibility of having to shelter and care for large numbers of prisoners for extended periods.

Even as the scope of the war widened, both sides assumed that a system of parole and exchange would be used much as it had fifty years earlier during the War of 1812. Under that system, enemy prisoners would be fed and housed for a few days at most, then released on parole to their own army. Indeed, in July 1861 the first Union prisoners arrived in Richmond, and after pledging on honor to remain prisoners at large, they were allowed to roam freely through the city.

However, the number of prisoners taken by both sides quickly grew to the point where an attempt was made to establish an official exchange program. At first, the North refused to enter into discussions, believing that to do so was tantamount to recognizing the Confederacy as a sovereign nation rather than a section in rebellion. However, in July 1862 General John A. Dix of the North and General D. H. Hill of the South agreed to an exchange cartel patterned upon that used between the United States and Britain in the War of 1812. Under its terms, all prisoners were to be paroled and returned to their own lines within ten days of capture.

Once returned, paroled prisoners were required to stay in special parole camps, guarded by their own men. While there, they were prohibited from participating in all military activities until formally exchanged. When similar amounts of parolees accumulated on each side, they were to be exchanged for enemy soldiers of equal rank. For example, a major was worth a major on the other side, and a private was worth a private.

Because of the imbalance in the numbers of officers and privates, an equivalency schedule was designed to facilitate exchanges. Under its terms, a commanding general was worth sixty privates; a colonel, fifteen privates; a captain, six privates; and a second lieutenant, three privates. Noncommissioned officers were worth two privates. A private was only worth another private. Excess prisoners who could not be accommodated had to wait until the next exchange.[9]

One immediate flaw in the cartel's plan was that it required each side to construct and maintain parole camps for their own men. Not only did an army temporarily lose the use of their parolees as active soldiers, they also had to build parole camps and assign unencumbered men to guard them. As Cornwell noted earlier in his letter of October 6, 1862, discipline among the parolees on both sides was notoriously poor, and they were often the source of much petty crime in nearby civilian areas.

Although there was much bickering between officials on both sides, the prisoner exchange program continued in operation until December 23, 1862, when politics again intruded into the process. That day, President Jefferson Davis issued a proclamation declaring Union Maj. Gen. Benjamin F. Butler (1818–1893) an outlaw for executing a New Orleans civilian named William B. Mumford. The situation regarding Butler had been simmering in the South since he captured the city of New Orleans on May 1.

At age forty-four, Butler was a bald, squat, goggle-eyed, former Massachusetts lawyer and politician. He had been a brigadier general in the Massachusetts militia, and used his political connections to obtain a major generalship in the volunteers. Interestingly, he had been a delegate to the 1860 Democratic Party convention in Charleston, where he voted fifty-seven times in succession to nominate Jefferson Davis as the party's presidential candidate.[10]

Butler's problems began with his arrival in New Orleans after he occupied the city on May 1, 1862. Although Butler had some talent as an administrator, he seemed genuinely amazed by the less than friendly welcome accorded to his troops by the residents of the city. Ladies snubbed the occupying Union soldiers, refusing to talk to them, leaving churches if they entered, and crossing the street to avoid having to pass near them. The situation worsened when a lady poured the contents of a chamber pot on the head of Admiral David Farragut (she claimed she did not see him passing under her window), and another spat in the face of two Union officers. In response, Butler issued his infamous "Woman Order." It said that any woman who insulted or acted contemptuously toward a Union soldier would be regarded as a common prostitute.

The entire South reacted in fury when Butler's order was published, and criticism of Butler's insensitivity even came from as far away as England. Lord Palmerston, the prime minister, stood in the House of Commons and said, "An Englishman must blush to think that such an act has been committed by one belonging to the Anglo-Saxon race."

Butler's heavy handedness came into play again on May 10, when he seized $800,000 from the Dutch consulate in New Orleans. He claimed the consulate was going to spend the money on war supplies for the Confederacy. The general also earned the sobriquet of "Spoons," for allegedly stealing large quantities of silverware from helpless citizens. On June 7 Butler hanged Mumford, the act that caused Davis to brand Butler an outlaw. Mumford's crime was that two months earlier he pulled down the United States flag that flew over the New Orleans Mint.

Davis further ordered that until Butler was captured and hanged, no captured Union officers would be exchanged. On May 1, 1863, the Confederate Congress also ordered that captured Negro troops were to be returned to the Southern states where they were captured. White Union officers commanding Negroes were to be put to death or otherwise punished. With these actions, the exchange of officers effectively ceased in May, although enlisted prisoners continued to be exchanged.

In July, the Union army won key victories at Gettysburg, Vicksburg, and Port Hudson, taking some 41,150 Confederate prisoners in the process.[11] Those losses greatly weakened the Southern army, and combined with the ongoing argument between the exchange agents led the North to halt all prisoner exchanges. Although a compromise worked out in March 1864, allowed captured Negro prisoners who had been free before the war to be treated as bona fide prisoners of war, Ulysses S. Grant, the overall commander of the Union army, privately discouraged further exchanges of any prisoners. He reasoned that exchanged Confederates would return to their units and fight again, whereas if they were kept as prisoners the Confederate army would be further weakened, thus shortening the war.

Rather than reveal this plan directly, Union negotiators obfuscated it by demanding that talks focus upon one-for-one exchanges that also included captured ex-slaves. Grant certainly understood this tactic would doom Union prisoners to the rigors of longer captivity, and that some would die needlessly as a result.

Richmond's role as a major prisoner of war center was not intended. Before the war, the city was the capitol of Virginia and a large commercial and industrial center in its own right. Its population of 38,000 was well served by a network of highways and railroads, and they enjoyed such modern conveniences as pipelines for natural gas and water. However, the city's population exploded with the outbreak of the war, as thousands flocked there to work in government offices or the war industry.

In the early days of the war, Richmond was an ideal location to temporarily hold captured soldiers. The city was close to the battlefields, and its transportation network could be used to receive and deliver prisoners. At that point, little thought was given to the possibility that the city might one day become the long-term jailer for thousands of prisoners. Soon, however, more and more prisoners and civilians soon began streaming into Richmond, and by the middle of 1861 the city's population had tripled. With that influx came an increase in petty crime, accompanied by severe shortages of food and goods of all kind, and steadily rising prices for everything.

To combat the growing problem, John H. Winder (1800–1865, pronounced "wine-der") was appointed as provost marshal of Richmond. Winder, a Marylander, was a graduate of West Point and a career soldier who served in the Seminole and Mexican wars. He was still on active duty when he resigned his U.S. Army commission in April 1861 to accept a brigadier generalcy in the Confederate army.

Winder imposed a strict martial law in Richmond. It was very effective, and probably necessary, but gained him the immediate and lasting hatred of its citizens. One of his first tasks was to reorganize the city's jumbled prison system. At the time, the Henrico County Jail contained an increasing number of civilian prisoners and McDaniel's Negro Jail (soon renamed Castle Godwin) housed both civilian and Confederate military prisoners. Union military prisoners of war were kept at Harwood's Tobacco Factory.[12] However, the number of prisoners, particularly captured Union soldiers, was increasing rapidly and more space was needed. Winder impressed the use of Ligon's Warehouse and Tobacco Factory, and they soon housed six hundred Union prisoners of all ranks.

After observing the results of overcrowding in the military prisons, Winder concluded that escape attempts would be reduced if officers and civilians were separated from enlisted men. The next day, Howard's Factory was appropriated for the exclusive use of officers and civilians. There, the prisoners were allowed to purchase food and other items from outside vendors, and were supplied with some furniture and utensils.

The beginning of the exchange program slightly reduced the number of prisoners. However, by late October about 2,000 were still in Richmond and the number began to increase early in 1862. More space was needed for the new prisoners. One day in March the government gave forty-eight hours' notice to the owners before commandeering their large warehouse called Libby and Son, Ship Chandlers and Grocers.

Located at the corner of Cary and Twentieth Streets, the three-story, three-hundred-foot-long building was originally used as a tobacco warehouse. Its brick walls and tin roof gave it the appearance of being one large structure, but it was actually three identical interconnecting buildings, each with its own entrance. Major Isaac H. Carrington of the Confederate army inspected the prison and described it in a November 18, 1863, report:

> In the Libby Prison there are eight large rooms occupied by the prisoners, of which one is used as a hospital. These rooms are 103 by 42 feet. There is a water-closet [enclosed toilet] on each floor.[13] There is an ample supply of water on each floor, and there is also facility afforded for bathing....The officers are allowed to purchase such articles as they wish, ...a competent person is employed whose sole business it is to make these purchases.[14]

The height of the ceiling of the middle floor was about eight feet. The bottom floor's ceiling height was somewhat lower, and because of the pitch of the roof, the top floor was the most spacious. The washrooms were supplied with running water by pipes hooked into the water main, and the enclosed toilets were troughs built into closets.

The back wall of the prison was on a narrow lane called Dock Street. Immediately next to it was the Kanawha Canal, a prime commercial waterway for the city of Richmond. The James River ran parallel to the canal. A view of Richmond from within Libby was described by Lt. Col. Cavada:

> I look out the window on the James river. Immediately below is the [Kanawha] canal; beyond it flows the [James] river, with a rapid, murmuring current, reflecting here and there the purple flush of the morning clouds; there is a cluster of tall factories on the opposite bank; beyond these is the village of Manchester on one side, and on the other are broad fields, and the rolling hills which fringe a distant curve of the river. Looking up-stream, there is a lovely little island, three long white bridges which span the stream, half concealed by the thick foliage, and beyond these, a full mile off, is Belle Isle, with some white tents crowning an eminence....
>
> I pass to another window: this one looks down upon the street. Yonder building, with the barred windows, I am told is "Castle Thunder," and on the opposite side of the street may be seen the gable end of another prison, known by the significant title of the "Cage." Nearer is an antiquated Meeting House; then comes a negro shanty, a stable, a church, an empty lot, and a large warehouse

used as a convalescent hospital for Confederate soldiers; place behind these some rows of brick dwellings, by way of a horizon, and a pretty correct idea may be formed of what we are destined to behold every day during our sojourn here. This, with the group of tents, the headquarters of the guard, at the opposite corner of the street, and a row of sentries pacing up and down on the pavement below, is all that the windows of Libby offer in the way of an immediate prospect.[15]

The prison was run by a small staff. In overall command was twenty-three-year-old Thomas Pratt Turner. A Virginian, Turner had attended Virginia Military Institute but left after a year to obtain a lieutenant's commission in a state regiment. He had the unenviable responsibility for keeping thousands of men secure within Libby while at the same time trying to provide for them with the ever-diminishing supplies of the Confederacy. Those who took the trouble to know him, and there were not many among the prison population who did so, generally considered Turner to be a humane officer who did his best for the prisoners.

Richard R. Turner was the prison warden. Universally called "Dick" Turner, he was a former overseer, prison jailer, and private in the Confederate army. In contrast to Thomas Turner, to whom he was not related, Dick Turner was a large, powerful man with a ferocious temper. The two Turners were often confused in some of the later accounts that were written by Libby prisoners.

The prison registrar was twenty-one-year-old Erasmus Ross, despised by the prisoners because of his abusive personality. Ross had to enter the prison every day to take roll call, and he did so armed with two revolvers, a Bowie knife, and accompanied by two armed guards.

Dr. Edgar G. Higginbotham was chief surgeon, and Jackson Warner was in charge of providing the prisoners with the same rations supplied to soldiers in the Confederate army. Both men were regarded sympathetically by the prisoners for attempting to do their best under extremely difficult conditions.

At first, Libby accommodated both enlisted and officer Union prisoners, as well as Southern political detainees. At that time, the first floor also contained the offices for Richmond's military prison system and barracks for about sixty guards. Within three days of its opening it held more than seven hundred military and political prisoners. This overcrowding was alleviated in May, when the political prisoners were transferred to Castle Godwin and the military prisoners were either transferred to other prisons in Richmond or were exchanged. For most of that summer, Libby became a military hospital.

Richmond by now was dotted with prison buildings, mostly in the form of hastily converted warehouses. One of the most famous of these was Castle Thunder, located two blocks from Libby. The Castle was actually a compound of three buildings, a factory and two warehouses, which in total could hold about 1,400 prisoners. Castle Thunder was used primarily to hold political prisoners, deserters from the Confederate army, spies, and civilian malcontents. These prisoners were treated with extreme harshness.

The population of Union prisoners in Richmond ebbed and flowed in 1862. Confederate victories brought in new prisoners by the thousands, but the exchange program returned many of them to their own units within a short time. Some 5,000 new prisoners entered Richmond between August and September, alone, but almost 65 percent of them were exchanged by the end of September.

Meanwhile, Libby had resumed its status as a prison. By the end of December it was overcrowded with a collection of 1,447 Union soldiers, civilian miscreants, and Negroes. Two or three of the prisoners died every day.[16] Fortunately, during the early part of January 1863 most of the prisoners in Richmond were exchanged, including those at Libby. Almost two hundred more soldiers deserted the Union army and took jobs in the city. For a short time following this exchange Richmond enjoyed the luxury of having to care for relatively few military prisoners.

This changed, however, when 1,400 new captives entered the city in early May. These were followed in June by an additional 3,000 men captured in various actions, including the battle at Winchester described in Cornwell's diary. At this point, enlisted prisoners were kept on the first floor of Libby, and officers were on the second and third floors. Later, as the number of captured soldiers greatly increased, the enlisted men were transferred to Belle Isle, and Libby became an officers-only facility.

Not only were there about 1,000 inmates in Libby at this time, but for months the supply of food for the citizens of Richmond had been dwindling. Few could afford to buy what was available because the escalating inflation destroyed the purchasing power of Confederate money.

Except for the wealthy, most residents of the city lived in a condition of near starvation that grew worse with each passing week. On April 2 a civilian mob rioted in the streets for bread, and only skillful handling by President Davis and the City Battalion prevented it from spreading. On July 17 a resident named John Beauchamp Jones wrote in his diary that "we are in a half starving condition. I have lost twenty pounds, and my wife and children are emaciated to some extent."[17]

Jones had achieved some success before the war as an author. With the outbreak of war he and his family moved to Richmond where he took a job in the War Department, serving under all five secretaries of war. He kept an extensive diary that is now famous because of its insider's view of the workings of the Confederate government and the rigors of daily life for middle-class citizens of Richmond. His comments about the ever-dwindling supply of food in Richmond during this same period are a striking counterpoint to the rations provided to the Libby prisoners. A number of Jones's observations are in the endnotes of this book.

In addition to the burgeoning civilian population and the growing number of Union prisoners, government officials also had to provide for some 8,000 patients in Richmond's military hospitals. All these were in a sense competing with the Confederate army, itself on extremely short rations, for an ever-dwindling amount of food, clothing, and firewood. The addition of more Union prisoners of war strained the tottering supply system. Cornwell's arrival at Libby on August 6, 1863, came at the worst possible time.

He was evidently out of communication with Lillie for some time, which prompted her to contact Capt. William L. James, a Union officer to whom she was related. On August 17, James instituted an inquiry through the surprisingly effective prisoner exchange system. James sent the inquiry to Brigadier General Meredith, the Union exchange commissioner. Meredith endorsed the letter and referred it to Robert Ould, his Confederate counterpart. Ould then referred it to Brigadier General Winder, the provost marshal of Richmond. He in turn sent it to Lt. John LaTouche, the adjutant of Libby Prison. LaTouche verified that Cornwell was in Libby, and sent the letter back to General Meredith.

The one letter and its series of endorsements, referrals, and comments made the round trip through Union and Confederate governmental channels in only fourteen days. On August 31 Lillie was sent copies of all the correspondence, which assured her that Robert was indeed a prisoner and "quite well."

Asst. Quartermaster's Office
Fort Monroe, Va.[18] 31st. Aug. 1863.
MRS. LYDIA CORNWELL

Dear Madam,
I have the pleasure of sending you the following copy of correspondence. Trusting it may relieve your anxiety, I remain,

Your Obdt. Servt.
Jno. P. Jefferies

Fort Monroe, Va. 17th Aug. 1863.
Brig. Genl. Meredith[19]
Commissioner for Exchange of Prisoners
Ft. Monroe, Va.

GENERAL,
Capt. Robert Cornwell of the 67th Regt. P.V. is supposed to have been captured at Winchester and taken a prisoner to Richmond; but his family have as yet been unable to learn definitively of his whereabouts. His wife is a relative of mine and has written me to assist in finding him. I will consider it a personal favor if you will endeavor to have inquiry made if he is there and his condition by next "Flag of Truce" boat.

Very Respectfully
Your Obdt. Servt.
Wm. L. James
Capt. & A.Q.M.[20]

P.S. Since writing the above, I have been shown a New York paper in which his name appears as a prisoner in Libby Prison.

Resp.
W.L.J.

OFFICE [of the COMMISSION] for EXCHANGE [of PRISONERS]
Ft. Monroe, 19th Aug. 1863

Respectfully referred to Hon. R. Ould,[21] Comm[issioner] for Exchange.

S.A. Meredith
Brig. Genl. & Comm[issioner] for Exchange

OFFICE [for the] EXCG. [EXCHANGE] of PRISONERS
Richmond, Aug. 21, 1863.

Respectfully referred to Brig. Genl. Winder,[22] Commdg. &c. Official.

R. Ould,
Agent of Exchange

HEADQUARTERS, DEPT. [of] HENRICO [COUNTY]
Richmond, Aug. 25th 1863–

Respectfully referred to Lt. Latouche Comdg. [Commanding] C.S. Prison for a report.

By Order of Genl. Winder
W.S. Winder, A.A.G.[23]

C.S. MILITARY PRISON.
Richmond, Aug. 27/63.

Capt. Cornwell is confined in this prison and is *quite well.*

John Latouche[24]
Lt. Comdg.

OFFICE COMMR. [COMMISSIONER] for EXCH. [EXCHANGE] of PRISONERS
Fort Monroe, Va., Aug. 30Th. 1863.

Respectfully returned to Capt. Wm. L. James, with reference to above endorsement.

S.A. Meredith.
Brig. Genl. & Commr [Commissioner] of Exchange

There are no diary entries or letters from Cornwell until October 4, 1863. However, a close approximation of what his first two months in Libby Prison were like can be extracted from Cavada's *Libby Life: Experiences Of A Prisoner Of War in Richmond, Va. 1863–64.* It seems likely the two men must have a nodding acquaintance. In any event, their experiences, like those of the other officers in Libby at that time, were virtually identical. In addition to its many details of prison life, Cavada's book also has a wry sense of humor, a trait that no doubt made life more bearable within Libby's walls.

The room we are in is low, dingy, gloomy, and suffocating. Some two hundred officers are lying packed in rows along the floor, sleeping the heavy, dreamless sleep of exhaustion. ...We have received permission to purchase provisions outside the prison. We have elected an officer, of the quartermaster's Department, to be our "Commissary-in-Chief." He has divided us into messes of fifteen to twenty, and we are to do our own cooking;...An assistant commissary is elected for each mess: to these the chief commissary issues, and they in turn issue to the cooks....The prison authorities issue meat and rice, of which we will make soup; with the boiled meat from the soup a hash will be made for breakfast next morning. All extras will be at the expense of individuals. Rye Coffee sells at one dollar per pound; sugar three dollars; eggs, two dollars per dozen; butter, four dollars per pound.[25]

The prisoners' daily routine began in the morning, when a Negro nicknamed "The General" came into each room to fumigate it by swinging a brazier of tar and hot coals. This was followed with breakfast, eaten off whatever old plates and utensils could be scraped together. Then Dick Turner conducted the first of the day's two roll calls and those who were sick could go to the hospital. Captain Harry E. Wrigley, a Union army topographical engineer, described the hospital as it was in late 1863 when he was released from Libby:

> The hospital is the best conducted part of the prison. It contains 120 beds—each a straw palliasse—and pillow, sheets, and comfortable [*sic*], on a wooden cot. The fare is a shade better. The surgeons (three in number) are really very skillful men, and do all in their power to alleviate the condition of the sick in their charge. Stimulants of all kinds are difficult to obtain, but are furnished by the Confederates to the fullest extent of their capability.[26]

After the morning roll call, the prisoners went about straightening up their possessions. Those who were so inclined, and not all were, scrubbed their soiled clothing or took a bath. Both activities were performed in Libby's bathtub, a trough-like affair situated under a faucet of running water in an enclosed closet. It was not unusual for three of four men to bathe at the same time. An unwritten rule among the prisoners was that no bathing would take place after 9:00 P.M. so as not to incur the notorious ire of one officer whose sleeping area was near the entrance to the closet.

Richard Turner, the jailer, had the floors scrubbed on a daily basis. This, however, irritated many of the prisoners, who had to move their belongings and scamper out of the way of the washers. They complained that morning washings prevented them from sitting on the floors until late in the day, when the boards dried. Afternoon washings gave rise to complaints that the authorities were trying to cause pneumonia from sleeping on wet floors at night. Similarly, they complained about fresh whitewashing.

> ...[I was disturbed by the] sudden influx into the rooms by a dozen negroes carrying buckets and brooms. I know too well what this portends. It is scrubbing-day...there is no line of escape! Everything, pretty much, that you possess, your bed, your baggage, and your dinner, are on the floor, and that floor, will be in a few moments a tempestuous ocean of splashing, filthy water. There is only one other day, with us, which can, in any manner compare with the tortures and

the terrors of this: that is, "whitewashing" day....this fiendish ingenuity of some monster in human shape, for the express purpose of completing the ruin of your already dilapidated wardrobe. Your only coat is sure to come out of the ordeal spotted and streaked with white down the back; your only hat will look as if you had just come in from a severe snow-storm,....[27]

Since Libby lacked virtually any furniture, prisoners manufactured stools, chairs and tables from empty wooden boxes. Those who had a knack for carpentry were able to construct fair imitations of easy chairs. Barrel hoops made tolerable clothes hooks, and empty cans became lamps that burned lard lit by wicks made from cotton removed from the bottom of clothing.

An orchestra of sorts was organized in late 1863. It consisted of a violin, banjo, guitar, tambourine, and the bones. Performances were given in the "Libby Concert Room," and were very popular among the prisoners. Amateur theatrical productions were also staged.[28]

Food preparation was done by the prisoners themselves, who divided into small groups of "messes," each of which did its own cooking. One man within each mess was assigned the job of cooking the food for all the other members. This task was rotated among the members, so that each man took a turn at cooking for two to seven days. It was hard work, and no one liked to do it.

Two daily meals were prepared, noontime dinner and a late afternoon supper. The cook's first job was to determine what food he had available, and then how to prepare it. This required a great deal of culinary imagination, for the supplies on hand were limited in both variety and amount. Authorities tried to supply each man daily with two ounces of bacon or four ounces of beef, half a pound of bread, and some beans or rice,[29] but the amount and quality of these ingredients varied greatly. Corn bread was also a staple item. From these, and whatever else his mess may have bought or received from the outside, the cook had to decide if he wanted to make soup, hash, or something more creative.

Once the "menu" was decided upon, the hapless cook went down to the basement where wood-fired stoves were located. There, he was faced with jostling men, the cooks from the other messes, all vying to get their humble food cooked before the supply of firewood was exhausted.

Supper had to be prepared and consumed before the day's second roll call at five o'clock in the afternoon. After both meals the mess cooks also had to clean their utensils with soap and hot water. Moreover, they were responsible for the safekeeping of the utensils. Dippers, spoons, coffee pots and plates, not to mention food itself, were in such short supply that much unauthorized "borrowing" was attempted. After supper and the last roll call, men were left to their own devices until the following morning.

To help alleviate the lack of food, Confederate authorities permitted relatives in the North to send prisoners large crates containing food, clothing, and other items. Confederate prisoners in the North were also permitted to receive containers from home. Cornwell vividly describes the contents of the "boxes," as they were called, that he and the others received. They undoubtedly saved the lives of many men who would have perished without them.

Libby prisoners received their boxes via so-called "Flag of Truce" boats which plied regularly between Richmond and City Point, the large Union supply depot on the Virginia peninsula. The prisoners were dependent upon the arrival of their boxes and it was a severe hardship to body and mind when Confederate authorities periodically withdrew the privilege of receiving them.

A problem came to a head on January 18, 1864, when the authorities ceased the delivery of any more boxes to prisoners. During ongoing discussions between the exchange agents of both sides, Confederate officials were accused of diverting Northern relief boxes to Robert E. Lee's Army of Northern Virginia. They in turn charged that Union authorities refused to deliver relief boxes to Confederate prisoners in the North. As a result, both sides agreed to prohibit the sending or delivering of boxes, and that Union prisoners in the South would subsist on the same scanty rations provided to Confederate soldiers in the field.

Libby's prison population soared to more than 1,000 in the summer of 1863. Because so many officers were captured together in groups, the names of the rooms they were assigned to were changed. Previously, the rooms had been named for their locations, such as "upper East" or "lower West." Henceforth, they would be known by the names of battles or captured commanders, such as "Chickamauga" or "Streight's."[30] The former upper and lower west rooms were given to the men of General Milroy's and Colonel Streight's commands. Among the men occupying those rooms was Captain Robert T. Cornwell.

———

October 4, 1863
Libby Prison
DEAREST LILLIE,

This occasion is taken to acknowledge the receipt of the box you sent me. I received it on the 26th ult., but did not write sooner for two reasons: first, I was awaiting a letter concerning it and, second, I was awaiting the arrival of a Flag of Truce boat. I cannot tell you how much pleasure the reception of the box gave me, nor how much satisfaction I am taking from it daily. Everything is so nice and good. I cannot enumerate. You sent me just what I wanted. The flour is very valuable to me. Nothing spoiled except the bread and melons, nor was anything damaged. Butter and peaches are delightful. The hay with Sallie's shirt for a tick [mattress ticking] makes a good bed for me. I am gaining in flesh now quite rapidly. Give my love to all friends and relations.

Fondly your own:—
R.T. Cornwell
Capt. Co. "I" 67 Reg.

———

Oct. 26th, 1863

Libby Prison, Richmond, Va.

DEAR LYDIA,

My health is quite restored. My weight and strength has increased during the past two weeks remarkably. I must ask you to send me another Box. By the time it arrives, the first will or nearly or quite exhausted. Let it contain about as follows:

1 large canvass ham, I hank dried beef, 15 lbs. sugar, 1 gal. syrup, molasses, 20 lbs. cheese, 15 or 20 lbs. butter, 10 lbs. lard, 1/2 doz. cans condensed milk, 1 sack corn meal, I peck lima beans, 1/2 lb. ground pepper, I box mustard, 1 box leaven, 1 doz. nutmegs & a grater, some chocolate, settling for coffee, ground ginger, pickles, chestnuts, butter crackers, army soap, a tin cooking boiler with lid & handle holding about a gallon, a half gallon tin bake pan, small frying pan, quart cup, tin plate, knife, fork & spoon, skein [of] black thread, quire [of] letter paper, 2 packs envelopes, small bottle [of] ink, pen holder and pens, tooth brush, small looking glass, comb, hair brush, 1 doz. paper collars (15 in.), 1 enameled steel collar, 1 pair woolen drawers, a hasp, two staples, padlock & key, 2 hinges & screws.

Put up also in a separate box 1 1/2 bushels of potatoes & 1/2 bushel of onions. I leave the rest to your own discretion. Give my regards to Grandfather, Mother, Sallie. To my Jane and other friends. Kiss Gibbie for me,

Affectionately Yours

Robert T. Cornwell

P.S. Put in the box a pocket diary for 64 [1864] and a pair of suspenders. R.T.C.

Nov. 6, 1863

Libby Prison

Richmond, Va.

DEAR LILLIE:—

Your very kind letter of the 21st ult. was not received until yesterday. I rejoice to know that you are all well and that dear little Gibbie is so interesting, and feel assured that under your careful guidance a noble disposition will be developed [in him].

I have written two letters since receiving the box, and do not understand why the 1st of them was not received by you before the indicting of your last. In my last, I requested another box, but thinking that you will yet receive it [the first letter], I withhold a duplicate of that request. The $6 of Confederate currency sent in the 1st box was received. I am well and am not in especial need of any clothing except the drawers that I ordered in the letter above alluded to. I hope that Grandfather is better. Remember me to him.

I cannot ascertain that there is any such man as Mark Broomhall in this Prison. There are none but Officers here. Is he such? If not, he may be a prisoner elsewhere about this city. I cannot yet learn. Give my love to Mother & Sallie, and my regards to friends.

Affectionately Yours,
Robert T. Cornwell
Capt. Co. "I" 67 P.V.

December 2nd, 1863
Libby Prison
Richmond, Va.
DEAR LILLIE,

On the 14th ult. I received a very fine box from you, and in about a week after the one containing the potatoes & onions arrived. They contained all that I sent for and much more besides. Such boxes create quite a sensation in the prison & one has a crowd of inspectors about him while he unpacks and explores the contents of so great a treasure. The butter, cheese and pickles are especially fine. One jar of apple jam broke and its contents was lost. It however did no particular damage to the other things. The molasses, apples, and indeed all the things are very nice and very good.

I wish you could see some of my ginger cakes, corn bread & biscuit. The satisfaction I derive from from these things will I know sufficiently repay you for all your trouble in sending them. I received your letter. There is plenty of flour and the tin-boiler is just the thing. Indeed, all my wants, *that it is your power to relieve*, are satisfied. Through the kindness of Capt. Turner,[31] I will be allowed to distribute any boxes among the needy of this prison that the people of Chester Co.[unty] may bestow.

Received a letter from Westlake. He has been in Indiana [Pennsylvania] and says that B & A have sold the furniture you left them for $45, and will or have forwarded the money to you. He was drafted and paid $250 for a substitute.[32] Has sold his interest in the "Messenger" to Sam and his father. Sold his own furniture & our melodeon, etc. Ada is unusually well.

Carpenter & White[33] return their regards with many thanks for the "things in the box."

Fondly Yours & Gibbie's
Robert T. Cornwell
Capt. 67th Pa. Vols.

Dec. 9/63
Libby Prison
Richmond, Va.
DEAR LILLIE,

Take [this] occasion to send you another short message. My health is good. I enjoy boiled potatoes prodigiously. Tell Tommy I think of him and feel grateful nearly every meal. I try to content myself here as best I can; at times the desire to get my feet on Terra Firma again and enjoy a little more elbow room is almost uncontrollable, but it is astonishing what a wonderful amount of patience one can command when he has to.

Of course, time passes most rapidly when one's mind is employed. Have made you a present out of *bone*, valuable, if I ever get safely out of this, mainly from its associations. Devote some of my time to the study of German. One finds plenty of natives[34] here to talk with.

But it is getting near time to get dinner. My mess mate is slicing down some dried beef. We will not take the trouble, as it is so late, to get a very elaborate dinner today. Will have some dried beef, fried potatoes, etc., etc. How would you like to do the honor at our board? They tell me I am getting fat, and I guess it is true, for I hardly know myself when I look in that glass you sent me.

The Officers of our Regt. here are all well. White & Carpenter send regards. We use the last skirt sent for table cloths.

Fondly Yours & Gibbie's
R. T. Cornwell
Capt. 67 Pa. Vols.

January 1, 1864 (Diary)
Libby Prison

The new year dawned upon me in Libby prison. These walls contained few sleeping eyes[35] when the sentinels last night cried "twelve o'clock and all is well." At once the old building resounded with the good old national song of "The Union Forever." Libby is not a stranger now-a-days to strong union sentiments. John Morgan[36] arrived in Richmond today and received the slim hospitality of the city. His chief of staff visited the prison but received none of the attentions due to a chieftain from prisoners here. The day has been cold and cheerless. A ball tonight in the eating room.

January 2, 1864 (Diary)
Libby Prison

Last night was intensely cold. The water pipes were frozen up so we had no water with which to get breakfast until about 10 o'clock A. M., when the darkies carried some up to us in buckets from the canal, muddy and dirty as it could well be. Filth has accumulated today from the privies immensely. I have played today several games of chess, but it has been so cold that I could not enjoy them much. Carpenter today has been learning the game.

January 3, 1864 (Diary)
Libby Prison

Sunday [January 3] has passed without a rumor. How strange! The first since I have been here. Exchange stock is evidently very low.[37] Straight [sic] and Reed[38] are still in the cell. They have spent their Christmas and New Year's there. A rare way of spending the Holidays. We haven't yet heard from Maj. White. He was taken from here on Christmas day. He hollowed up to us as he went out of the door under guard that they were going to take him to Saulsbury [sic],[39] and asked us to write his friends. Why he is taken we do not yet know.

January 4, 1864 (Diary)
Libby Prison

Exchange stock low.[40] Some unfounded rumors of a boat with officers on board this evening. When there is any prospect of an exchange, it creates a terrible excitement and is the only thing talked of.[41] Letters were distributed today but I received none. Much disappointment. Preaching in our room this evening by a Reverend. Capt. Lieut. Flick & Capt. Carpenter[42] are playing chess by my side. Carpenter has just moved for checkmate and lost his *queen*. Cloudy and cold with much appearance of snow. "Lights out."

January 5, 1864 (Diary)

Libby Prison

Warmer. Spent the day in cooking and playing chess. Heard that Lieut. Frank Young was under arrest for disobedience of orders. Pretty general impression that we are "in" for the war. Understand that many of our regiment are reenlisting for three years. Get $400 bounty and the time from this till the expiration of the present term thrown in.[43] *Big thing!* Nine o'clock P. M. has come again. Oh but I am tired of putting down and sleeping on these dirty blankets in this close and crowded room. Must do it.

January 6, 1864 (Diary)

Libby Prison

The first snow of the season for this place has fallen today to the depth of about 1/2 an inch. But what is snow to us! No sleigh rides are ours. Whether the heavens smile of frown, it is all the same in this cheerless place. We were all sent today into the lower middle and east rooms, and allowed to pass back into the lower west and upper rooms as our names were called. There were many speculations as to the object of this alphabetical roll-call. I presume it was simply to verify the roll.

January 7, 1864 (Diary)

Libby Prison

Cold. No news. The papers speak very despondently. Adjt. LaTouche[44] said today he wished they could get rid of us, for they were unable to feed us. He says the guard have had no beef for 4 days. That at Camp Lee and in Lee's army they have had no meat or wood for some time. The guards around the prison ask us for bread. I am afraid the Confederacy will rot down over our heads. Capt. Ed. Forbes has been issuing Commissary stores to the officers here, who are to pay for them hereafter.

January 8, 1864 (Diary)

Libby Prison

Quite cold this evening but pleasant during the day. Col. Streight and Capt. Reed were released from the cell and came to their quarters in the room above us. Lieut. Ruff, my mess mate, a Col., Maj., two Capts. and another Lieut. Intend attempting to escape tonight by bribing the guard, who is to go with them. The guard talks alright and seems anxious to go. He says seven of his company here already crossed our lines. They suffer for something to eat. Their rations are a little cornmeal & sometimes a small piece of meat. The guards are so unreliable [that] it is a dangerous experiment to attempt escape.

January 9, 1864 (Diary)
Libby Prison
        Last night was very cold. Oh! What must our men on Bell Island [sic] have suffered without wood, few blankets, and only 1/4 rations.[45] I am creditably informed that three of our men froze to death last night. It pains me to think of it. Gen. John Morgan was expected here on New Year's day did not arrive until last night. He, General A. P. Hill and some members of Morgan's staff visited the prison today. Gen. M. looks to me very much like a black leg.[46] Dark hair and eyes, moustache & imperial. The party who expected to leave last night were frustrated in their designs by an attempt of other parties.

January 10, 1864 (Diary)
Libby Prison
        Sunday in Libby so far as any observances are concerned is not to be distinguished from any other day of the week. Chess, checkers and cards, with various other devices as on any other day, are resorted to pass away the time. I have spent the day reading the "Loiterings of Arthur O'Leary." Exchange is the prevalent topic of discussion this evening. Night before last three "*Fresh Fish*"[47] came in. They were Lieutenants and were very hungry. Had suffered much from cold on their way here. Some *fresh fish* came in this evening, but where from or how many I have not yet learned.

January 11, 1864 (Diary)
Libby Prison
        This evening Genl. Neal Dow[48] delivered a temperance lecture in the upper middle rooms. I did not attend. Was too much engaged with the "Loiterings of Arthur O'Leary." A few more "fresh fish" arrived this evening. Said they were captured at Ridgeville. No officers that I know of. I still hear that our men on Bell Island [sic] are absolutely freezing to

death. Last night was bitter cold. I cannot give expression to my feelings when I think of this terrible outrage on humanity. Have played chess today. Many people in Richmond are gathering ice today. It is worthy of record that our guards absolutely beg bread of the prisoners,—changing posts [so] that they can get near a window.

January 12, 1864 (Diary)
Libby Prison

Baked today—biscuit. Excellent. No news. No boat up but one, anxiously awaited. Most of my time consumed with "Arthur O'Leary." Dancing school in the dining room. Maj. Henry[49] attended tonight. I was down a short time. Attempted a few steps and exhausted myself wonderfully. Whether more from extra weight (for I am heavier now than ever before, something like 175 lbs.) or from the result of long confinement I cannot tell, but true it is that a few movements tires me out completely. I shall need a long leave of absence when I get out of here.

January 13–17, 1864 (Diary)
Libby Prison

[Cornwell devoted five full pages in his diary to the following poem. The author is unknown but Cornwell is mentioned in it by name.—T.M.B.]

The night was stormy, dark and cold.
It cramped the frames of young and old.
While north winds howl and tempers roar,
A thousand officers or more
Thin clad and shivering hug the floor
Of Libby prison. No sleep for them
Such nights as last. The fates condemn
That they shall scratch and quake away
The weary hours from dusk to day:—
For pinching cold and clothing thin,
Makes Libby lice hug close the skin
And plunge their proboscis the deeper in.
I washed today (I don't wear frocks)
My shirts and towels, drawers and socks.
Capt. Martin loaned his tub,
I borrowed a board on which to rub
Then washed with water scalding hot

My clothes are clean of stain and spot.
Some say hot water won't kill lice
Now it killed all mine "just like a mice."
I found while washing two or three
And they were dead as lice can be.
Barker swears will kill nitts too
For eggs won't hatch when boiled clear through.
Now Barker is the quaintest "genus"
Who e'er drained his bladder thru his penis.
He's a close observer of all that passes
And makes remarks about all classes.
An anecdote I here may tell
Will illustrate my meaning well.
One day while boarding here at Libby
He met Capt. C.[ornwell] perched on a privy.
Says Capt. to Barker sitting near
"I'm troubled with much diarreah."
Quoth Barker, "you'll be as bad I dare foretell,"
As for your fellow Captain, Capt. Cornwell.
For to tell the truth without hair-splitting
He's always cooking, eating or s—ting.
I washed today from head to foot
Put on clean clothes and shaved to boot,
Closed a rent with with needle and thread
And baked a loaf of sweet cornbread.
Ruff cooked a mess of pork & beans
And loused his clothes thru all the seams.
Lieutenant Flick is sick a-bed
Prayer meeting here by Caldwell led
A dance down stairs in the dining hall
It looks like rain and that is all.
At midnight last a sly arrangement
Long planned with care approached
The Colonel of the eighth Kentucky,
Deaf Lieutenant-Colonel Ely.
And so on down in rank descendant.
A Major, Captain and Lieutenant.
And lieutenant Ruff my chum in mess:
Six souls in all-no more, no less,
Composed the party. For full a week
negotiations all discreet
Were going on with two or three

Of the prison guard, who did agree,
That for a small consideration
Which means a watch or two and money ration,
To pass them out and e'en to go
Along with them to—well, you know,
Where blessings come but never go,
Where plenty reigns and greenbacks grow.
To tell the truth our friends were loathe
To trust the scamps e'en on their oath,
The more since promise quite as fair
Caught Streight and Reed in the dungeon snare.
Reassurances given and sent
At length convinced of pure intent.
These guards were on the second relief,
Posts five, six, seven enclosed their beat,
'Twixt eleven & twelve the party met
To undertake the fatal step.
Each well supplied with bread and meat,
Our dried beef ham Joe had to eat.
They had a rope to make descent
From window sill to street pavement,
And silver watches two in number
To give the guard to hold their thunder.
Then came the point of all the worst,
Who shall run the gauntlet first.
For plain it was for he who did
Of the enterprise its danger hid,
If the guards intent was them to slay
Or otherwise the plot betray.
Why *he* it was, was shot or struck
Or in a dungeon mourned his luck,
While all unharmed in safety's nook
They from his fate their warning took,
When Ruff found all would have dispersed
before they'd ventured going first,
He volunteered to make descent
And pump the guard on their intent.
So with the rope they dropped him down
His conduct merits fair renown,
When satisfied that all was right
They drew him up the story height;
He made report and downward straight

He went again to make escape.
Just as affairs were in this fix,
The guard on *nine* came down to *six*
And seeing Joe stand near the door,
He gave a yell, half cry, half roar
"Whose there?" and then (fe-fi-fo-fun!)
He came to a charge and cocked his gun.
"Don't shoot! Don't shoot!" cried Joe, "Damn the luck"
"Lower the rope! Draw me up! Draw me up!"
The guard on six was just in time
In seizing the gun of number nine
And crying, "don't shoot! Oh, don't shoot, Dan,
Jesus Christ, don't kill the man!"
A dozen voices till then mute
Rang out, "don't shoot! Oh, don't shoot!"
Meantime Joe's friends hard pulled the rope,
Joe saw I was his only hope,
They jerked him over the window sill
And skinned his knee, he's living still.

January 18, 1864 (Diary)
Libby Prison

A boat arrived on last Friday bringing with it a mail and a large number of boxes variously estimated in the papers at from twenty to seventy tons. We were informed by the "Examiner"[50] this morning that the boxes are all confiscated. How bitter about it we all feel! Unless they relent on the subject of our receiving boxes or we are exchanged, there is certainly before us gloomy forebodings of hungry times. My stock of provisions is growing fearfully less, and I am afraid my large box here will never be gifted with the miraculous powers of the Widow's "cruise of oil." The recent interim between boats is the longest (three weeks) that has transpired since negotiations commenced.

January 19, 1864 (Diary)
Libby Prison

Scarcity of wood for warming and cooking purposes. The result is that the partition between the kitchen and the privy rapidly disappeared to boil coffee and meat. I received a letter towards evening from Lillie. Oh, how anxiously expected and it came. What shall I say of it? It was like her and what can I say more in its praise. It contained a photograph of Grandfather which was also most strikingly like him. What a dear old man he looks. He seems to be thinking about and mourning our country's trying difficulties and praying that he may be spared to see her relieved from the thralldom of fraternal war and discord.

January 20/64
Libby Prison, Richmond, Va.
MY DEAREST LYDIA:—

I received a letter from you last evening and read and re-read it. It is like you, and I am sure I could not say more in its praise. Indeed, it is not less like its loving author than the striking photograph it contained is like its dear old original! What a deep, even solemn, pleasure I take in contemplating that countenance, so steeped in life's experience!

I fancy as my eyes dwell upon it, and my heart drinks in its subdued melancholy language, that his heart's prayer is that his life may be spared to see his country out of this cruel, fraternal strife. May his prayer be answered, and his most sanguine hopes realized!

I lay his face by the side of yours and Gibbie's and Sallie's. Three generations! What a gallery of love! What a chain of affection! But there is a picture in the gallery, a link in the chain—out. Send me Mother's sweet face, and I have the four consecutive generations—the entire household.

I suppose you wonder, my dear, that I have delayed writing you so long. It is in consequence of the non-arrival of a truce boat for an unusually long period. As no small recompense for the tortures of long-continued confinement, with its attendant unpleasant circumstances, I have yet the blessing of good health and plenty to eat to be thankful for. My potatoes and onions, however, are all gone. Have still some corn meal, flour, sugar, coffee, tea, ham, and a few etceteras.

There seems to be an misunderstanding between the Federal and Confederate authorities on the subject of receiving Boxes. The prevailing opinion here seems to be that *private* boxes will be allowed to come. If we are to remain here much longer (and there seems to be no other prospect at present), I sincerely hope this is the true state of the case. Received another of your letters this morning of an earlier date (Dec. 2nd) than the one received yesterday. Give my love to all. Fondly Yours,

Capt. R. T. Cornwell
67th Pa. Vols.

January 20, 1864 (Diary)

Libby Prison, Richmond, Va.

I received another letter this morning of an earlier date (Dec. 2nd) than the one received yesterday. These letters do me so much good, and though they remind me forcibly of my dear little family at home and make me long to be in their midst once more, yet they in some way impart strength to me to bear against my thronged yet solitary condition. I have today reconfined[?] my spare time in completing "David Copperfield," which I read when quite a boy but did not then appreciated [*sic*]. I have been at this reading much interested with it.

Lieut. Ruff is quite sick today. Symptoms of Typhoid Fever.

January 21, 1864 (Diary)

Libby Prison, Richmond, Va.

Lieut. Ruff is today somewhat better. He got up about 4 o'clock P. M. and partook of some hot biscuits and tea which I prepared for him. I wrote two letters today—this morning one to Lillie, which I gave to George[51] at Roll-call. The other to Prof. Brooks this evening, which I will hand to George to-morrow.

Weather pleasant. Rumors of a force of federal troops landing at "White House." Capt. Carpenter and myself promenaded in the dining hall two hours after lights were out, entertaining one another with various scenes in the history of each. C. entertained with experiences at College in the state of Ohio.

January 22, 1864 (Diary)

Libby Prison, Richmond, Va.

We have become today the victims of a new grief. Heretofore, we have been permitted to pass through all the six rooms of this building in which prisoners are confined. But today, with no other apparent motive than to render us the more uncomfortable, the doors communicating between the three departments have been nailed up and this small gratification denied us. No rations have been issued for the past eight days except half a loaf of corn bread, very coarse and as hard and heavy as lead. Once in a while a hand full of rice to a man.

January 23, 1864 (Diary)
Libby Prison, Richmond, Va.

My candles are all consumed. Hence, I resort to-night to another mode for producing light. I take one of my empty leaven [lard] cans, cut a hole through the lid, make and insert a wick of muslin rag, fill the can with ham fat and lard, put on the lid, light, and behold a good lamp. To-night a number of officers, among whom is Maj. Henry, went down into the dining hall making [a] considerable [amount of] noise, when lo! a guard marched in, and they are kept standing on the floor in line from which comfortable position they are not yet released.

January 24, 1864 (Diary)
Libby Prison, Richmond, Va.

The party kept standing on the floor last evening in the dining room were not released until 10 o'clock at night. We had considerable of sport over the matter with Maj. Henry today. Meat was issued for the first time in ten days. When we will get any more it is hard to tell. I baked today four plates of biscuit and had very good success. Pursued my German.[52] Learned to conjugate "Haben"–to have, "Sein"–to be, and "Werden"–to become. Formed a resolution to learn two pages every day. My evenings are most irksome, having not grease enough to spare to keep my lamp going.

January 25, 1864 (Diary)
Libby Prison, Richmond, Va.

My two pages of German were duly committed. Lieut. Ruff is much better today. Lieut. Weeks quite sick. Affected very much as Ruff was. Scarcely any thing has transpired today out of the regular routine of prison life. Some of the officers got in some whiskey of [from] the guard. The guard tied a string to the bottle and handed it up to one of the windows on the point of his bayonet. It cost the officers who got it $20 a bottle. Not so dear, however, as it would seem. Only about one dollar in our money. Still, had I any money I think I could use it better.

January 26, 1864 (Diary)
Libby Prison, Richmond, Va.

Weather fair. Received another ration of meat. Lieut. Weeks passed a very restless night, tossing about very hot with fever. He and I slept under the same blankets. My pantaloons too small since corporouty [*sic,* his weight] has so much increased are irrepairably [*sic*] bursted out. And I have been obliged to get a pair of Lieut. Anderson of the 122nd Ohio. The Rebs perpetuated a great outrage on the officers in our corner of the room by nailing up the two front windows. Didn't they get a blessing [cursing] though, from some of our tongues while they were doing it! Other officers don't come to our corner to [de] louse now.

January 27, 1864 (Diary)
Libby Prison, Richmond, Va.

Lieut. Weeks much better. Capt. Sawyer and Lieut. Wood[53] with two or three other officers were up to Judge Ould's[54] office this morning, and asked him something about being exchanged. He told them to go back to their quarters. "If our [Federal] government would parole the excess, we would be exchanged; if not, we never would be." We have heard enough of such talk, however, to feel much affected by it, and all believe, as Capt. C. says, that Judge Ould is an constitutional liar. Received nothing to eat today but half a loaf of corn bread. Senator [unclear] said the other day down here that the bread was not fit for a white man to eat.[55]

January 28, 1864 (Diary)
Libby Prison, Richmond, Va.

Weather fair. Not much has today transpired out of the regular routine. Rations were bread only. Committed about three pages in German. After lights were put out took an evening promenade with Carpenter in the lower part of the room above the stove. Heard that Col. Powell[56] was exchanged and several other officers with him, but who they were we could not learn. Understand that they are to go tomorrow morning at half past six o'clock. Powell feels good this evening and will not sleep much tonight in anticipation of so happy an event. He is a very worthy man and I am glad to know that his Libby sorrows are soon to be passed.

January 29, 1864 (Diary)
Libby Prison
Richmond, Va.

I am twenty-nine years old today. What a place to spend one's birthday! Col. Powell and three other officers unknown to me left this morning per exchange (special). The Rebs have been busy today putting iron bars in all the windows. They have finished this room. This afternoon they were working downstairs in the eastern part of the building with their coats off. Maj. Bates of Streight's command and a Capt. Porter[57] saw the coats and an idea struck them. Smearing their faces with dirt and slipping on the coats, they walked out the door in post number "1" with the air of "all right" in their manner and made their escape. Hush! I dare hardly write it yet. The Rebs have not missed them.

January 30, 1864 (Diary)
Libby Prison, Richmond, Va.

The successful exit of Maj. Bates and Capt. Porter induced three other officers—Lieuts. King, Carothers and Cupp,[58] to make a similar effort. The latter went out of the back door and down the steps about the time for "sick call." He passed Inspector (Dick) Turner on the pavement by the side of the prison and went out at post "No. 1" without exciting suspicion. Shortly after he left, some death-deserving *traitor* among our number (Lieut. Myers, *the Jew* is suspected) informed the prison authorities of the escape, and pursuit was commenced immediately. The roll was called and all the missing ones ascertained. None have as yet been caught. A boat load of boxes arrived this morning. Will not order any more until I see whether they are issued or not.

January 31, 1864 (Diary)
Libby Prison, Richmond, Va.

Cloudy. No meat. Ross[59] and Dick Turner were busy all day yesterday calling roll, but could not be satisfied with the result. Maj. Bates was brought in last night. Was caught four miles beyond Bottom Ridge, about 16 miles from here. Became exhausted from travel after so long confinement, and called at a house for something to eat, where he was betrayed. King was brought in this morning. They are both in the cell. It is now about noon and the Rebs are calling the roll for the second time since morning. Ross, it seems, can't make head or tail of it. Inspector Turner tried it and he made twenty-four men more than they ever had. Now Maj. Turner, after taking every precaution against the Yankees cheating him, is trying it. It remains to be seen how he will succeed. They send us all into the east room and count us as we come out.

Captain Robert Thompson Cornwell and his wife, Lydia "Lillie" Jackson Cornwell. He is wearing a fatigue jacket similar to the one described in a letter to Lillie.

Daily Local News

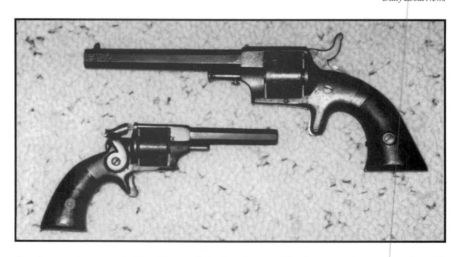

Service revolvers carried by Cornwell during the war. The large revolver on top is a .31 calibre 5-shot manufactured by the Bacon Arms Company of Norwich, Conn. The other is a .32 calibre Allen and Wheelock.

Courtesy of Richard Cornwell

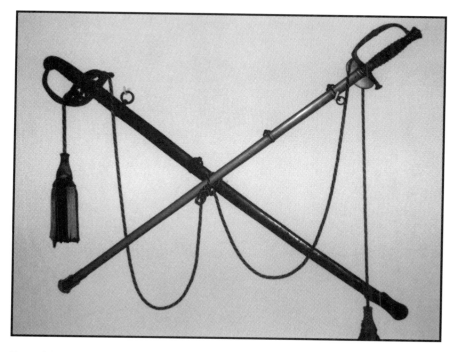

Draped by a banner tassel from a regimental flag are two swords owned by Robert T. Cornwell. He carried the large sword on the left after his release from Libby Prison. It was manufactured by W. Clauberg of Solingen, Germany and is typical of the imported swords often purchased by Union officers. The other is a Model 1860 staff officer's sword presented to Cornwell by members of his postwar Pennsylvania national guard unit. The blade is inscribed: "Capt. R. T. Cornwell by the Wayne Fencibles, Co. "I," 11th Regiment N. G. P., 1877."

Courtesy of Richard Cornwell

The destroyed armory at Harpers Ferry

The town of Harpers Ferry in ruins. In the foreground are the piers of the Baltimore & Ohio Railroad bridge, all that remained of the 900-foot covered structure.

Libby Prison as seen from the front in an 1864 sketch drawn by W. C. Schwartzburg, a soldier in Company "A," 24th Wisconsin Volunteers. The Confederate Second National flag flies from the roof. The prison's offices were located in rooms behind the awning in the ground floor area at the bottom right of the sketch.

Library of Congress

Side view of Libby Prison taken shortly after the Union occupation of Richmond in April 1865. The tunnel through which the 109 prisoners escaped opened into the field in the foreground. After the escape, the lower part of the building's walls was whitewashed in an attempt to make it easier for the guards to see men in the windows.

The Photographic History of the Civil War

The rear of Libby Prison, showing a boat in the Kanawha Canal unloading supplies for the prison. Between the canal and the prison wall was a narrow lane called Dock Street.

The Photographic History of the Civil War

Brig. Gen. John H. Winder. A West Point graduate and professional soldier (and son of the general who commanded American forces at the battle of Bladensburg during the War of 1812), Winder was assigned two of the most thankless tasks in the Confederate government. As provost marshal of Richmond from 1862 to 1864, he earned the enmity of the civilian population because of his strict enforcement of the laws. Union army prisoners, who were under his overall control throughout the war, hated him despite the fact that the inadequacy of food, medicine, and clothing in the Confederacy made it virtually impossible for him to supply their needs.

The Photographic History of the Civil War

The massive Union supply and prisoner exchange base at City Point on the James River in Virginia

Battles & Leaders

Period sketch of U.S. Colored Troops beginning their charge into the Crater at Petersburg. Cornwell referred to this action in a letter to Lillie.

Battles & Leaders

Maj. Gen. Benjamin F. Butler (*top*) and Col. Robert Ould, the Union and Confederate exchange agents, respectively, at the time of Cornwell's release from Libby Prison.

Top, Library of Congress; *Bottom*, *The Photographic History of the Civil War*

The "flag-of-truce boat" *New York*. Frequently mentioned by Cornwell, this boat was a familiar sight to Union prisoners in Richmond. Sailing regularly from City Point, it brought supplies and letters to prisoners in Richmond and returned with exchanged prisoners, including Cornwell.

Library of Congress

The fortifications around Washington, D.C., in 1864

Battles & Leaders

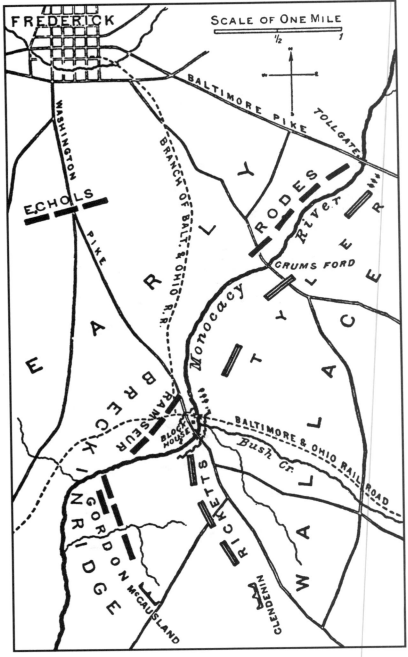

Positions of the opposing armies at the battle of Monocacy, July 9, 1864

Battles & Leaders

Four provost marshals of the Union III Army Corps in winter quarters at Brandy Station, December 1863–April 1864. The gold staff officer's cording, mentioned by Cornwell, is visible on the outside trouser seams of three of the officers.

Library of Congress

Maj. Gen. James Brewerton Ricketts as he appeared in the November 12, 1864, issue of *Harper's Weekly*.

Harper's Weekly

"Old Jube," Maj. Gen. Jubal Anderson Early

Battles & Leaders

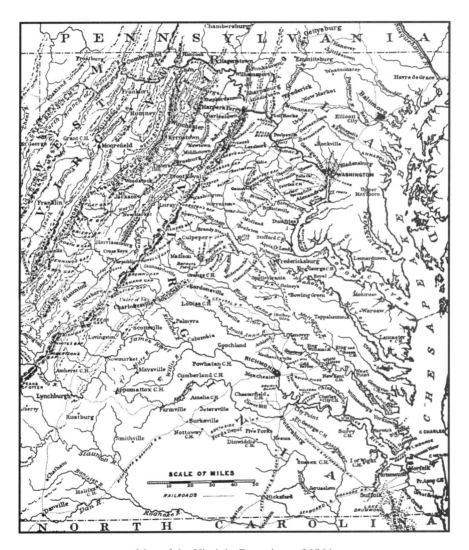

Map of the Virginia Campaigns of 1864

Battle & Leaders

Ricketts attacks Rode's division during the third battle of Winchester, September 19, 1864. Cornwell described the fighting in his letter of September 23.

Battles & Leaders

Maj. Gen. Philip H. Sheridan
Battles & Leaders

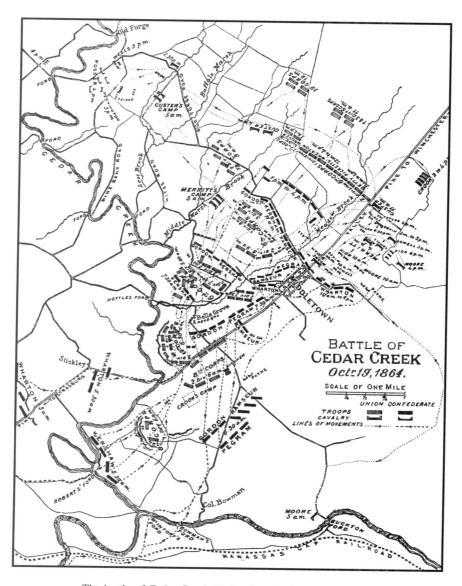

The battle of Cedar Creek (Belle Grove), October 19, 1864

Battles & Leaders

Headquarters Third Division, Sixth Corps,

Office Assistant Adjutant General,

October 20 1864.

My Dearest

Your letter of the ___ has just come to hand. We have just ended another terrible fight and glorious victory. Rather the fighting ended last night. But the numerous dead are not all buried yet. Nor are all the wounded yet cared for. It was a terrible day, but it ended gloriously. General Ricketts was wounded, but a short distance from me. He was struck by a ball in the left breast near the shoulder. It is thought that he will recover. Genl Bidwell of the 2nd Div 6th Corps, Comdg a brigade was killed. Very many valuable officers and men are among the killed and wounded. Now for a brief outline of the affair. The Rebels about 25,000 strong have been lying in our front at Fisher's Hill for several days. Night before last under cover of fog and darkness, their whole force was moved over against the side of the mountain and passed single file along a mountain path around our left flank. Our force laid in the following order. Eigth Corps on the left, Nineteenth Corps in

The first page of Robert T. Cornwell's October 20, 1864, letter to Lillie, describing the battle of Cedar Creek.

Courtesy of Daniel Cornwell

93

ENCAMPMENT OF UNION PRISONERS AT BELLE ISLE, RICHMOND, VIRGINIA.—[From a Sketch by Captain Harry E. Wrigley, Topographical Engineer.]

Captain Harry E. Wrigley sketched this view of Belle Isle, the camp for enlisted Union prisoners on an island in the James River.

Harper's Weekly

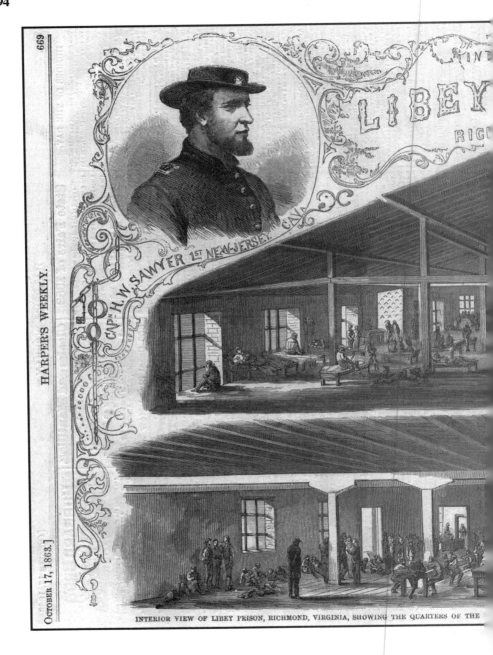

CAP^T H. W. SAWYER 1ST NEW-JERSEY CAV^Y.

INTERIOR VIEW OF LIBEY PRISON, RICHMOND, VIRGINIA, SHOWING THE QUARTERS OF THE

CONFINED THERE.—SKETCHED BY CAPTAIN HARRY E. WRIGLEY, TOPOGRAPHICAL ENGINEERS.—[SEE PAGE 667.]

An interior view of "Libey [sic] Prison" that appeared in the October 17, 1863, issue of *Harper's Weekly*. The sketch was made by Captain Harry E. Wrigley, who was imprisoned there for several months. Also shown are illustrations of Captains Flynn [sic] and Sawyer, the officers threatened with retaliatory execution.

Harper's Weekly

This 1863 view of the exterior of Libby Prison was based upon a photograph. The tents were for the detachment of guards, some of whom can be seen in formation in the background. The adults in the foreground are believed to be the prison's senior staff: (*left to right*) William D. Turner, the young son of Richard Turner; Erasmus Ross, clerk; Richard Turner, jailer; and Thomas P. Turner, commandant.

Harper's Weekly

4

Libby Prison: The Great Escape
February 1–February 29, 1864

In many respects, the month of February 1864 was the most difficult for Cornwell. The weather was cold, severe new restrictions were imposed upon the prisoners, and food was in short supply. But it was also an interesting time in Libby's history, and he was an eyewitness.

On February 1, new regulations went into effect regarding letters sent by prisoners. Henceforth, they could send only one letter north each week. It had to be written on just one page, could not have more than six lines of writing, and could discuss only topics that were strictly personal in nature.

The letter to be mailed was placed inside two envelopes, the larger outside envelope being addressed to the Commissioner for Exchange in Richmond. There, it was read by a member of the commissioner's staff. If approved, it was inserted into the smaller envelope that was addressed to the letter's recipient. That envelope was then sent to Fortress Monroe, from where it entered the regular United States postal system for delivery to the addressee. All this was accomplished for the same three cents charged by the Federal post office to deliver any letter weighing under one-half ounce. Letters to prisoners had to follow the same procedure in reverse.[1]

Cornwell records the most daring event in Libby's history, the escape of more than one hundred prisoners through a tunnel on the night of February 9. The escape was planned by Col. Thomas E. Rose of the 77th Pennsylvania Infantry and Maj. Andrew Hamilton of the 12th Kentucky (U.S.) Cavalry. The two officers found a fireplace in "Rat Hell," a little-used section of the basement so called because of the swarms of rats that inhabited the area. They determined that a tunnel could be dug in the earth surrounding the prison if the bottom of the fireplace was lifted out and some bricks were removed from the back of the flue.

Rose, Hamilton, and a small group of officers sworn to secrecy started working using nothing but more than an old chisel, a wooden box to carry away the dug dirt, and a candle for illumination. Groups of ten to fifteen officers worked at night when the other prisoners were sleeping. While some dug, others supplied air into the tunnel by fanning their hats into opening. The remainder dumped the rubble into Rat Hell. Each man worked one night and took the next two off so as to not arouse suspicion.

The first attempt was abandoned after their route mistakenly took the tunnel into an open field. The second attempt cut into a sewer line, which rapidly filled the tunnel with water. Finally, after almost three weeks of digging, a tunnel was completed. It was fifty-three feet long and about two feet wide and eighteen inches high. It sloped downward for the first twelve feet, then rose slightly for another twelve feet before leveling off and exiting into a field next to Kerr's Warehouse, where the prisoners' boxes were stored.

Colonel Rose was apparently the first officer to enter the tunnel on the night of the escape. He was followed by the rest of the secret group, the last of whom was to inform the rest of the prison population of the existence of the tunnel. Those among the latter who wished to escape lined up by the entrance to await their turn to squirm through the tunnel. In all, one hundred and nine officers escaped. Of those, fifty-nine reached the safety of Union lines, forty-eight were recaptured, and two drowned. The only officer of the 67th Pennsylvania to escape was 1st Lt. Charles L. Edmonds of Company "D." Cornwell was in the line of prisoners waiting to escape, but was prevented from doing so when the guards finally raised an alarm.

Colonel Streight, who had been complaining about the lack of food at Libby, caused a problem when he entered the tunnel and became wedged in its narrow confines. He was forced to remove most of his clothing in order to continue moving through it. Once out, he and three other escapees were given refuge in a house owned by Elizabeth Van Lew (1818–1900), one of the characters in the murky world of Richmond's prison system.

Van Lew was an abolitionist and ardent supporter of the Union. Her odd clothing and strange behavior earned her the nickname of "Crazy Bet," but her oddities were designed to be a cover for her other activities. She was well known to the Libby prisoners as a frequent visitor who brought them books, food, and other supplies. Van Lew also operated a successful spy ring, and went so far as to have an operative placed in the Confederate White House as a servant. The information obtained was then passed on to her Union contacts. Confederate authorities were deeply suspicious of her activities, but she was never arrested.

Streight remained at Van Lew's house for a few days, then used the reduced security to make his way to an island in the Potomac River, where he was rescued by a Union warship. He returned to duty three months later and was promoted to brigadier general. He is frequently, but incorrectly, mentioned as being the leader of the escape plan.[2]

There were other significant events at Libby during the month. In his diary for February 20 Cornwell mentions the hanging of Spencer Deaton and two other Union army captains. The situation is worth examining, as it shows the retaliatory attitude of governmental authorities on both sides.

In May 1863 Union Maj. Gen. Ambrose Burnside (1824–1881) executed as spies William F. Corbin and T. G. McGraw. Both were Confederate army captains who were recruiting soldiers in parts of Kentucky under Union control. Several months later, Confederate officials announced that two Union captains, selected from among prisoners at Libby, would be executed in retaliation. The name of each captain in Libby was written on a piece of paper and another prisoner, a chaplain, drew out two names at random. The men chosen were captains John M. Flinn, 51st Indiana, and Henry W. Sawyer, 1st New Jersey Cavalry. Federal authorities reacted quickly to this threat, saying that if those two officers were put to death, they would execute two more Confederate officers.

The stakes were high, because the announced victims held in captivity by Union authorities were two prominent Southerners: Brig. Gen. W. H. F. "Rooney" Lee, a son of Robert E. Lee, and Lt. William S. Winder, the son of Richmond's provost marshal. None of the four men themselves had any involvement with espionage, and were simply being used for political purposes. Fortunately for all of them, as Cornwell mentions, the Confederate government relented and released Flinn and Sawyer. Lee and Winder were released shortly thereafter.[3]

Cornwell mentions two other Union captains who were hanged, and describes the death of one of them, an officer named Spencer Deaton. The other captain was Spencer Kellogg. In late 1862 Kellogg appeared on a boat floating in the Mississippi River off Columbus, Kentucky, an area held by the Confederates. He announced that he was a Union deserter and convinced local Confederate military authorities that he wanted to join their side.

Kellogg was first assigned to a Confederate floating battery of artillery, then to a gunboat, and finally to the engineer corps at Island No. 10. There, he made sketches of the defenses and returned to Union lines with his drawings. In exchange for his information he received a promotion to the rank of fourth master of the Union gunboat *Essex*.

On March 5, 1863, Kellogg was captured by the Confederates and charged with being a spy, a role he had clearly filled despite official Union protests to the contrary. On August 4, Commodore W. D. Porter of the Union navy wrote that Kellogg "performed valuable services for the [U. S.] Government…of a character which could only be trusted to a brave and faithful officer." Kellogg was hanged at Camp Lee, near Richmond, on September 25, 1863. He was a brave man, and just before his execution wrote a touching letter to his family.[4]

On February 25 Cornwell copied in his diary the wording of a general order that appeared in a Richmond newspaper. It announced the appointment of Braxton Bragg (1817–1876) as military advisor to President Jefferson Davis. No doubt Cornwell was as amazed at Bragg's appointment as were the people in the South.

Bragg was a West Point graduate who had served with distinction in the Seminole Wars, then retired from the military and became a successful sugar planter in Louisiana. He was also a personal friend of Jefferson Davis, who appointed him a brigadier general in the Confederate army in early 1861. It was a case of an officer being promoted above the level of his capabilities. Given command of the Army of Tennessee in June 1862, he led it in a series of inept campaigns at

Murfreesboro, Chickamauga, and Chattanooga. Bragg lost the confidence of his officers and men, and was held in low esteem by the public. He offered his resignation on November 29, and it was readily accepted by Davis.

Therefore, Bragg's return in February 1864 as military advisor to Davis was greeted with derision by many in the South. Bragg, however, possessed administrative skills and energy, and he performed well in his new role, making some needed and useful changes in the military bureaucracy. Unfortunately for the Confederates, the final event in his career resulted in another disaster.

He was returned to active command in late 1864 in a pivotal role. President Davis sent him to protect Wilmington, North Carolina, the last port still open to blockade runners. Bragg once again demonstrated his inability to command in the field. In January 1865 a Union amphibious force of 8,000 men assaulted Fort Fisher, which guarded the entrance to the Cape Fear River and Wilmington. Bragg and 6,000 men were safely posted just several miles away. Despite pleas from the 1,500 beleaguered defenders within the fort, Bragg refused to send his men to their aid. The fort was overrun and captured, and with its fall the Confederacy was cut off from outside supply.

February 1, 1864 (Diary)
Libby Prison, Richmond, Va.

The statement that Lieut. King was yesterday retaken proves to be a mistake. Some unfortunate citizen on the road was dragged here supposed to be, by the Rebs, the above mentioned Lieutenant. We had roll call this morning about 6 1/2 o'clock. The Rebs had considerable trouble getting us up and over into the East room. The authorities of this Prison read in all the rooms this morning the following order-to wit-

C. S. Milt. Prison

Richmond Feb. 1st/64

From this date no Federal officer will be allowed to send to the *so-called* United States *no* more than one letter each week, said letter not to contain more than six (6) lines-Letters must delivered to the sargeant on Mondays & no other days.

Signed

Th. P. Turner, Maj. Comdg.

February 2, 1864 (Diary)
Libby Prison, Richmond, Va.

Still cloudy, without rain or snow. Lieut. King was brought in yesterday afternoon. The authorities here did not know they had the right man, for none

PERSONAL CATALOG REQUEST and RELEASE INFORMATION

White Mane Publishing Company, Inc. would be happy to add you to our growing list of readers. For your personal copy of our book release information please return this card with your complete mailing address information.

FROM: _____

_____

_____

I purchased this book through:
A. Direct Mail
B. Bookstore
C. Book Club

I chose this book because of:
A. Book Reviews
B. Magazine Ads
C. WM Catalog Release
D. Friends Recommendation
Other: _____

I prefer to purchase books through:
A. Direct Mail
B. Book Store
C. Book Club

5123 X

White Mane Publishing Company, Inc.

P.O. Box 152

Shippensburg, PA 17257-0152

recognized him. So, they called down Col. Streight who, without suspecting the true state of this case, walked up to King, spoke to him by calling him by name. They immediately sent Streight back and consigned King to a cell. We have had two roll calls this morning already. A mistake made the first time. The prevailing opinion is that the meat issued to us today was horse flesh. Lieut. Kupp was brought in today. Where he was caught we have not yet learned. He is a powerfully stout man, and it was thought that no one guard could take him.

February 3, 1864 (Diary)
Libby Prison, Richmond, Va.

Cloudy & much colder. Last evening Maj. Henry of the 5th Ohio Cavalry entertained the officers with an address on spiritualism. He is quite a talker. Spoke first of the probability of spiritual manifestations, secondly of the many manifestations that he had witnessed, and lastly of the doctrine of spiritualism. Lieut. Kupp was taken 36 miles from here within 14 miles of Williamsburg. Lieut. Carothers was brought in this afternoon. There is but one man now out (Lieut. Porter) of all that attempted escape. There perhaps could not be a more unfavorable time to escape, for the whole country is filled with patrols to arrest conscripts fleeing to our lines. Every citizen is a policeman.

February 4, 1864 (Diary)
Libby Prison, Richmond, Va.

Colder, Colder grows the weather,
Filth, Hunger, Cold confined together.
With "Milroy's Thieves" in all their glory
In western room and second story,
Fifteen windows large and bleak
Four by six when spanned in feet.
Four whistling winds and driving rain
From North & West across the plain,
Of Libby's Western second floor
To Southeast corner entrance door,
Drenching sleepers, opening peepers
Alarming screechers, startling creepers.

February 5, 1864 (Diary)
Libby Prison, Richmond, Va.

Still cloudy but not so cold. It would seem that the Rebs suspected that some of us had attempted to escape last night. There were frequent gun shots heard during the night, and this morning we were all sent into the East room and allowed to pass out as our names were called. Breakfast was much delayed on that account. Quite a number of "fresh fish" arrived in Richmond this morning, and among them five or six officers. Understand they were captured at New Bern, N. C. It is six months today since I arrived at Libby. Since the 31st of Jan. the doors communicating between the three departments of the building have been left open. I wish they would close them again to stop the rush to our cook stoves. No bread today. Turnips instead.

February 6, 1864 (Diary)
Libby Prison, Richmond, Va.[5]

A wise and patriotic Reb, a ways and means provider,
In breaking up the odious web of the bloody Yankee spider
A raw material gatherer, with talent rare therefore,
A powder manufacturer, a parasite of war.
Tho Richmond's papers ask from all in high and lowly station,
From male and female great and small, the urea of the nation.
We know full well they eat mule soup, of it not half a ration
But oh! that F. F. V.s should stoop to such humiliation.
Now matron fair and lovely miss, here's something you can do,
More worthy far than bless and kiss,
To help your country thru
Your ammunition's nature's gift, and costs not e'en a thankee,
For every time you lift your shift, you shoot a bloody Yankee.

February 7, 1864 (Diary)
Libby Prison, Richmond, Va.

Three roll calls—last one by name. Yesterday, Capt. Reed, Capt. Ives & Major Sterling were taken from here to go to Saulsbury [sic] as hostages.[6] There is quite a "scare on" here in Richmond this morning. Rumor has it that a large force from Butler's command are at Bottom's Bridge. The bells rang for an hour this morning, calling out the militia and shortly after were to be seen Jack Ass batteries[7] and squads of militia in all garbs of dress, directing their way down the James [river].[8] Have had but one roll call today. Rations were turnips, corned-beef and bread. Made a fine pot of soup of turnips, beans, rice & corned beef.

February 8, 1864 (Diary)
Libby Prison, Richmond, Va.

Started a six line letter to Lillie, requesting her to draw some of the money due me from the U. S. Government, also requesting some *virus*[9] for vaccination. The *scare* of yesterday seems in a great measure to have subsided. Many of the militia returned last evening. Some very bad corned beef issued today, but I did not get any. Have been reading "Bleak House" for some days past. Am about halfway through it this evening. Quite interested in "Easter's Narrative." Stoves are so crowded and wood so bad that I did not get any dinner until nearly night. The boxes (several boat loads) have not been issued, except now and then one as a *special* favor. We cannot understand why they refuse to issue them all.

February 9, 1864 (Diary)
Libby Prison, Richmond, Va.

The wintry morn looks with clouded and sullen face through the window bars of our prison. A few boxes were issued this morning, but to whom and under what pretext I do not know. Occupied most of my time reading "Bleak House." The day has been barren of any unusual incidents. Nothing out of the various devices and employments to pass away the time. Time here is a burden, a tormentor, a bore. There are few officers here who would not willingly have stricken from their lives the portion that is still to be spent in this hole. Received no meat today. Nothing but bread and water issued.

February 10, 1864 (Diary)
Libby Prison, Richmond, Va.

The first news that greeted my ears this morning when I awoke was the startling intelligence that on last night Libby had sprung a very big *leak*, and so it was—one hundred and two officers made their escape. Thru an underground passage from the dining hall on the first floor by cutting with knives a hole thru a brick chimney, and descending thru the chimney with a ladder they obtained access to the basement. Thru the Eastern basement wall a hole was cut neatly to mother earth, and a hole burrowed for 50 ft. under the sentinels' post to an adjoining lot where their exit was secluded by a board fence. 51 days the work has been in progress. The guard are all under arrest this morning & undergoing an examination.

February 11, 1864 (Diary)
Libby Prison, Richmond, Va.

An article in the "Richmond *Examiner*" with the following caption appeared this morning. "Escape of one hundred Yankee officers from the Libby prison—A scientific tunnel—Their underground route to liberty." For article entire, see *side pocket* [of diary]. Lieut. Edmonds was the only one who left from our regiment. He was brought in this evening; during yesterday four were brought in. Today 17 have been returned to the prison. They are all put in the dungeon below as fast as they are recaptured. Eighty nine are still out. But one field officer[10]—Col. Spofford[11]—has yet been recaptured. The Rebs are very anxious to catch Col. Streight. I think however they will miss him.

February 12, 1864 (Diary)
Libby Prison, Richmond, Va.

Eight more officers have been brought in today. Among them, I was very sorry to see Maj. Henry. There are eighty-one still out. It is rumored today that Col. Streight had been overtaken and ordered to halt, refusing to do which he was shot and wounded. I do not rely on the statement.

The remnants of some boxes have been issued today. The Reb officers say they will issue from the boxes only such articles as are "*perishable*." They keep butter, coffee, tea, sugar, molasses, ham, dried beef, indeed everything except the articles as bread, cake and rotten apples. I will not attempt to express my indignation at such conduct.

February 13, 1864 (Diary)
Libby Prison, Richmond, Va.

Damp and chilly. Am painfully afflicted with a severe cold caught yesterday from sitting about two hours without my pants on [while I was] mending them. Went to bed immediately after roll call. Took five cathartic pills about 8 o'clock P. M. Operated [they took effect] about one o'clock this morning. Felt relieved immediately after, and slept some before daylight. The Rebs have now captured forty-one of the Federal *escapades* [*sic*]. Sixty-nine still out. Several of the recaptured officers, among them Lieut. Edmonds, were sent upstairs this evening. The cells,[12] I suppose, are over-full. Received a letter from Lillie. [I am] Reassured that my little family are all well.

February 14, 1864 (Diary)
Libby Prison, Richmond, Va.

Much better this morning. Day pleasant. Wrote a six line letter to Lillie—addressed to Sallie. Six more officers recaptured arrived here. Forty-seven in all. Sixty-three still out. The Reb papers state that they fear the "famous or rather the infamous Streight"[13] is out of their reach, and now under the protection of the Stars and Stripes. Commenced reading today Bulwer Lytton's "Harold" or, "The Last of the Saxon Kings." Like it very much. Ruff cut his hand quite badly today while cutting corn bread with a case knife. Lieut. Myers and another officer in the 9th Md. [Maryland] after shaving were fooling by daubing one another with lather when Myers, striking at the other with the lather brush, struck him with the razor, cutting quite a large gash in the chin, which bled profusely.

Feb. 15th, 1864
Libby Prison, Richmond, Va.
MY DEAR LILLIE:—

Am still quite well. Received a letter from you dated Jan. 24th last evening. Feel happy in the reassurance that are all well, and that our dear little darling is doing so well in his way. I frequently find myself imagining how you all look. My supply of commissaries [food] is getting very low. Boxes arrive here by the boat load, but for months none have been issued, save now and then one as a special favor. Last Friday, the farce of allowing the owners to receive the "perishable" articles (already perished) in a few of them was gravely enacted. My love to all.

Robert

February 15, 1864 (Diary)
Libby Prison, Richmond, Va.

Did not sleep more than half an hour last night. Heard the sentinel every semi-hourly cry of "Post no. —Hour of night" and all is well. Still, I rested quite comfortably. Suppose my wakefulness was owing to my having slept or dozed about fifteen hours the day before. Gave the letter to the sargent [*sic*] this morning. Routed Joe out for breakfast shortly after daylight before roll call. The day is much colder than any weather we have had for some time back. Could not be comfortable even while briskly walking. If we attempted a little "double quick"[14] by way of getting up a little heat, an order was received instanter from Maj. Turner to "*stop that noise.*" Two escapades [*sic*] were recaptured today.

February 16, 1864 (Diary)
Libby Prison, Richmond, Va.

The weather is still colder—too cold to sit down to write even for a few minutes. We cannot resist cold here as we can when out—for our systems have in a great measure lost the power of reacting against it. Neither does our food enable us to resist cold. Hundreds here are obliged to eat nothing but the worst of corn-bread and a little rice. I understand there have been fifty-two of the *escapades* brought in all, so that there are now more than half still out. Nearly all of whom, it is quite reasonable to suppose, have made good their escape. I do trust that such is the case. Happy men.

February 17, 1864 (Diary)
Libby Prison, Richmond, Va.

Did not sleep more than half an hour last night. Heard the sentinels every semi-hourly cry of "Post No."—hour of night & "all is well." Still I rested quite comfortably. Suppose my wakefulness was owing to my having slept or dozed about fifteen hours the day before. Still colder. Many a poor soldier has suffered intensely last night. What our poor fellow prisoners suffered last night on the island—very scantily fed and clothed and no protection from the weather, it would be difficult to realize without experiencing the same hardships. Brig. Gen. Scammon was brought in yesterday to share our quarters from the Dept. of the Cumberland.

February 18, 1864 (Diary)
Libby Prison, Richmond, Va.

Still colder. The James River is partially frozen over. The papers state that the weather is unusually cold for this latitude.[15] It is hardly possible to keep warm even after wrapping one's self with all the clothing he has. We have a stove, but for the great portion of the time no wood. [Union general] Neal Dow has been kicking up a smoke about our rations, and the result is that we now get double the bread we did before—a small loaf apiece instead of half a one. We had some meat yesterday, the first for a long time; today—none. Nothing else out of the usual routine. I think it must be too cold for much to occur.

February 19, 1864 (Diary)
Libby Prison, Richmond, Va.

Still colder! The papers state that their conscripts are freezing to death in Camp Lee—what must be the condition of our fellow prisoners in Belle Island. A truce boat arrived at City Point[16] last night with some twenty tons of boxes aboard of our necessities. Why in the name of sense do our authorities send boxes here by the boatload when they must know they seldom reach the prisoners for whom they are intended, but are appropriated to feed the Confederacy. Spencer Deaton of "Co. B," 6th East Tenn. "Renegade" was executed today in the yard of Castle Thunder on charge of being a spy. His execution was to have taken place last Friday but Jeff [Davis] granted him a week's respite. Senator Wigfall was here today.

February 20, 1864 (Diary)
Libby Prison, Richmond, VA.

I think it was still colder last night than [the] night before. The "*Examiner*" of this morning, in relating the incidents of the execution of yesterday, says that Spencer Deaton when brought to the gallows was unable to stand alone and had to be held up while the rope was adjusted. He has been so weak from long and close confinement and poor food that for some time previous to his execution he was only kept alive through the instrumentality of stimulants. Saw a letter today from Gen. Lee to a Rev. Moore of the 1st Presbyterian Church in Richmond, in which it was stated that the Confederate government had released Sawyer & Flinn as they had already hung two Capts. for the two that Burnside hung and for the same offense. Charge of being a spy. His execution was to have taken place last Friday, but Jeff. [Jefferson Davis] granted him a week's respite. Senator Wigfall[17] was here today.

February 21, 1864 (Diary)

Libby Prison, Richmond, Va.

Weather much moderated. Rather cloudy but the air feels quite like Spring. Quite an excitement has been aroused here by the account of four hundred officers (Confed.) having been removed by our government from Johnston's Island[18] to Baltimore and handed over to Maj. Mulford. It looks as though they were to be put on board a truce boat for exchange. Wrote a six line letter to Lillie. Rations were bread and black beans, full of worm holes. Grated up two loaves of corn bread, mixed the meal with an equal amount of flour, put in some salt and condensed milk, butter and soda, baked and had three loaves of elegant bread, fit for a king. Our beans I soaked parboiled and baked with a piece of fat ham.

February 22, 1864 (Diary)

Libby Prison, Richmond, VA.

Weather much moderated. Last night, Lieut. Weeks took his two blankets and left the old quarters by the old North West post for other parts. Where he slept last night I do not know. He has said *nothing* to me about the matter. The Richmond papers state this morning that twenty-two more escaped prisoners from Libby have arrived at Fortress Monroe [in the Union lines]. This makes forty in all that have arrived at that place. There are about seventeen more still to be heard from. Played several games of chess and read Bulwer's "Harold." Spent the evening very restfully doing nothing.

Feb. 22/64

Libby Prison, Richmond, Va.

MY DEAR LILLIE:—

The weather here for the past week has been intensely cold. My health is still good. I have said nothing to you of the great *escapade* from Libby. You will have seen e'er this an account in the Northern papers. It was quite an episode in the intolerable monotony of this place. About one-half have been recaptured. Expect to receive a letter from you soon, i.e., the letters that came up on the last truce boat are distributed. Tell Sallie I have a bone present[19] for her. Kiss Gibbie for me, and give my love to all.

Fondly,

Robert

February 23, 1864 (Diary)
Libby Prison, Richmond, Va.

Morning pleasant. There was a large fire last night in the city. Ben[20] cries this morning, "Great news in the papers! Great news from Florida. Confederate victory!"[21] Gen. Scammon[22] feels very much mortified at finding himself caged at Libby. Lieut. Weeks and Capt. Carpenter received their boxes today, almost or quite entire. They were God-sends to their respective messes, whose stock of commissaries have been exhausted for some time, and they were reduced to the petty allowance issued each day. A *Messenger*[23] in Carpenter's box was perused by we Indianians with great avidity.

February 24, 1864 (Diary)
Libby Prison, Richmond, Va.

Pleasant and Spring-like. Spent almost the whole day playing chess with Lieut. Schuyler of the 123rd Ohio, with varying success. I think we quit at about even games. Am much in want of a German reader [textbook]. There are some in the building, but I cannot get hold of one. My interest in German flags from want of one. I have been through the Grammar and partially reviewed it. No news, few rumors. General stagnation. Received beef today. Quite a number of boxes have been issued today, among them one to Lieut. Weeks from Sappington. Baked three loaves of bread.

February 25, 1864 (Diary)
Libby Prison, Richmond, Va.

Called up last night at eleven o'clock for roll call from some suspicion that some had escaped. Turner and LaTouche had been seen examining the sewers with a lantern a short time before. We have had two roll calls this morning. The following general order appears in the papers this morning:

War Department
Adj'tant Insp. Genl's Office
Richmond, Feb. 24/64
Genl. Order No. 23
Genl. Braxton Bragg is assigned to duty at the seat of government and, under direction of the president, is charged with the conduct of military operations in the armies of the Confederacy. By orders of the secretary of War.
S. Cooper
Adj't and Insptr. General.

February 26, 1864 (Diary)

Libby Prison, Richmond, Va.

Air cool and bracing, and I love to get my nose inserted between two window bars and hold it there by the hour to enjoy the luxury of fresh air. In the room, the air is so full of smoke & dust that we can scarcely see through it, and we are obliged to cough at nearly every breath. Letters were distributed yesterday afternoon, but I got none. The letters from the North are very discouraging to us. Henry Winter Davis and others wrote that no more exchanges under the cartel will take place, that the U. S. Government will exchange man for man & rank for rank and in no other means. I am very reluctantly coming to the conclusion that we are to be smoked and stifled and choked during the remainder of the war as hostages for about three times our number, who are held for an uncertain number of Negroes who may hereafter be captured.

February 27, 1864 (Diary)

Libby Prison, Richmond, Va.

This morning another terrible outrage was practiced upon us. Roll call was announced while we were still under our blankets. But instead of going into the two East rooms as usual, we were all crammed down at the point of the bayonet into the dining room, as full of smoke as it could be. The room was so full that the men were fairly wedged together & the bayonet had to be forcibly applied to the backs of several officers before the steps could be cleared. We were then informed that the building was to be searched, and the keys were called for. Thus were the officers held until about noon, when the search was completed. Fire arms I believe they were after. Don't think they found any. A search was proper enough, but there is a proper time and way to make it. A boat load of boxes arrived.[24]

February 28, 1864 (Diary)

Libby Prison, Richmond, Va.

Morning pleasant and Spring-like. Oh! How I would like to be out enjoying it. Received a letter from Lillie day before yesterday, informing me of the very dangerous illness of Grandmother Jackson[25] with apoplexy. Wrote a letter also for Joe to his brother for a box. Wrote a letter to Sister Mary signed Thompson.[26] We are all coming to the conclusion, and many of us write it to our friends, that exchange is hopeless, except for a favored few who have friends near the throne. Whatever may be said *for* the No

Exchange policy, it cannot be denied that it is barbarously inhuman. It is rumored that another truce boat is up. Negotiations of some character seem to be going on.

Feb. 29, 1864
Libby Prison, Richmond, Va.
MY DEAR LILLIE:—

Received yours of the 2nd. inst. on the 26th. Regret much to hear that Grandmother's life is dispaired of. Would give anything to see her even for a few moments. Received a letter from Mary.[27] My Dear, I must trouble you again for a box, to contain about as follows:—20 lbs. butter, 20 lbs. sugar, 10 lbs. cheese, 2 new hams, 2 gals. syrup, 7 lbs. coffee, 7 lbs. tea, 10 lbs. candles, 10 lbs. lard, sack [of] flour, doz. [cans of] condensed milk, 1 pk. [peck] beans, soap (bars), pickles, baking soda, dried apples & peaches, crackers, 2 brown linen shirts for Summer, Adler's German Reader and a set [of] chess men. The syrup had better be put in tin to ensure against *breakage*. Private boxes arrive here with every boat. Am quite well.

Fondly Yours,
Robert T. Cornwell
Capt. 67Th Pa. Vols.
P. S. Send also 1 bbl. potatoes & onions.
RTC

February 29, 1864 (Diary)
Libby Prison, Richmond, Va.

Gave my letters to the sergeant this evening. Found for the first time Lieut. Col. Piper, who proves to be my old pupil at Millersville. Had a long talk with him. He belongs to the 77th Pa. Vols. Col. Rose well—acquainted with Morris Wickersham of the 79th. Col. [unclear]. Morris has had difficulty with his Col. And has scarcely been with his command at all since entering the service. Damp and cloudy all days. Played chess almost continually, but tire of everything. Subscribed for three copies of a beautiful lithograph of Libby and scenes with the names of all the officers here, by a Lieut. in the East Room. A fine memento of the war.

5

Libby Prison: Dahlgren's Raid
March 1–May 5, 1864

Cornwell's diary entry for March 2 refers to a "raiding party under command of Kilpatrick." The raid was actually a bold but doomed attempt to free all the Union prisoners held in Richmond.

It began on February 28, when Brig. Gen. Hugh J. "Kill Cavalry" Kilpatrick (1836–1881) put into action a plan of his design that had Lincoln's approval. It called for Kilpatrick, with 3,500 picked cavalrymen and some artillery, to strike weakly defended Richmond from the north. Col. Ulric Dahlgren, the son of Rear Admiral John Dahlgren, and five hundred more cavalrymen were to attack the city from the south. Once in Richmond, they would free all the Union prisoners and cause as much damage as possible to the city.

On the evening of February 28, the entire command began moving southeast toward Ely's Ford, where they engaged in a minor fight with some Confederates. The column split the next day. Kilpatrick and the bulk of his men moved toward Richmond, while Dahlgren and his five hundred men headed toward Goochland, about thirty miles from Richmond.

Confederate authorities, however, had long expected such a raid and were prepared for it. When spies alerted the city of the approaching danger, militia, bureaucrats, and office workers were called out to man the city's defenses. These armed civilians were trained to some extent, and had been called out on previous occasions. They were led by Brig. Gen. George Washington Custis Lee, eldest child of Robert E. Lee.

On March 1, Kilpatrick reached Richmond's northern outer defenses, five miles from the city, where he encountered very stiff resistance from Lee's waiting home guards. After fighting for several hours, Kilpatrick realized that Confederate resistance was much stronger than he had anticipated. He abandoned the raid and began withdrawing eastward toward the Union lines, but was soon attacked from the rear by a small force of Confederate cavalry. Kilpatrick's troopers, now thoroughly exhausted, fought for several more hours before they could resume their retreat.

In the meantime, the swollen condition of the James River forced Dahlgren to switch his attack to the west of Richmond. He got within two miles of that side of the city before being halted by strong defenses. Confederate opposition was commanded by Custis Lee's brother, Maj. Gen. William Henry Fitzhugh "Rooney" Lee. His troops consisted of some cavalry, and infantry company of young boys, and the "Department Battalion," composed of clerks from the various Richmond government offices.

Dahlgren began retreating late in the night of March 1, but the next evening he and his men rode into a trap set by home guards and some of Rooney Lee's men. A volley was fired at the Union cavalry and Dahlgren was among those killed. About one hundred of his men were captured.

Although Dahlgren's raid was stopped in its tracks, it threw Richmond into a frenzy of concern, particularly regarding the possibility of thousands of Union prisoners being released in the city. Security for the prisons was greatly tightened as a result, and rumors swirled within the Libby community. Cornwell's diary for March 3 records that commandant Turner supposedly threatened to blow up the prison if necessary, and had buried a thousand pounds of gunpowder under the building for that purpose.

Whether this was merely a ploy by Turner is open to question. Cavada said there was "well-authenticated information" that the prison was mined, and that the Richmond newspapers stated that "measures not necessary to mention" were in place to prevent the liberation of Libby's prisoners. However, he also said there were a "rumored two hundred," not one thousand, pounds of gunpowder. Furthermore, Cavada was told by another prisoner, who "had it from the best authority," that a guard "was sent down to where the kegs of powder were buried, regularly every half hour during the night, *with a lighted candle* [italics Cavada's], to see that the fuse was all right!"[1] Cornwell states that his information came from Negro workers who had "been digging a large hole in the cellar."

Jones, the civilian war clerk who was in a better position to know, simply said that an unidentified captain procured "several hundred" pounds of powder and "placed them in readiness." He did not say where. In any event, one must question whether Major Turner would tempt fate by allowing unskilled workers to bury such a large quantity of unstable black powder under the area of the prison that contained the cooking stoves. Also, it seems unlikely that Confederate authorities actually intended to explode a large building located in a built-up area of Richmond.[2]

The so-called "Dahlgren Papers" mentioned in Cornwell's diary for March 5 have been controversial since the day they were found on Dahlgren's body by a boy named William Littlepage. Supposedly written by Dahlgren, they called for the terroristic acts mentioned by Cornwell, acts which were considered barbarous by mid-nineteenth century standards. Northern authorities quickly branded the papers as forgeries, but Union general George C. Meade (1815–1872), among others, believed them to be true. The papers have been studied for years, and the prevailing view of modern historians is that they are genuine.[3] The salient points in the papers are shown in Appendix B.

The authorities recognized the growing problem in holding so many prisoners in the city, and began transferring them to camps in other areas. Provost marshal Winder announced that enlisted Union prisoners would be removed from Belle Isle to a new camp at Americus, Georgia.

Beginning on February 7, some of the prisoners were transferred in groups of about four hundred, and by March 24 Belle Isle was empty.[4] Others were directly paroled due to the lack of food to feed them during the continuing impasse in exchange negotiations. Cornwell's diary for March 23 innocently records the fact that some of the Richmond prisoners had been "sent to Americus, Georgia." That camp soon became infamous by another name: Andersonville.

The size of the Libby population was not reduced, however, because those prisoners were officers. They began to create new diversions to while away their time. As Cornwell shows, for a time debating became all the rage. Cavada also described the new activity:

> ...we have among other pastimes, organized a Lyceum, or Debating Club. The chairman sits on the floor *a la* Turque, the "chair" itself being an empty name, without any local substance. The members sit in a circle on the floor, like Indian Chiefs at a war council. The debates are very spirited, and grave questions, involving the destinies of the whole human race, and the future destiny of our "Great Country," are discussed with intense enthusiasm, sometimes even with political virulence, and not seldom with very bad grammar. [5]

Cornwell's entries of March 1, March 20–21, and April 12 describe three incidents of prisoners being fired upon by guards. The first incident took place at Castle Thunder and resulted in the death of a Confederate officer who went to investigate the shooting. The second was the deliberate firing upon Cornwell and two other prisoners who were standing together near an open window in the prison. Cornwell escaped injury, but one of the others was seriously wounded. The third incident was the accidental discharge of a guard's musket, which killed a Libby prisoner. Uncharacteristically, Cornwell failed to note the March 28 killing of a Union prisoner held elsewhere in Richmond. The official report of the event, submitted by Lt. John LaTouche, does much to explain the adversarial relationship between the guards and prisoners in all the military prisons in the city:

> [The guard stated] A prisoner put his head and shoulders out of the window. I told him to go away several times, but he paid no regard to it. I then drew on him and the cap snapped [his musket misfired]. He then made fun of me and laughed at me. I could not understand the words he said, but again refusing to take his head back, I recapped my gun and fired on him.

LaTouche's account also included the statement of the officer in charge of the guard detail:

> [I] was around the corner when I heard the report of a gun; came back and asked the sentry on post No. 2 if he had fired. He replied that he had, but did not know whether he hit him or not; went upstairs and found the prisoner dying. The ball had passed through his head. One of the prisoners told me that they had

warned him that if he persisted in keeping his head out of the window he would be fired upon, but he paid no regard to it.[6]

Discussions about prisoner exchanges began again in March, albeit haltingly. On the 29th, Col. Robert Ould, a Richmond judge and the Confederate agent for exchange, sailed to Ft. Monroe to meet with the new Union agent, Gen. Benjamin F. Butler. Once again, talks broke down over the question of captured Negro soldiers. However, Butler agreed that "In all other respects, [the] cartel [is] to be carried out, and exchange and parole [are] to go forward according to provisions." Jones, the government clerk, reported "it is announced that arrangements have been made for the immediate resumption of the exchange of prisoners on the old footing."[7]

This news revived the spirits of the men in Libby, and the possibility of exchange became, as Cornwell shows, the great subject of conversation and speculation among them. The picture brightened on April 9 when Butler sent "400 and odd" wounded and sick Confederate prisoners to Richmond on a flag of truce boat. Grant, however, urged Butler to take a very hard stance during his negotiations with Ould regarding the status of the Negroes.

On April 17 he instructed Butler that "no distinction whatever will be made in the exchange between white and colored prisoners; the only question being, were they at the time of their capture in the military service of the United States."[8] Progress continued slowly on the exchange talks, and the prisoners were alert to every scrap of news or rumor regarding developments.

Cornwell was by now running low on food. He was partially sustained by friends who shared some of the contents of their boxes. His diary entries reflect his discouragement at the slow progress of the talks, and of his seemingly poor chance of being exchanged. Quite unexpectedly, on April 30 he was exchanged and put aboard a flag of truce boat bound for City Point.

March 1, 1864 (Diary)
Libby Prison, Richmond, Va.

We would fain hail the glad Spring time, but the circumstances are very unpropitious. The day is rainy as been the night just past. The air with fog and smoke and dust and poisonous exhalations is bitterly thick. Altogether, the advent of spring is a very unpromising day. Today, an [Confederate] officer by the name of Wootters was shot and mortally wounded at Castle Thunder. A sentinel shot at a Yankee prisoner,[9] but did not hit him. The Reb official, hearing the report, went upstairs, and finding no one hurt stuck his head out of the window cried out, "All right, Sergeant." Scarcely had he uttered the words when another sentinel, without stopping to see who it was, shot him, the ball taking effect in the right eye and lodging in the left temple.

March 2, 1864 (Diary)

Libby Prison, Richmond, Va.

Yesterday we heard the alarm bells ringing, and this morning learn that a raiding party under command of Kilpatrick has been within three miles of Richmond. Brig. Gen. Henry A. Wise narrowly missed being captured. He was at the house of his son-in-law a few miles out of the city, spending a furlough, when the alarm was given him that the Yankees were within 500 yards of the house. Paying little attention to formalities, he rushed for his horse and made for Richmond and was the first to give the alarm of danger. Something like one hundred Yankee cavalrymen have been brought in today as prisoners. If Kilpatrick succeeds in getting safely away again, he can boast of being nearer to Richmond than any other Yankee commander.

March 3, 1864 (Diary)

Libby Prison, Richmond, Va.

"Gunpowder on the brain" is a very prevalent but not very alarming disease in Libby just at present. The disease takes its name from the following circumstances: Maj. Turner, we learned from some niggers, has been digging a large hole in the cellar. Yesterday afternoon he sent for Adj't. Nuggs and told him he wished him to inform the officers that he had a thousand pounds of [gun] powder buried under the building and that at the first intimation of revolt he would "blow you all to Hell." Their fears arise from the close proximity of our raiding force. The raiders have made good their escape. A batch of letters arrived today, but I received none. Capt. [unclear] knocked down my jug of molasses today. The jug broke, and I lost my syrup.

March 4, 1864 (Diary)

Libby Prison, Richmond, Va.

Cool but pleasant. Very little news this morning. An advance up the Peninsula by a portion of Butler's command was made yesterday, which created some excitement in Richmond, but its whole object seems to have been to cover the retreat of Kilpatrick's raiding party. We understand from a wounded Yankee Lieut. in the hospital under the East Room that the object of the raid was to capture Richmond, etc., etc. and that Kilpatrick's command was divided. The portion under his own command was to attack the town on the N. W. The other portion under Col. Dahlgren were to cross the James River and attack from the south side, while Butler was to attack from the Chickahominy side. Dahlgren missed his way and reached the James at a point where he could not cross.

March 5, 1864 (Diary)
Libby Prison, Richmond, Va.

Thus delayed, he [Dahlgren] found it necessary to abandon that course of attack. He then attacked the fortification on the southeast side of the town and drove away the garrison and captured fourteen Confederate officers in a whore house. Kilpatrick signaled him to withdraw as Butler had failed to cooperate. This is the Lieut's story.[10] This morning's papers say that Col. Dahlgren was killed and that papers found on his person disclose the whole project. Richmond was to be taken. The prisoners on Belle Isle released. Davis and his cabinet killed, and the city burned. The Reb cabinet held a meeting to determine what to do with the Yankee officers captured from the raiding party. It was decided to put them in cells. Dahlgren's body is to be brought to Richmond today. The *Examiner* urged that it be hung in the capitol yard, and buried with all the dishonors of war.

March 6, 1864 (Diary)
Libby Prison, Richmond, Va.

The privies which have heretofore been in a boarded column appended to the outside of the building next to the [Kanawha] Canal are now being changed and brought inside of the brick wall. The friends had better wait until the change is effected before they imperil a man's life whenever he enters them. Yesterday afternoon a Lieut.[11] belonging to the [unclear], while in the privy and doing nothing to provoke the outrage, was fired at by one of the guard. The ball carried away part of one ear and riddled his hat. Such a statement seems too improbable to be believed, but it is strictly true. Today, 64 Rebel officers and 800 men landed at City Point and came to Richmond. About 600 Federal prisoners were sent to City Point in return.

March 7, 1864 (Diary)
Libby Prison, Richmond, Va.

This morning forty eight Federal prisoners-officers were selected [and] notified. Paroled and sent to City Point in return for the Reb. Officers who came up yesterday. Happy men.—Oh! that I had been one of them. Col. Sanderson, Capts. Rowan, Forbes, Jones, etc. were among them. The prospect is that exchange will be resumed; and that our government paroles 25 percent of the excess. Today, the body of Col. Ulric Dahlgren was brought to Richmond for identification. When the body was found, it was lying in a field, stark naked with the exception of the stockings, stripped, robbed, the fingers cut off for the sake of the diamond rings that encircled them. The body had been thrown over a fence from the [turn]pike to save it from the hogs. The artificial leg worn by Dahlgren was removed and it is now at Gen. Elzey's[12] headquarters. It is of the most beautiful design and finish.

March 7th, 1864
Libby Prison, Richmond, Va.
MY DEAR LILLIE:—

Am still quite well. How is Grandmother? If still living, give her my love and tell her how ardently I hope to see her again. I am very glad to hear that our Gibbie is growing to be so fine a boy. Kiss him for me. Ordered a box in my letter last week: lest you should not receive it, I repeat the order.—20 lbs. butter, 20 lbs. sugar, 15 lbs. cheese, 2 new hams, 2 gals. syrup, 7 lbs. coffee, 1 lb. tea, 10 lbs. candles, 10 lbs. lard, sack [of] flour, doz. [cans of] condensed milk, [peck] beans, soap (bar), pickles, baking soda, dried apples & peaches, crackers, set [of] chess men, Adler's German reader, & 2 brown linen shirts for Summer. Send also I bbl. potatoes & onions. Put the syrup in tin to ensure against breakage. [Capt.] Carpenter sends regards. Give my love to all.

Fondly Yours,
Robert T. Cornwell
Capt. 67Th Pa. Vols.

March 8, 1864 (Diary)
Libby Prison, Richmond, Va.

Where the body of Col. Dahlgren was buried no one except those concerned in the burial know. He was buried in a plain flat topped white pine coffin, dressed in a clean coarse white cotton shirt, dark blue pants, and enveloped in a dark military blanket. He was quite a young man, not more than 28 yrs., about 5 ft. 10 in. in stature, long cadaverous face, light hair, slight beard, closely shaven, and had a small goatee very light in color.[13] We learn from Northern papers that Col. Streight has arrived safely at Washington, that his reported arrival at Fortress Monroe was a hoax of his own device. That he requested those who left the prison with him, if they should reach Fort Monroe, to report his arrival there to deceive the authorities here. He remained in or around Richmond for seven days after *emerging* from the famous *hole*.

March 9, 1864 (Diary)
Libby Prison, Richmond, Va.

We learn from the papers of this morning that an arrest and lodgment in Castle Thunder of an important Confederate official took place on the day that the Federal prisoners were taken to City Point. Philip Cashmeyer, chief detective to Gen. Winder, commander of the Department of the Henrico, a man in whom Gen. Winder and "all others in authority" had reposed the most implicit confidence for two years, was noticed to be in confidential conversation with two or three Yankee officers on board the *Schultz* on the way from here to City Point. At the latter place he was observed to hand a package to one of the Yankee officers, who put it in his bosom. The Yankee officer was immediately told that he would be sent back to Richmond unless he delivered up the package, which he immediately did. It consisted of an English & a German document. The former, the late orders of Gen. W [inder]. The latter, so far as translated, highly treasonable. Capt. Hatch put Cashmeyer under arrest.

March 10, 1864 (Diary)
Libby Prison, Richmond, Va.

The papers of this morning state that Philip Cashmeyer was arrested on mistaken suspicions. That the documents which he was detected in handing to the Yankee prisoner were sent to Mr. Aylett—District Attorney for the Confederate states—who pronounced them not of a treasonable character & that there was no legal impropriety in sending them to his wife in Baltimore, & that he was only culpable in the manner of sending them. The act indicated a little vanity on the part of Cashmeyer, who seemed to desire to show his wife in what an important relation he stood to the Confederacy. Yesterday, the Lieut. in charge of the prisons at Saulsbury [sic] was here. He claims to be the confidential friend of Major. W[inder].

March 11, 1864 (Diary)

Libby Prison, Richmond, Va.

The day is fine. Lieut. [Martin] Flick joined our Mess on the 5th inst. Lieut. Weeks having left here and gone upstairs to join the Map & Welch crowd. Since Flick has joined us we have cooked day about.[14] Tomorrow is my day again. There has been considerable emulation among us to see who could get up the best meals. The stock in our larder is getting so low that I hardly know what to attempt to get tomorrow. Think I will have some baked beans, self-made bread & boiled potatoes (some that Flick bought) for breakfast & some pancakes, rice pudding and soup for dinner. We have but two meals per day. Autographs are all the rage here now. Rumors are rife of exchange.

March 12, 1864 (Diary)

Libby Prison, Richmond, Va.

All on the qui vive [heightened alertness] today about a boat and their chances for exchange. Bed time has come again, but no boat heard from. Our condition will be a hundred times worse than before if we are disappointed in the prospect of exchange. Two Southern ladies under charge of the young commissariat came through the building today. I don't wonder that they are curious to look into this [unclear] of Yankees. To one who has never seen a thousand officers confined as it were in one room for nine months, and especially to a lady, such a visit would be intensely interesting, amusing & perhaps instructive.[15] They caught no one skirmishing, I believe.

March 13, 1864 (Diary)

Libby Prison, Richmond, Va.

Rumors are rife this morning of a boat & prisoners. A boat without prisoners— 15 officers to go, &c., &c. Dick Turner came up and took Col. Wilson's[16] name this morning. Understand Lt. Col. Northcott's name is down. Of all the men I know, Capt. Sawyer & Maj. Henry exhibit the most fearful symptoms of Exchange Fever. Maj. Henry had a positive assurance of going from Col. Ould,[17] but when he reminded him of it about a week ago, Ould told him "that was before he attempted to escape through the hole." Bed time again and still we have Libby life continued. I can scarcely imagine how I will feel when my old liberties are restored. Wrote a letter to Lillie.

March 13, 1864
Libby Prison, Richmond, Va.
MY DEAR LILLIE:—

Your letter of the 28th ult. reached me last week. Your statements concerning our dear son's illness have excited considerable concern in my mind. He is in good hands, and I hope for the best. There is but one topic, one hope, one consideration here now, and that is *Exchange* (or Parole): for which there really appears to be some prospect, one load [of exchanged prisoners] having already left. If we are sent away according to date of capture, I will probably enjoy the extreme felicity of being with you again before a great while. If, however, my fate is dependent on the friendly influence I can bring to bear in the matter, my prospects for an early release are poor.

Fondly Yours,
T. T. Cornwell
Capt. 67th Pa. Vols.

March 14, 1864 (Diary)
Libby Prison, Richmond, Va.

All excitement again this morning. Forty officers[18] were taken to City Point to go North. Col. Wilson, 123rd Ohio; Lt. Col. Nichols, 18th Conn.; Lt. Col. Northcott, 12th Va.; Capt. Carpenter, 67th Pa. Vol.; Capt. Douglass, Capt. Martin, Lieut. Rush, Lt. Higginson &c. were among them. Carpenter got his name on the list through Maj. Henry, who induced Rev. McCabe of this city to solicit Judge Ould to put his name on the list. But why this dribbling work of forty officers per week, and they selected not according to date of capture but by rebel favoritism. If this course is continued, it will be five months before we all get off. I wait as patiently as possible for the next boat.

March 15, 1864 (Diary)
Libby Prison, Richmond, Va.

Pleasant. No particular news. My day for cooking. Had fried potatoes, dried beef fried with flour, gravy, pancakes & tea for breakfast. Boiled potatoes, rice pudding, pancakes & tea for dinner.— Only two meals. Played several games of chess. Quite a batch of Yankee prisoners passed here on their way from the [Belle] Island to Americus, Georgia.[19] They looked hard, and some were hardly able to waddle. An attempted demonstration took place today in honor of the returned Confederate prisoners, but we learn that though strongly guarded, more than half of them slipped the ranks before reaching Camp Lee. There is a great contrast between the appearance of the Confed. & Yankee prisoners.

March 16, 1864 (Diary)

Libby Prison, Richmond, Va.

Pleasant and Spring-like. Our fare is becoming quite plain: no *butter*, no *lard*, no meat, corn meal or bread & rice. Since Lieut. Flick joined our mess, he has purchased $20 Confederate dollars' worth of potatoes & $8 worth of eggs. But we have consumed all the potatoes except about one mess, and have left only eggs enough for about two more nice puddings. Potatoes are $10 per bucket full & eggs are $5 per dozen.[20] Lieut. Flick's money is all out now, and we concentrate all our hopes on an early exchange. No news. All quiet along the lines.

March 17, 1864 (Diary)

Libby Prison, Richmond, Va.

St. Patrick's Day is unobserved by any one here that I observe. Though I scarcely know how we would go about observing such a day here. One thing is certain, there would seem little danger of doing it violence by eating meat, for we can get none to eat. 10 o'clock A. M. A lot of meat has just arrived, the first we have had during the present month.[21] A number of Confederate officers[22] were in today, talking to us. They were returned prisoners from the North. All speak well of their treatment. While indignant at our own treatment, I feel proud that they acknowledge that the U. S. had done better.

March 18, 1864 (Diary)

Libby Prison, Richmond, Va.

Cool. My day again for cooking. Had three meals. A self-made loaf of corn bread & tea for breakfast. Rice soup (we had meat again today) and tea and another loaf of corn bread for dinner, and rice pudding and pancakes & tea for supper. To make a rice pudding, I take about 2 quarts of boiled rice and stir into it three eggs & three spoons full of sugar, well beaten together, and add about two thirds of a nutmeg. Bake well. The new privies were completed today. The occupants of the lower and upper West rooms are glad of it.

March 19, 1864 (Diary)
Libby Prison, Richmond, Va.

Pleasant. Two alarms of fire last night in the city. Nothing issued today but corn bread and some of the hardest looking soap ever you saw, whoever you may be. A batch of letters were distributed today, but I received none. Carpenter wrote a letter, it seems while at City Point, to Capt. Borchers, which he read today. It contained nothing in particular except assurances that all was right. Played several games of cribbage this evening, a game in which I have had very little experience. Capt. Zender was my partner.

March 20, 1864 (Diary)
Libby Prison, Richmond, Va.

Quite cool. There is said to be another boat up, containing about 1,100 prisoners, but how many officers rumor sayeth not. A Reb. officer in here yesterday says that our government is purposely delaying exchange till after the 1st of April when, if they are paroled, they will not be declared exchanged according to the terms of the cartel until after the 1st of July, three months thereafter. This interpretation of the tardy manner in which exchange is going on seems to receive considerable credence here. 4 P. M. Just now narrowly escaped being shot. Lieut. Kupp, Lieut. Brownell[23] & myself were standing near a window in [continued on March 21.—TMB]

March 21, 1864 (Diary)
Libby Prison, Richmond, Va.

the kitchen, cooking & looking down the river at the truce boat coming up the river, when the sentinel, unobserved by any of us, fired at us through the window with a charge of ball & buckshot. The ball missed, passing through the upper story and out the roof. One buckshot took effect on the right side of Lieut. Kupp's face, below the cheek bone & coming out at the temple; pieces of another shot broken by one of the window bars, which it struck, entered his neck, nose, forehead & cheek. Brownell and myself escaped uninjured. Sixty or more officers left this morning,[24] among them Col. De Cesnola, Lt. Col. Piper, and every man of the ninth Md. [Maryland].[25]

March 21, 1864
Libby Prison, Richmond, Va.
MY DEAR LILLIE:—

During the past week our immunities in the way of correspondence with our friends have been extended from *six lines to one page*, once a week. You are doubtless watching anxiously at the arrival of prisoners at Annapolis from this place. About eighty-eight officers have left here for a flag of truce [boat], and others are expecting to leave today. About forty left last week, and forty-eight the week before. Carpenter left with the last lot, through the solicitation of a friend here. Like every other officer here, I am waiting anxiously for my turn to come, if there is any such thing as *turn* about the matter.

Am quite well, though I fear from long confinement am sadly incapacitated for field service. A batch of letters was distributed among us yesterday but I received none, which was of course quite a disappointment. You spoke of Gibbie's illness in your last, and I have felt some uneasiness to hear from him again. How is Grandmother? Did you draw any of the money[26] due me? I directed you how to proceed, in a previous letter, to do so, but have no assurance that you received it. Wonder if there is any possibility of my going today? Could scarcely give expression to my gratification if my name should happen to be on that eventful, all-important, happy list. But expectations are groundless and should not be encouraged. I will strive to *bide my time*. Remember me to affectionately to Mother, Sallie and Grandfather, and give my kindest regards to all our friends.

Fondly Yours,
R. T. Cornwell
Capt. 67th P. V.

March 22, 1864 (Diary)
Libby Prison, Richmond, Va.

Today we have had the greatest snowstorm of the season. During the winter we had no snow over an inch deep. It is now 6 inches deep and still falling rapidly, accompanied by a squally wind. The snow drives in at our large barred windows[27] and flies over the whole floor, wetting it and rendering the place more than usually disagreeable. The sentinels are so covered with snow that [when] we look down on them they can scarcely be distinguished from the ground on which they walk. Too cold to sit down; we who are not cooking, tramp about to keep warm. The day has been [a] very disagreeable one to me.

March 23, 1864 (Diary)
Libby Prison, Richmond, Va.

I think last night was the most disagreeable I have ever spent in Libby. The floor was wet, and the howling wind drove the snow into my face all night. My covering was insufficient to keep me warm. So busy was I fighting the cold all night that I slept but very little. This morning the snow was ten or eleven inches deep, much drifted. We have had another very uncomfortable day. Many a poor soul has suffered last night. I am glad to know that very few of our men (about three hundred) are now on the [Belle] Island, and they are working in shops as tradesmen and tolerably comfortable. The rest have been paroled or sent to Americus, Georgia.

March 24, 1864 (Diary)
Libby Prison, Richmond, Va.

My day again for cooking. Maj. Turner has supplied the stoves with cups anew and issued an order to the effect that if we do not keep them on the stoves, he will take the stoves down and issue cooked rations to us. Quite a large number of boxes have been issued today. Lieut. J.C. Hagenbush[28] received one. It had been confiscated because a bottle of liquor was found in it, but he made application personally to Turner for it, and was successful. A debate was held in this room last evening. Capt. & Lt. White, Blair, Anderson & Armstrong participated.

March 25, 1864 (Diary)
Libby Prison, Richmond, Va.

Today, fifteen deserters were to be executed, but the president, Jeff Davis, has reprieved them during the past week, much to their satisfaction. Rained considerably during the day. Presume the storm was snow at the North. Occupied considerable of my time playing "Crib" [cribbage] with Col. Hunter, Lieut. Schuyler [*sic*] & Lieut. Culver.[29] A debate was held this evening in this room on the following question: "Resolved, that a

Republican form of government like that of the United States is better than a Limited Monarchy like Great Britain." Lieut. Sibley of the 123rd Ohio made an able speech in the affirmative. The question is to be resumed on tomorrow evening.

March 26, 1864 (Diary)
Libby Prison, Richmond, Va.

Pleasant. All full of expectation of a truce boat with prisoners. Came near losing our cook stoves today. The wood was all cut, poor as it is, and with nothing to cook with. Some of the officers tore off several boards along with side of the door from the partition between this room and the kitchen. Inspector [Dick] Turner came up, and seeing the havoc, swore he would take down all the stoves and issue us cooked rations. Better council, however, prevailed, and after threatening us through Col. Hunter if the offense was repeated, some wood was sent up. Debate resumed this evening. Capts. Hamlin & McKee[30] made able speeches.

March 27, 1864 (Diary)
Libby Prison, Richmond, Va.

Pleasant. My day again for cooking. Which made it a laborious one for me. Wood very green, so much so that it will not burn at all unless split into very small sticks, which we are obliged to do with case knives, everything in the shape of an axe or hatchet having been taken from us for fear that we may use them for something else than splitting wood. Some rumors but no evidence that there is yet a boat up. We are waiting for one with great impatience. Great solicitude is felt that something yet will turn up to arrest exchange. Phillip Cashmeyer is released and restored to his position as special detective to General Winder.

March 28, 1864 (Diary)
Libby Prison, Richmond, Va.

On Saturday, a batch of letters arrived here and were distributed, but I received none, at which I was considerably surprised, for in the last received Lillie spoke of Gibbie's sickness and she must know I am anxious to hear from him again. Still there is no boat up that we can learn. What can be the reason? Major Henry tonight summed up the arguments very ably given on the aff. [affirmative] & neg. [negative] of the question that was under discussion several evenings of last week, and decided for the affirmative. The day without has been very pleasant and Spring-like.

March 29, 1864 (Diary)
Libby Prison, Richmond, Va.

Stormy.—Rain. Rumors of a boat being up, but the general impression thus evening seems to be that they are false. Many are very much depressed in spirits from the impression that there is [sic] some difficulties between the governments which has arrested exchange. These fears, I think, have little foundation. Have spent most of my time today playing chess & "Crib." For the latter game I have formed quite a relish. Is quite a mental culture and facilitates calculation. Maj. Henry resigned his seat as chairman of the debating society this evening, and Maj. Clark[31] succeeded him.

March 30, 1864 (Diary)
Libby Prison, Richmond, Va.

Little has transpired to break the monotony of the life we had today. Weather cool. This evening the following resolution was discussed by several officers in this and other rooms. Resolved,—that the Periodical Press has a greater influence over mankind than the Pulpit. Myself and two officers were appointed a committee of decision on the merits of the argument. Able speeches were made by Lieut. Sibley, White Anderson, & others. On motion, the resolution was held over for discussion on tomorrow evening.

March 31, 1864 (Diary)
Libby Prison, Richmond, Va.

Received quite a fine present from Lieut. Blanchard's[32] mess of some coffee, sugar, tea, beef tongue, can[ned] roast beef, two slices of ham &c., for all of which we were very much obliged, as for some time back we have been reduced to dry corn bread and rice, morning, noon & night. The Resolution decided on last evening was continued this evening, a number of new speakers participating. The decision of the committee for judges was called for and given in the Negative, though the Committee were not unanimous.

April 1, 1864 (Diary)

Libby Prison, Richmond, Va.

Genl. [Braxton] Bragg visited the prison. A new Resolution was discussed this evening, and one to which many officers objected, claiming that it was not a proper question for discussion. Resolved,—that the right of suffrage ought to be extended to all male colored persons over 21 yrs. of age that can read and write. Lieut. Sibley & White made able speeches on the Aff. Capt. White and others on the Neg. On motion, the discussion was carried over till tomorrow evening. A new committee for decision was appointed.

April 2, 1864 (Diary)

Libby Prison, Richmond, Va.

A very severe snow storm all day. Rain all last night. James River very high. The discussion of the Negro question was resumed this evening. It excites much interest. Lieut. McKay & Capt. Lee from the East room made very able speeches on the Aff., Capt. Monroe & others on the Neg. The disputants still unsatisfied voted to continue the discussion on Monday [April 4] evening. There are many exciting side discussions on the question during the daytime. Many are so indignant at even the mention of such a thing [Negro suffrage] as to scarcely restrain their temper.

April 3, 1864 (Diary)

Libby Prison, Richmond, Va.

Cold and unpleasant. A day of rumors. We hear Judge Ould has returned from Fortress Monroe and says he has been unable to effect an exchange. Again, that the arrangements are all completed and soon we will see our homes. Most of these rumors come from the hospital. I place no confidence in any of them, and am in no manner certain even that Judge Ould has either gone to Fortress Monroe or that he has returned. Am too impatient about this matter to think or do anything else.

April 4, 1864 (Diary)

Libby Prison, Richmond, Va.

Still quite cold. Good News! The papers all state that Judge Ould has returned from Fortress Monroe where he has had an interview with Genl. Butler that all difficulties between them on the subject of exchange are adjusted, and that the work will go briskly on immediately. A boat is expected on Wednesday with prisoners. The river is so high that no water can be pumped from the river to the reservoir, and we get no water or very little carried to us with buckets and that very muddy. It was nine o'clock this morning before I could wash.

April 5, 1864 (Diary)
Libby Prison, Richmond, Va.

River falling. The prison is still supplied with water from buckets. The negroes carry it to the barrels stationed at the dining room front door & at intervals of an hour or so we are allowed to go down with our tin vessels for a supply of water. The debate has been discontinued. The negro suffrage question has been decided in the negative. The papers state that two boats are expected up tomorrow with sick and wounded and a similar number to be sent back. The sick room in the Hospital room downstairs are big with expectation.

April 6, 1864 (Diary)
Libby Prison, Richmond, Va.

The day is quite pleasant and the river still falling. No news of a boat. We are still obliged to use the muddy water from the canal. Our corn ration was today somewhat reduced. Molasses was issued to us for the first time since I have been [here]. Each man receives about 1/4 of a gill. This is constructed as a favorable omen. Quite a large number of boxes were issued today, but nearly all have suffered more or less from plundering hands.

April 7, 1864 (Diary)
Libby Prison, Richmond, Va.

Ruff is quite sick today and I cook in his place. Boiled a lot of stock beans and baked them with a piece of pork that Flick obtained from Capt. White. Quite warm and Spring-like. River still falling. Understand there is a boat up with four prisoners on and nineteen ladies. We cannot understand why more prisoners have not been sent up. The boats are the *New York* and the *Express*. Many of the officers still think there is some difficulty in the way of exchange.

April 8, 1864 (Diary)
Libby Prison, Richmond, Va.

Rainy all day. The papers state that the *New York* and *Express* are up with four prisoners and nineteen ladies; but say that several hundred sick and wounded are to be sent back with them. We cannot learn why the boats have been sent here comparatively empty. All sorts of surmises are rife. "The water is too high to send a load up," "Our government won't have our men put into the same beds aboard the boat that rebel sick have just got out of," Our government won't trust them with advanced prisoners," &c, &c, &c.

April 9, 1864 (Diary)
Libby Prison, Richmond, Va.

Very heavy rain all night. Many say the heaviest they ever knew. River rising rapidly. A drizzling rain still continues. 6 o'clock P. M. The river is nearly as high as it has ever been since we have been here. Lacks only about a foot of running over into the canal. Has rained quite continually all day. No news about exchange. The river I presume is too high to send off the sick here that it is said are meant to be sent. Washed all my clothes today, including my pants.

April 10, 1864 (Diary)
Libby Prison, Richmond, Va.

Raining hard and such has been the case nearly all day. The river & canal are one. The water was started in the pipes today. Got hold of a number of the *Atlantic Monthly* and read it through. Very little news of exchange. Some rumors. Think it must be the policy downstairs [Confederate authorities] to dupe us as much as possible. The *Wm. Allison* and another steamer ran up opposite the prison in the river and anchored under shelter of the island.

April 11, 1864 (Diary)
Libby Prison, Richmond, Va.

Sun shining brightly this morning. Dock Street is under water and the James River is a foot to eighteen inches deep in the basement of Libby Prison. The guard is driven from their posts on the South side of the prison, and we look out the windows on that side with impunity. 6 o'clock P. M. The river has fallen rapidly today. Already it is below the level of Dock

Street. God speed its decline, for with it comes the prospect of an early return to our country and homes.

April 12, 1864 (Diary)
Libby Prison, Richmond, Va.

Anniversary of the attack on Fort Sumter in '61. Cloudy with the appearance of more rain. A sad casualty occurred this morning about 9 o'clock. The new guard as usual drew up in front of the prison in the middle of Cary Street to relieve the old. In this position they were commanded to *load* [their muskets]. One of the men while priming his gun carelessly discharged it. The ball and buck[33] with which it was loaded passed through the middle window of the Upper Middle room, killing Lieut. George L. Forsythe (of the 100th O.V.I. [Ohio Volunteer Infantry], from Toledo, Ohio) instantly, and wounding a Lt. Wells in the neck severely and another officer slightly in the hand. The ball took effect in the left eye of Lt. Forsythe and passed out the back of his head. He was sitting on a bench about 4 ft. from the window at the time. Buck shot struck him in the side and hand.

April 13, 1864 (Diary)
Libby Prison, Richmond, Va.

At a meeting of the officers last evening in the U.M.R. [Upper Middle Room], of which Maj. Henry was chairman, the following Com. [Committee] was appointed to draft resolutions to be sent to the relatives and Regiment of Lieut. Forsythe, expressive of our sentiment with regard to said officer and his violent death. The com. was as follows:—

Lt. Col. Hunter—Ohio	Maj. Clark—Mich.
Capt. Pillsbury—Maine	Capt. Mann—Ill.
Capt. Davis—N. H.	Maj. Walker—Ind.
Maj. Hall—Vt.	Lt. Col. McNew—Kan.
Lt. Col. Josselynn—Mass.	Maj. Johnston—Tenn.
Lt. Peterson—R. I.	Capt. Smith—Al.
Capt. Bowen—Ct.	" Wilcox—Missouri
Capt. Pennfield—N. Y.	Maj. Marshall—Iowa
Capt. Bradford—N. J.	Capt. Love—Kan.
Capt. Uswiler [sp.?]—Penn.	Adj. Jenkins—Wis.
Lt. Sullivan—Del.	Lt. Nucus—Col.
Capt. Menunit [sp.?]—Md.	Capt. Smith—U. S. A,

Capt. White—W. V.
Capt. Fentrip [Fentriss?]—U. S. N.

The "Masons"[34] and members of his own Regt. held meetings for a similar purpose.

April 14, 1864 (Diary)

Libby Prison, Richmond, Va.

Very pleasant. The com. appointed yesterday submitted this evening the following preamble & Resolutions which were adopted:

Whereas:—by a most unfortunate and deplorable occurrence, 1st Lt. George Duncan Forsythe of the 100th regt. O. V. I. has been stricken down in the bloom and vigor of an early and promising manhood; and whereas we his fellow prisoners and brethren in arms feel it a privilege to give expressions on this solemn and mournful occasion to our feelings toward our deceased brother:—Therefore be it resolved by the U. S. Officers in Libby Prison:

1st. That while we submit with becoming reverence to this mysterious dispensation of divine providence, yet we cannot but lament that our service has lost a brave, determined and efficient officer in our cause, a popular, fearless and eloquent advocate; Society, an ornament and support, and the stricken friends of the deceased a heart warmed with noble impulses and moved by exalted aspirations for his country's good.

April 14, 1864 [Diary, continued on a sheet of paper.—T.M.B.]

Resolved:—that we hereby tender to the relatives and friends of our deceased brother our heartfelt commiseration and condolence in the irreparable loss they sustain in his untimely death, and hope that the remembrance of the manly virtues which graced his character and secured the friendship and respect of numerous acquaintances may in some degree mitigate this poignancy of their grief. Resolved:—That in his death we recognize this fact that his life was given up and his blood as truly shed in the defense of the cause so dear to us all as though he had fallen in deeds of valor on the fields of Battle. Resolved:—That the proceedings of this meeting be published in the Toledo papers and a copy of these resolutions sent to the relatives and Regiment of the deceased.

April 15, 1864 (Diary)

Libby Prison, Richmond, Va.

Cloudy and at intervals rain. The Rebs are placing our sick aboard the *Schultz* and *Allison* preparatory to transporting them to Fortress Monroe, or rather to City Point where they will be reshipped on board our boats and taken to the former named place. An effort was made yesterday to raise money enough among the officers to procure a coffin (metallic) for the body of Lieut. Forsythe. The rebels express a willingness to send his body to his friends in Ohio.

April 16, 1864 (Diary)
Libby Prison, Richmond, Va.

Pleasant. Capt. Chase[35] arrived from Saulsbury [*sic*]. At Gen'l. Winder's office he was told he was exchanged. He brought a letter for the officers of the 67th here from Maj. White. Says White is well and fatter than while here. Major says in his letter that his disappointment on last Christmas when he learned that instead of going home he was to be sent further South was very bitter. Thinks he has been exceedingly unfortunate. Chase looks well, and says Saulsbury [*sic*] is much to be preferred to Libby. Says the numerous Union people there befriend the prisoners greatly. Capt. Sneed accompanied him here.

April 17, 1864 (Diary)
Libby Prison, Richmond, Va.

Cool. Wrote a letter to Major White. The reporter of the *Richmond Examiner* visited the prison this morning. A clergyman was here this morning to see Lieut. White in the East Room. He states that the officers will certainly leave here this week. That Judge Ould expects a boat up tomorrow. That their prisoners are ready to start for City Point as soon as ours arrive at Fortress Monroe. Our coffee and tea are all out. We now have nothing but cornbread and cold water.

April 18, 1864 (Diary)
Libby Prison, Richmond, Va.

Pleasant. The [Richmond] *Whig* states that a boat is expected up today. All interest here are now swallowed up in this one momentous one of Exchange. Should we be doomed to disappointment, despair would overwhelm every heart. The harrowing suspense is scarcely less destructive to our peace of mind and health than the actual hardships of close confinement on rations only sufficient to prolong the agonies of starvation. We got no meat at all— nothing but a little cornbread and water regularly, rice in a number of days, and a few black beans. I have nothing on hand that I received from home, and am reduced to my rations. Hundreds of others are in my fix.[36]

April 19, 1864 (Diary)
Libby Prison, Richmond, Va.

Cool but pleasant. The papers contain an account of the capture of Ft. Pillow and the savage butchery of its garrison.[37] It is enough to make one's blood run cold to read the boastful account of the most inhuman murder of five hundred officers and men after they had surrendered, and that, too, by a force ten times as great as that of the garrison. As sure as there is a God in Heaven and brave hearts in the land of the free, there is a great day of retribution coming. Anniversary of the assault on Baltimore.[38]

April 20, 1864 (Diary)
Libby Prison, Richmond, Va.

Weather unchanged. A number of boxes were issued today. Lieut. Flick received one. Though small, it is a God-send to our mess. It contained one ham, about a pound of dried apples, 9 peaches, 1/2 lb. sugar, 2 lbs. butter and a few onions. This evening we enjoyed a very good meal on some stewed peaches, tea, ham, and bread & butter. Got up from around our big box on which we spread our unassuming meal, satisfied for the first time for several weeks. Expecting hourly to hear of a truce boat being up.

April 21, 1864
Libby Prison, Richmond, Va.

Still pleasant though rather cool. This afternoon a large box full of letters was sent up for distribution. They came to City Point about 3 weeks ago. I received a *six line* letter from Lillie. She has understood me to mean that her letters were also restricted to the above limit. She does not acknowledge the receipt of my letter of the 8th of February, in which I suggested that she should draw some of my pay. Carpenter writes to Capt. Borchers. Says he saw my *friend* at Fortress Monroe, and supposes I am exchanged ere this. He writes from [Manor?] Station. Has 20 days *leave*.

April 22, 1864
Libby Prison, Richmond, Va.

Air softer and more balmy. Decidedly Spring-like. The papers contain an account of the capture of Plymouth, Washington County, near the mouth of the Roanoke River, N.C. He [the reporter] reports the capture of a brig. general and some sixteen hundred prisoners.[39] There is certainly someone to blame for the succession of misfortunes that we have been experiencing.

Miss Mary E. Walker, M.D., U. S. A. [United States Army], extra assistant surgeon of the 52nd Ohio Vols. arrived yesterday as prisoner of war at Castle Thunder, where she is confined. She is dressed in male attire, wearing a low-crowned fur hat with black feather, high boots encasing her pretty feet, blue army pants and jacket and blue cloth coat, the latter trimmed with small gilt-coated buttons, the former without ornaments, and hanging talma-fashion over her shoulders and down to her knees.[40]

April 23, 1864 (Diary)
Libby Prison, Richmond, Va.

Day delightful. The truce boat is still expected. Last night a body of prisoners from Danville[41] passed the prison. An officer was overheard to ask at the prison door if there was a boat up. The reply was *no*, but one is hourly expected. He than asked if the other batch had left yet—from which we conclude that the prisoners who passed here three nights ago were also from Danville. A train of ambulances[42] accompanied each lot.

April 24, 1864 (Diary)
Libby Prison, Richmond, Va.

Day delightful. The flag of truce [boat] *Grayhound* came up to City Point about 6 o'clock this afternoon, bearing dispatches from Butler to the commander of the French fleet lying there waiting for tobacco, and reminding him the time fixed upon by the U. S. & French conventions for the fleet to leave the river had arrived. The *Grayhound* returned immediately to Fortress Monroe. And the same afternoon the French fleet started for Hampton Roads. Wrote a letter to Lillie.

April 25, 1864 (Diary)

Libby Prison, Richmond, Va.

Warm. Showers in the morning after which the sun shone out warm and delightfully all day. Cooked today. Consumed the last of Lieut. Flick's box, when I stewed the last of the dried apples this evening. With what impatient anxiety does every prisoner in this building await the arrival of a Truce boat. The [unclear] idea of remaining in this stench house another summer is intolerable.

April 26, 1864 (Diary)

Libby Prison, Richmond, Va.

Fresh fish! Fresh fish! 19 officers from the captured Plymouth garrison arrived here this morning. Among them as they entered the room I almost immediately recognized Surgeon Frick, formerly of the Lancaster County Normal School. He did not recognize me so readily, but was greatly surprised when the truth burst upon him. Among the arrivals were: Brig. General Wessels, Dr. Rush (of Lancaster Co.), Staff Surgeon; Capt. A. Stewart; Lt. D.F. Bergh; Lt. M.G. Font; Capt. Cook; Lt. Col. S.S. Moffitt; Col. Frank Beach, 16 Conn.; Major H.L. Pasco, 16 Conn.; Capt. J.D. Wheeler, 17 Conn.

April 27, 1864 (Diary)

Libby Prison, Richmond, Va.

[Continued—T.M.B.] Lt. A.P. Day, 13 Conn.; Lt. Gordon Robins, 16 Conn.; J.H. Rowlings , chap[lain] 103 Pa.; chap[lain] A.S. Billingsly, 101 Pa.; Lt. O.M. McCall, 103 Pa.; J.D. Lewis, Surg.[eon] 85 N.Y.; A.P. Frick, Surg. 108 Pa.; & N. Mayor, Surg. 16 Conn. The day is quite pleasant. I have spent the day quite pleasantly in the company of Dr. Frick and Dr. Rush. The latter is a fine and talented gentleman and brother of the Rush who attended the Lancaster Normal School during my connection with that institution.

April 28, 1864 (Diary)

Libby Prison, Richmond, Va.

Weather still fine. Vegetation has so put forth that the fields and forests begin to look quite green. I have very much longed today for something good to eat. When I pass a shelf containing crackers & cheese belonging to more fortunate prisoners I can hardly keep my hands off of them. This miserable cornbread all alone does not satisfy me, and though I feel relieved in a measure from hunger after eating it, it is an absolute punishment to do so.

April 29, 1864 (Diary)
Libby Prison, Richmond, Va.

Day delightful. Today we have good news. The news has reached us that there is a boat up with sick prisoners and a very uncertain number of officers. Major Henry informs me this evening that he has a positive assurance of going on the return boat. Oh! What an enviable privilege. Though I cannot reasonably expect to go myself, yet I am glad even with this evidence that the good work is still going on, though it is at a snail's pace.

April 30, 1864 (Diary)
Aboard the *New York*

Flag of truce boat *New York* 9 o'clock P.M. What inconceivable transport of mind and body have I experienced today. I am out of Libby and riding at peaceful anchor in the cabin of the *New York* in the middle of the James River opposite City Point. So unexpected! So desirable. Thirty-four officers, including the Chaplains and doctors of the Plymouth capture and 300 sick. Captain Memmert, Lieut. Remington, Capt. King, Col. Rose, Lt. Cripp, &c., &c. are with us. The Stars and Stripes float over me again for the first time in more than ten months.

May 1, 1864 (Diary)
Aboard the *City of New York*

Off Fortress Monroe. Major Mulford has gone ashore.[43] Left City Point at 10 1/2 A.M. Weather cloudy. The officers on board paroled are as follows: Col. T.E. Rose, 77th Pa.; Col. Frank Beach, 16th Conn.; Lt. Col. James H. Wing, 3rd Ohio; Maj. T.N. Walker, 73rd Ind.; Maj. Henry, 5th O. V. C. [Ohio Volunteer Cavalry]; Surg. D.G. Rush (Genl. Wessel's staff); Surg. A.P. Frick, 103rd Pa.; Surg. N. Mayer, 16th Conn.; Surg. J.D. Lewis 4th Ky. Cav.; Chap. J.H. Rowlings, 103rd Pa.; Chap. A.S. Billingsly, 101st Pa.; Capt. R.T. Cornwell, 67th P. V.[Pennsylvania Volunteers]; Capt. F. Memmert, 5th Md.; Capt. Sam'l. McKee, 14th K. C.[Kentucky Cavalry]; Capt. S.B. King, 12th Pa.; Capt. Robt. Pollock, 14th Pa. Cav.; Capt. J.W.

Lewis, 4th K. C. [Kentucky Cavalry]; Capt. J.B. Fay, 154th N. Y.; Capt. Seth Cole [unclear]; Lt. L.B. Comins[sp.], 17th Mass.;

May 2, 1864 (Diary, continued.—T.M.B.)

Lt. E. M. B. [McBaron] Timony, 15th U. S. I.[Infantry]; Lt. Thos. S. Harris, 3rd Pa.; Lt. H.S. Bevington, 12th U. S. Infantry[?]; Lt. J.M. Holloway, 6th Ind. Cav.; Lt. D.P. Rennie, 73rd O.V.I. [Ohio Volunteer Infantry]; Lt. G. Good, 84th Pa.; Lt. Wm. Stewart, 16th U. S. I.[Infantry]; Lt. G. Cilly [sp.]; Lt. M. Kupp, 167th Pa.; Lt. H. Hubbard, 12th N. Y. C. [Cavalry]; Adjt. W.P. Pierce, 11th Ky. C.[Cavalry]; Adjt. J.B. Wilson, 5th Md.; Adjt. M.R. Small, 6th Md.; Adjt. H.W. Camp, 10th Conn. Reached Annapolis at about 10 o'clock this morning. Met Carpenter and numerous others of our Libby friends in the navy yard. Reported at Barracks on old Camp Ground. Had on a complete new outfit in less than an hour.

May 3, 1864 (Diary)

Camp Parole,[44] Annapolis, Md.

Telegraphed to Lillie to know how many months pay she had received. Last evening attended a reception supper given by our predecessors from Libby. Went this afternoon to parole camp by rail. At depot, met Dr. Petinis on his way to Baltimore, where he is to be tried by court martial on charges preferred by Col. Root of Parole Camp. Met at Camp Private Patterson of my own company. He looks hearty and seemed very glad to see me. Went to hospital to see James Innis, who is now hospital steward in regular army. He was absent on a twenty day leave.

May 4, 1864 (Diary)

Camp Parole, Annapolis, Md.

Received this morning a dispatch from Lillie, informing me that she had drawn six months pay from March 1st [18]63. No orders yet for us from Washington. We are waiting [for] our leaves [to be granted] quite impatiently, such is our anxiety to get home once more. Walked down to the Yard to see the paymaster. Found his office closed. Maj. Wilson appointed while our regiment was on duty here is paymaster. Several officers, among whom Col. Rose & Capt. Memmert, took a *French* [leave] to Baltimore.

May 5, 1864 (Diary)

Camp Parole, Annapolis, Md.

Still no leaves from Washington, and no money from the paymaster. Col. Rose & Capt. Memmert returned from B—[Baltimore]. Called this afternoon on Mrs. Ambler in Cornhill Street. Had quite a pleasant time— the first ladies I have talked with for more than ten months. Josie is not with her mother, but in New Jersey. Well, I suppose I cannot spend my time better than in enjoying the luxury of a decent bed. I will therefore retire.

6

Staff Officer at Monocacy
June 6–August 7, 1864

The page for May 6 in Robert Cornwell's diary is blank. Perhaps it was not necessary to put words on paper that day. He was going home to West Chester.

The War Department granted him a twenty-day leave, commencing on May 5.[1] That wonderful news must have been delivered to him either after he retired that same evening or early the next morning. His joy must have been boundless, and he no doubt rushed to pack his belongings and arrange for transportation to take him to West Chester. We can only imagine his happiness during this time spent in the company of Libby and family and friends; Cornwell the faithful writer left the pages of his diary untouched throughout his leave. How interesting his observations of civilian life would have been.

However, we do know that Cornwell suffered from the effects of his internment in Libby Prison. He was not fully recovered on May 25, the day his leave expired, and wrote to the Secretary of War requesting an extension of his leave. A Surgeon's Certificate describing Cornwell's condition accompanied the letter:

West Chester, Pa. May 25th. 1864.
To Edwin M. Stanton, Secretary of War:—

I have the honor to report that, on account of Physical Disability as set forth in the enclosed Surgeon's Certificate, I am unable to report in person at Annapolis, Md. at the expiration of my *Leave* of *Absence*, but will account for myself to the Commandant at that Post by letter & sending him a duplicate of the enclosed certificate. My address is West Chester, Pa.

Very Respectfully,
Your Ob't Serv't.
R. T. Cornwell
Capt. Co. "I" 67th Pa. Vols.

West Chester, Pa. 25th May 1864
To All whom it may Concern.

Capt. R. T. Cornwell of the 67th Reg. Penna. Vols. having applied for a certificate for leave of absence, I do hereby certify that I have carefully examined this officer and find that he is laboring under *"Physical Disability"* with diaerhoea [sic]. He was evidently very much debilitated by the former condition when I first saw him about ten days ago. I consider him wholly unfit to travel and entirely unfit for Military duty. I would recommend him to be absent from duty, for three weeks from next Friday, May 27th, the time[2] at which his present leave of absence expires. The probabilities are that he will be fit for duty at that time. Capt. Cornwell was an inmate of "Libby Prison" for about ten months, had been very ill with Typhoid fever before his incarceration and his condition is somewhat precarious—he is Anemic and will require medical treatment. I give you as reference the Hon. Jno. M. Broomalt and the Hon. Jos. J. Linis, Commissioner of Internal Revenue. I have the pleasure of a personal acquaintance with both these gentlemen and have been engaged in the practice of my profession in this town for about 27 years.

J. B. Brinton, M. D.

The extension was granted; on his regiment's return dated May 31 he is shown as "Absent with leave by order War Department."[3] While he continued his recovery at home, the 67th Regiment would soon engage in some of the memorable battles of the Civil War.

The veterans of the 67th returned from their furloughs in April, and the regiment was then temporarily attached to the 138th Pennsylvania Volunteer Infantry.[4] They formed part of some 122,000 men under Grant's overall command situated on the north side of the Rapidan River in Virginia. Grant's aim was to open a campaign that would cross the Rapidan, pass by Lee's right flank, and aim directly toward Richmond. At the same time, Benjamin F. Butler and his Army of the James would drive westward between Richmond and Petersburg after landing at Bermuda Hundred.

Opposing Grant was Lee's Army of Northern Virginia, outnumbered almost two to one. The campaign opened with the inconclusive battle of the Wilderness May 5–7, and during the next five weeks the 67th fought at Spotsylvania Courthouse, North Anna River, Totopotomy Creek, and Cold Harbor.[5] By the end of this series of battles Lee had managed to divert Grant from Richmond and inflicted heavy losses on the Army of the Potomac. Butler was ineffective. After being defeated by Brig. Gen. P.G.T. Beauregard (1818–1873) at Drewry's Bluff in mid-May, the Army of the James was bottled up between the Appomattox and James Rivers.

Although he had blunted Grant's challenge to Richmond, Lee was now in defensive positions around Petersburg, a key transportation hub located about twenty miles south of the Confederate capitol. Despite its losses the Army of the Potomac was still formidable, and by mid-June Grant changed his strategy and began digging in for a siege around Petersburg.

In the meantime, Cornwell reported to Camp Parole, near Annapolis, sometime during the month of June. His extended leave at home was over, but officially he was still a paroled prisoner awaiting exchange. Cornwell therefore spent the next few days as a prisoner in the camp he was once assigned to guard earlier in his career.

He was exchanged late in June, and evidently rejoined the regiment in the vicinity of Petersburg.[6] On June 29 he accepted an invitation to go on the staff of the Third Division, VI Corps as provost marshal. Orders to that effect were issued the next day.[7]

The Union army Provost Marshal General's Department was organized in March 1863. It provided each army in the field with its own provost marshal, who was the senior officer in charge of enforcing military law. Lower commands appointed provost marshals from among their own officers. Cornwell, therefore, became the chief military police officer for the several thousand men in the VI Corps' Third Division, commanded by Brig. Gen. James Brewerton Ricketts (1817–1887).

As provost marshal, he would have been assigned some troops, probably cavalry, to assist in carrying out his wide range of duties. These routinely included maintaining discipline among the troops, arresting those who broke military law, administering martial law in occupied civilian areas, and apprehending deserters.

On the march, one of Cornwell's primary duties would have been to reduce straggling, a constant problem in Civil War armies, and to make sure that those who did fall behind eventually rejoined their units. In battle, Cornwell and his provost guards prevented soldiers from leaving the firing line without good reason, arrested those who abandoned their posts, and took charge of captured enemy soldiers.[8]

The role of provost marshal was difficult but important, and required both intelligence and good judgment on the part of the officer assigned to it. It was also a compliment to Cornwell's military and personal skills that he was selected, because provost marshal was a staff position.

Staff officers, who were typically experienced captains or majors, reported directly to their general and assisted him with the operations of his command. They formed the general's military family and had to work well together in order to achieve maximum effectiveness. Moreover, the better commands, and the Third Division was one of them, made do with a relative handful of staff officers. Therefore, the selection of a new officer was a matter of some importance.

Cornwell's August 5 letter lists his fellow staff officers by rank, name, and staff position. The August 4 letter is a fine description of life in camp for the Third Division's staff officers and the pleasantries associated with the visit of Frances Ricketts, the wife of the division's popular commanding officer.

General Ricketts was born New York. He graduated from West Point in 1839 and married the following year. Unfortunately, his wife died soon after, leaving Ricketts to raise their infant child. He served as an artillery captain in the Mexican War, and in 1856 married his second wife, Frances Lawrence. Cornwell erred when he wrote that Mrs. Ricketts accompanied her husband in Mexico.

"Fanny," as everyone called her, was described as being less than beautiful and taller than her husband. She was, however, truly a soldier's wife and Ricketts relied heavily upon her. She was accustomed to military camp life, and made herself useful while accompanying her husband. One officer commented that ever since her marriage she always made out Ricketts' regimental muster rolls and reports.[9]

Ricketts began the Civil War as a captain in the artillery. He was wounded and captured at First Manassas (Bull Run) in July 1861, after a conspicuous display of bravery. Ricketts spent the next five months in Libby Prison, returning to duty in April 1862 as a brigadier general of volunteers commanding the First Brigade of Ord's Division, Army of the Rappahannock. Two months later he was given command of the Second Division, III Corps, leading them at the battles of South Mountain and Antietam.[10]

A serious wound at Antietam forced Ricketts to leave his command. He recuperated in Washington, where he served on courts-martial boards during his recovery. In April 1864 he was given command of the Third Division, VI Corps, Army of the Potomac, which he led at The Wilderness and Spotsylvania.

Cornwell's July 6 letter refers to his division being sent from Petersburg to Harpers Ferry "to check a raid of Rebs into Maryland." Rather than a raid, it was the beginning of Robert E. Lee's twofold strategy to obtain control of the Shenandoah Valley and relieve pressure on the siege of Petersburg.

"The Valley," as it was generally called, runs 165 miles in a southeasterly direction from Harpers Ferry in the north to Lexington in the south. It averages about thirty miles in width, and is bordered on the east by the Blue Ridge Mountains and by the Alleghenies on the west.[11] Because the Valley rises in altitude as it runs north to south, the usual traveler's terms are reversed. Moving south is going "up" the Valley, and vice-versa. The lush farmland produced bounteous amounts of grain, cattle, fruit, and vegetables. It was the major source of food for the Army of Northern Virginia and, strategically, the Valley was a natural portal into both the North and the South.

The first part of Lee's plan was to wrest control of the Valley from the enemy and secure its fall harvest for the Army of Northern Virginia, now virtually entirely dependent upon the Valley for its sustenance. Then, he intended to relieve pressure on besieged Petersburg by marching down the Valley and menacing Washington. This he believed would force Grant to release troops from Petersburg for the defense of the capitol. Lee was also aware that the capture of Washington, although not a part of his overall strategy, might revive the possibility of overseas recognition of the Confederacy.[12]

Lee assigned these tasks to Lt. Gen. Jubal Anderson Early (1816–1894), then commanding the Second Corps of the Army of Northern Virginia at Petersburg. It was Stonewall Jackson's old command, composed of some 12,000 veteran soldiers. Early, a Virginian and West Point graduate, was an experienced soldier who served in the Seminole and Mexican wars. After resigning from the army he established a successful career as a lawyer and was active in local politics.

Early offered his services to Virginia the day after the state seceded, and he was immediately commissioned as a colonel in the state's forces.

Although nearly six feet tall, Early suffered from painful arthritis which at times caused him to be bent almost double. The pain of that affliction may have been the cause of his irritable personality, which tinged his wit with biting sarcasm and filled his conversation with a stream of loud profanity. Lee seemed to enjoy Early's company despite the differences in their personalities, calling him "my bad old man." Another officer who knew Early said his "keen glance drove home the wit or humour, and everyone who ventured upon word-combats with Lieutenant-General Early sustained a 'palpable hit.'"[13]

While not particularly popular among his fellow officers, Early was respected as a highly competent soldier. A staff officer described him as "one of the ablest soldiers in the army. Intellectually, he was perhaps the peer of the best for strategic combinations, but he lacked ability to handle troops effectively in the field; that is, he was deficient in tactical skill."[14] His troops called him "Old Jube" or "Old Jubilee," and they fought like wildcats for him.

Lee's order to begin moving arrived late on the night of June 12. The next day, the Second Corps left Petersburg and began marching toward Lynchburg, Virginia, to prevent its seizure by Union Maj. Gen. David Hunter (1802–1886). Hunter and his 18,000 men blocked the lower part of the Valley and were attempting to cut the strategically important Southside Railroad at Lynchburg. After several blighted attacks, Hunter broke off his attempt and retreated into West Virginia. As Early entered Lynchburg on the 18th, he shouted in the direction of the receding backs of Hunter's men: "No buttermilk rangers after you now, you God-damned Blue-Butts!"[15]

The entire Valley was now open, and Early began moving down in it, reaching Winchester on July 2. The next day he was near Harpers Ferry, skirmishing against the inept Brig. Gen. Franz Sigel (1824–1902). All along the route from Lynchburg Early noticed the devastation wrought by Hunter's men on the countryside. "Houses had been burned, ...At Lexington Hunter had burned the [Virginia] Military Institute, with all its contents, including its library and scientific apparatus; and Washington College [now Washington & Lee] had been plundered and the statue of Washington taken."[16]

Early's goal was to take Harpers Ferry and then move directly to Washington, and his powerful movement began to worry the residents of Baltimore and Washington. However, because Union forces in the vicinity of Harpers Ferry were in strong defensive positions, Early decided to cross the Potomac River near Shepherdstown, W.Va. on July 5. Fighting soon broke out in the vicinity.

He captured Hagerstown the next day and levied a $20,000 ransom on the city to pay for part of Hunter's destruction of property in the Valley. The Second Corps' march was halted for three hours while the city fathers raised the money. Baltimore and Washington were in a growing state of panic; although the capitol had an immensely strong defensive network of fortifications, there were not enough soldiers in Washington to man them. The artillery and infantry regiments that had occupied the fortifications had been sent to reinforce the Army of the Potomac earlier in the year, and relatively few combat-ready soldiers were in the city.

As Lee hoped, Early's approach toward Washington forced Grant to release units from Petersburg and send them to reinforce the capitol. Among these was the VI Corps' Third Division, in which Cornwell served. At the same time, the states of New York and Pennsylvania were asked to send 20,000 militia to the scene. They would be joined by a hodgepodge of War Department clerks, "100 day men," Veterans Reserve Corps soldiers and citizen volunteers. This scratch force of about 6,000 was put under the command of Maj. Gen. Lew Wallace (1827–1905), who later achieved fame as the author of *Ben-Hur*.

In an attempt to delay Early until Union reinforcements arrived from Petersburg, Wallace, then at Frederick City, Maryland, retired southward and took a strong defensive position at Monocacy Junction, along the Monocacy River. Early entered Frederick City on July 9. The battle of Monocacy that Cornwell describes in his letters and diary commenced early in the morning.

The fighting was severe everywhere, but particularly so on Wallace's left flank, where Ricketts' Third Division was placed. Cornwell attended a reunion at the Monocacy battlefield twenty-five years later and told a newspaper reporter about the battle. According to Cornwell's account, on the morning of the battle he was acting as an aide to General Ricketts, commanding the two brigades of the just-arrived Third Division of the VI Corps. Ricketts told Cornwell to ride to Wallace and ask how he wanted the Third Division positioned in the line. Cornwell returned with the information that Wallace wanted it put on the left flank of the Union line. Cornwell and Captain Damon, Ricketts' aide-de-camp, were then ordered to form the brigades on the left, across a bridge and on the bank of the river. Cornwell recalled that fighting commenced as soon as the Union troops were posted, and it was soon evident that Early was going to cross the river below the bridge and turn the outnumbered and outgunned Union left flank. He finished his account by describing how Union soldiers thereupon burned the bridge and an adjacent house and changed their front to meet the attack.[17]

Wallace held his position until late in the afternoon, when his left flank began to weaken and he was ordered to retire. He had put up a brave fight and lost 2,000 men. Early's losses were fewer, about seven hundred, but Wallace had delayed Early's march toward Washington for almost an entire day.

The only Union impediment was now out of the way. Washington was only about forty miles away and the road to it was open. As he did with Hagerstown, Early also imposed a ransom on Frederick City, this time in the amount of $200,000. On the morning of July 9 Early began moving toward the capitol. That day and the next he was fighting in the outskirts of Washington, but had to stop his advance in order to rest his exhausted men. Battle casualties, sunstroke, and other effects of the intense campaign had reduced Early's effective strength to about 8,000 men. Meanwhile, Union reinforcements were finally arriving in Washington. By July 12 Early was outnumbered. He viewed the city's now fully manned defenses and described them as being:

> ...exceedingly strong, and consisted of what appeared to be enclosed
> forts of heavy artillery, with a tier of lower works in front of each pierced for an

immense number of guns, the whole being connected by curtains with ditches in front, and strengthened by palisades and abattis....every possible approach was raked by artillery....as far as the eye could reach, the works appeared to be of the same impregnable character....every appliance of science and unlimited means had been used to render the fortifications around Washington as strong as possible.[18]

Early concluded that the defenses were too strong for him to assault. After demonstrating at Ft. Stevens, he withdrew back across the Potomac River that evening. Although he did not capture Washington, his attack nevertheless sent shock waves through the North: after four years of fighting, the Confederate army was still able to strike closer to its enemy's capitol than the Union army could at Richmond. Moreover, Early cleared the Union army out the Valley and had gathered large amounts of supplies in Maryland.

After disengaging at Washington, Early's army moved through Rockville on its way to Leesburg, Virginia. The Union VI and XIX Corps and men from Hunter's command pursued in an attempt to locate and drive Early out of the Valley. Cornwell's August 1 letter vividly describes the worn-out condition of the Union soldiers at this time.

In the same letter he mentions that Confederate forces were in Pennsylvania and had burned the town of Chambersburg. That event occurred on July 30, when Confederate cavalry, acting under Early's direct orders,[19] demanded a ransom from the town of $500,000 in currency or $100,000 in gold. The local officials refused to pay, erroneously believing that a body of Union cavalry was on its way to save the town. Chambersburg was put to the torch and most of its buildings were destroyed. Damages exceeded $1.5 million, much of which was not covered by insurance.

The burning of Chambersburg and the nearby presence of Confederate troops threw the rest of southeastern Pennsylvania into panic. Lillie, who lived less than one hundred miles east of Chambersburg, must have been worried that West Chester might also be visited by these elements of Early's army.

June 27, 1864 (Diary)

Near Petersburg, Va.

Nothing new. Saw a report of our officers who had arrived in Richmond in a Richmond paper. All prisoners had to go around that way.[20]

June 28, 1864 (Diary)

Near Petersburg, Va.

Troubled much with Diarreah [*sic*]. Took some powders to check it.

June 29, 1864 (Diary)

Near Petersburg, Va.

Received note from Capt. Burnham. Rode his horse up to the front. Was not with his train. Returned about 4 o'clock. Went to Div. Hd. Qrs. [Division Headquarters]. Saw Capt. King A. Adj. [Assistant Adjutant]. Offered me a position on staff. Accepted. Saw Staunton in the evening. Reported to him as he reported [unclear] to his Regt. at Div. Hd. Qrs.

June 30, 1864 (Diary)

Near Petersburg, Va.

Stayed last night with Capt. B.[Burnham?]. Visited [Dr.] Barr with Mr. Smith. Rec'd. my orders as Provost Marshal, 3rd Div. 6 A.C. [VI Army Corps] about noon. Reported. Moved with the Corps to [unclear, probably Reams'] Station on Weldon [and Petersburg] Railroad—8 miles. No obstacles.

July 1, 1864 (Diary)

Reams' Station, Va.

Corps moved from Reams' Station after destroying effectively many miles of the Weldon R. R. At about 7 o'clock P.M. came back to Jerusalem Plank Road. Where we arrived about 11 P.M. Encamped.

[There are no diary entries for July 2 through 5.—TMB.]

July 6, 1864 (Diary)

Near Petersburg, Va.

This morning our Division received orders to pack up and move to Harpers Ferry to check a raid of Rebs into Maryland. A very severe march to City Point. Reached there about 10 o'clock P.M. Genl. Rickett's & Staff with Provost Guard and Pioneers and Head Quarter horses were loaded in the *Sylvan Shore* [transport boat]. We anticipated a rapid run for Baltimore in advance of the troops. We were much disappointed. The boat was a "tub." Ran slow. Most of the other boats passed us. Left 18 Hd. Qr. horses at Fortress Monroe.

July 7, 1864 (Diary)

Baltimore, Md.

Arrived at Baltimore about 10 o'clock P. M. after quite a pleasant time on the [Chesapeake Bay]. We were obliged to board ourselves on the boat.

July 8, 1864 (Diary)

Baltimore, Md.

Took cars from Camden Station to Monocacy Bridge. Took cars in the afternoon for Monocacy where we arrived about 5 o'clock next morning. The 69th [unclear] and 6th Md. and part of another Reg't. did not arrive at Baltimore in time to go to Monocacy with us. Col. Staunton was left back to send them up as soon as they can. Arrived at Ellicotts Mills and encamped.

July 9, 1864 (Diary)

Monocacy, Md.

Formal line of battle of Monocacy. Formed line of battle in the morning at about 7 o'clock A.M. Fought until about 3 1/2 P.M., when we fell back under orders to Baltimore Pike and marched to Ellicotts Mills. Took cars for Baltimore.

July 10, 1864 (Diary)

Monocacy, Md.

Arrived at Ellicotts Mills and encamped.

July 11, 1864 (Diary)

Monocacy, Md.

Took cars for Baltimore.

July 12, 1864 (Diary)

Baltimore, Md.

Marched to Druid Hill Park and encamped.

July 13, 1864 (Diary)

Baltimore, Md.

    Marched to Mt. Clair Station and took cars to Washington.

July 14, 1864 (Diary)

Washington, D. C.

    Marched from depot to several miles beyond [unclear].

July 15, 1864 (Diary)

Washington, D. C.

    Marched to Edwards Ferry. Forded and found line of battle on the south side of Goose Creek.

[There are no diary entries for July 16–24. This may be due to the extensive movements of the army during those days, which are described in Cornwell's July 25 letter.—TMB.]

July 25th/64

Hd. Qrs. 3Rd Div. 6th A.[rmy] Corps.

Near Georgetown, D. C.

MY OWN DEAR LILLIE:—

    Once more we have stopped an "immediate movement is expected." I had better write while a moment offers respite. We arrived here day before yesterday evening. I rode into Washington yesterday afternoon and spent the balance of the day with Mr. Westlake. He is well—has had some experience as a soldier. Was out with all the rest of the emergency population of the city for a few days guarding the defenses. I cannot perhaps give you a better summary of our doings for some time back than by extracting from my diary. So here goes—July 6, 3rd Div. 6th A.C. marched from the point of Petersburg to City Point—12 miles, and taking transports, started down the James.

    July 7th, on the Chesapeake Bay. July 8th arrived at Baltimore about 2 o'clock A.M. Took cars about 4 P.M. from Camden Station for Monocacy Bridge. July 9th, arrived at Monocacy Bridge about 2 o'clock A.M. Prepared and ate some breakfast, formed line of battle—the enemy drove in our pickets about 8 o'clock A.M. General fight commenced about 9 A.M.

Terrible fight (in which we lost very many brave men and officers and during which I came out unscathed, though I rode thru a most terrific shower of bullitts [*sic*] just in rear of our line several times) until about 4 P.M., when we fell back by order to the Baltimore Pike on which we retreated until nearly daylight next morning.

July 10th—arrived at Ellicotts Mills. The ladies treated our wounded and footsore soldiers with the most delicate consideration. I think when wars are no more, I would like to live in such a place as Ellicotts Mills. July 11th, about 1 o'clock P.M. Took cars for Baltimore, where we arrived in the evening. Stayed at Mt. Clair station, Baltimore, overnight. July 12th, marched to Druid Hill Park and remained in camp there all day. July 13th, took cars for Washington, where we arrived in the evening. July 14th, marched towards Edwards Ferry on [the] Potomac, about 15 miles. July 15th, proceeded to the Potomac—forded it and marched to Goose Creek. July 16th, marched from Goose Creek about 4 miles beyond Leesburg, where we overtook the other two Divisions of our Corps, the 19th Corps & Hunter's troops under command of Genl. Crook.[21]

July 17th, marched about 16 miles to the Heights on the South side of the Shenandoah near Snickers Ferry. Crook's command undertook to cross before we came up, but the Rebs advanced in force from the other side to contest their crossing and repulsed them.[22] July 18th, in camp on the Heights. July 19th, the whole forces crossed the river (waded) and marched nearly to Berryville without opposition, and received orders to return to Washington. July 20th, marched 25 miles in return to Goose Creek. July 21st, proceeded to Difficult Creek. July 22nd, reached this point.

Our men are much worn out, and an effort is being made to allow us to remain here for a few days to recuperate. Whether it will be successful or not is doubtful. We expect to be shipped back to City Point and had orders to be ready this morning. But the storms (how strange to speak of a storm of rain) interfered in our behalf, and the order to move was countermanded. If I can have any reasonable ground for supposing that we will remain here a few days, I will telegraph for you to come to Washington where I will meet you. I do wish they would let us stay here a little while. Should I do so, you must bring Gibbie along. My health is very good. Westlake thinks I look well. Genl. Ricketts and most of his staff are in Washington today. The Genl. is there with his wife. I wish I was there or somewhere else with mine. Mrs. Ricketts makes her home in Washington.

Capt. Carpenter is not wounded but *is said* to be sick. He is trying very hard to get out of the service. It is very amusing to read his letters. He has not been with his Reg't. at all since he was released from prison. Adj't. Young is going to try to get out while here at Washington. It remains to be seen whether he will succeed or not. I think he will.[23] He can get a Surgeon's Certificate & this with the influence of Foster at Greensburg & William Stewart[24] of Indiana will probably get him through. You ought to see my horse, or rather, mare. I call her Mary, and we have a fine gallop. I have had several horses for myself since I have been provost Marshal. Whenever I can seize a better one [horse] than I have, I make an exchange and turn the old one over to the Quarter Master.

Mary is only about 6 yrs. old and is a very good beast. I have her well taken care of. If I keep on as I have been, I will soon be one of the best-mounted men in the service. Give my love to Sallie, Mother & Grandfather. I received the towels and handkerchiefs night before last. They are very good. Tell Gibbie Papa always thinks of him, wants to see him and loves him. Tell him he must not forget Papa.

Fondly Your Own,

Robert

Excuse the red [ink], I had no black.

July 26, 1864 (Diary)

Rockville, Md.

Left the vicinity of Georgetown and marched to Rockville. Order of march for Corps—3rd Div., 1st Div., 2nd Div. Reached Rockville about 5 o'clock P.M. Many of the Corps back to Washington. Col. Hyde sent to Washington with a Regiment to bring up stragglers.

July 27, 1864 (Diary)

Hyattstown, Md.

Left Rockville at 4 A. M. Order of march—1st Div., 3rd Div., 3rd Div.,—1st Brig., 2nd Brig. Reached Hyattstown at about 1 1/2 o'clock P.M. Head Qrs. at a house owned by one Teigler. Quite an entertainment in the evening by band and glee club. Arrested two citizens by the names of Thomas & Eli Price. Charged with disloyalty and piloting Rebels during the recent raid of the latter.

July 28, 1864 (Diary)

Monocacy Bridge, Md.

Left Hyattstown at 5 o'clock A.M. Order of march for Corps.— 1st–2nd Div., Gen'l. Getty; 2nd–3rd Div., Gen'l. Wheaton; 3rd–1st Div., Gen'l.

Russell.[25] [unclear]. Released Thomas & Eli Price for want of sufficient evidence against them. Arrived at Monocacy Bridge, the scene of the fight of the 9th inst. [unclear] . Rested about 4 hours and resumed the march, fording [the] Monocacy [and] leaving Frederick to our right. Reached Jefferson at 10 1/2 P.M.

July 29, 1864 (Diary)
Harpers Ferry, Va.

Left Jefferson at 5 o'clock A.M. Order of march the same as on yesterday so far as Divisions are concerned. Ruben Cochran's house was our Hd. Qrs. Arrived at Harpers Ferry about 1 1/2 o'clock P.M. Called at Mrs. Rowe's in Bolivar. Mrs. Rowe was not at home. Saw Nellie and ate some dinner with her. Visited Mrs. Fosset and saw Mattie. Marched on to Halltown, when we overtook Crook's command and encamped for the night.

July 30, 1864 (Diary)
Halltown, Va.

11 o'clock A.M. Strange today we have been allowed to be still thus far today. No orders are yet issued for a movement. 3 o'clock P.M. Received orders to march immediately back toward Frederick City. While the artillery of the 2nd Div. was crossing the Pontoon bridge, it (the bridge) broke, delaying our progress so that the 3rd Div. did not cross the bridge before 3 o'clock A.M. of [the] 31st.

July 31, 1864 (Diary)
Frederick, Md.

Crossed the pontoon over the Potomac and marched on to Jefferson (12 miles) from the Ferry, where we stopped for dinner. The day intensely warm. Many died on the road from exhaustion and *sun stroke*. Very dirty. Found it impossible to keep the Division closed up. Reached the vicinity of Frederick City about 6 o'clock P.M. and encamped for the night.

August 1, 1864 (Diary)
Frederick, Md.

Remained in camp during the day. Visited Frederick City during the forenoon. Bought some socks, shaving apparatus, gloves, riding whip, stationery, etc. Col. Truax of 1st N.J., formerly commanding 1st Brig., dismissed the service of the U. S. for disloyal sentiments, breach of arrest, etc. Was dismissed by order of Gen'l. Hunter.

August 1st/64
Hd. Qrs. 3rd Div. 6th A. Corps
Frederick City, Md.
MY OWN DEAR LILLIE,

We are resting today. Oh! How much we need it. Our Corps and particularly our Division has had a very severe campaign since we left Petersburg, Va. I have been making a little calculation, and find our Division has marched over 300 miles since landing at Baltimore on the 8th of July. It must be remembered that this marching has been done in the hottest of weather and over roads so dusty that when the column is in motion the dust is suffocating. A dense cloud rises over the men to a great height, so thick that the column is invisible at 20 yards distance.

Day before yesterday afternoon we were suddenly ordered back from Halltown in Va. (A position we had just reached after marching from Washington). Starting about 4 o'clock P.M. [we] marched all night and all the following day, reaching our present position last evening. Yesterday was the hottest, and in every way the worst, day for marching I ever experienced. A number of our men fell dead on the road, and cases of *sun stroke* were very numerous. You know, it is my business [as provost marshal] to keep up stragglers. Yesterday, I could not do it [as] the men gave out in such numbers; and indeed, my guard had all they could do to keep up themselves. To give you an idea of what we have been doing since I last wrote you, I will make some extracts from my diary.

July 26th, left the vicinity of Georgetown, D.C. and marched to Rockville, Md. July 27th, marched from Rockville to Hyattstown. Left Hyattstown about 5 o'clock A.M. and reached Jefferson about 11 P.M. On the way, we passed over the battle ground at Monocacy Bridge fought on the 9th of the same month. The numerous graves both of our own men and rebels, the dead horses, the houses and fences perforated with bullets and shell, tell the tale of the terrible strife I witnessed there a few weeks before. July 27th, left Jefferson and passing through Harpers Ferry reached Halltown, Va. I have told you our doings since.

We hear that the rebels are in Pennsylvania in considerable force. That they have burned Chambersburg, etc. I presume that great excitement prevails in Southern Pa. again. We expect to move toward Hagerstown from here. At least, *I* expect we will. I wonder how you all do. Whether you are greatly alarmed or not. I do not think there is much occasion for it [alarm]. I wish they would take us by rail to Pennsylvania to meet them. P. of Wickersham [unidentified] will have an opportunity for another emergency reg't. He can use those bright swords. I suppose he will claim to be a veteran now, on the strength of his former experience.

How is our dear Gibbie and Mother and Sallie? Give them my love.

I forgot to tell you that I saw Miss Nellie Row[e] when I was at Harpers Ferry. She was well, and I had the pleasure of taking dinner with her. She sends her love to you and Gibbie. Mrs. Row[e] was not at home. I also called at Mrs. Fossett's. Saw their daughter, Mattie, for the first time, though she said she felt as though she was acquainted with me.[26] They were considerably surprised to see me, for they had heard of my capture but had not heard of my release. Of course, I had a great many questions to answer. They have had a very hard time of it there. On last Fourth of July a fight between our men and the rebels took place in the streets of Bolivar, and the town was shelled from Maryland Heights. Several houses were burned and several women killed. Mrs. Fossett's and Mrs. Row[e]'s families stuck to their houses, though those terrible shells burst around them and many bullets passed through the doors and windows.

It is about 10 o'clock P.M. and we still have no orders to move. I just learned that Gen'l. Hunter is sending all disloyal citizens in Frederick [to the] South. I was in Frederick City today; this is the town from which the rebels squeezed $200,000. It was paid by the banks and the Corporation [the city government] to save the town from destruction. The loyal citizens declare they will not pay it. I must close. I am tenting with Dr. Barr. He is well, and sends his regards.

Very Fondly Yours,
Robert

August 2, 1864 (Diary)
Frederick City, Md.

Ordered to move in the morning. Order countermanded. Remained in camp all day. In the evening visited Frederick City with Gen'l. Wheaton, Capt. Clendenning, Capt. Oaks, Dr. Barr, Capt. Snodgrass, Charles Eckendon & the [New York] *Herald* correspondent—Mr. Hannam. Orders issued in the evening restoring Gen. Wright[27] to [command of] the Corps and Ricketts to the Division, etc.

August 3, 1864 (Diary)

Near Monocacy Junction, Md.

The Corps struck tents and took the road for Buckeystown at 6 A. M. Encamped on the banks of the Monocacy Junction, our old battleground. Our Hd. Qrs. in A.M. —Thomas' Orchard. Gen'l. Ricketts telegraphed to Washington for his wife. Capt. Burnham in consideration of the preparations to stay awhile, discussed the propriety of sending for *ours*, but could find no place for them to board and was discouraged, moreover, by the uncertain period of our stay.

Aug. 3rd/64

Hd. Qrs. 3rd Div. 6th A. Corps.

Near Monocacy Junction, Md.

MY OWN VERY DEAR LILLIE:—

Received your nice letter, including Gibbie's self-executed and expressed message on the 2nd inst. I remember distinctly my surroundings and feelings at the time of its reception and sending. Here is the picture. Division Hd. Qrs. in a beautiful orchard, carpeted with a cool, rich green sod, on the east side of a hill commanding a beautiful view of Frederick City. Dr. Barr lounging by my side in our tent after having refreshed himself with a thorough wash. The *Herald* correspondent stretched on the grass at the tent door,—the General on his couch, asleep. My Provost Guard encamped under two large trees in a field on our left and front, lazily dreaming the sultry hours away. The Pioneers encamped on a hill to our left and rear, employed in a work very similar to that of my Guard. Our horses tied to trees and stakes on the North side of the orchard, switching and stamping off flies that seem very destructive to their peace of body.

And orderlies lounging about under different trees with their horses saddled and always holding themselves in readiness for the familiar call of "Orderly" when some message is to be carried to any part of the Corps or Division. Such were my surroundings when the mail carrier rode up with a letter for *me*. Of course I knew who it was from a soon as I saw it.

My Dear Lillie, a man who has a sweet wife and child has no business in the army so far as any personal considerations are concerned. That is my proposition. I would advise a military man never to love a woman. I am no Captain. I am entirely unfit to command men, to say nothing of holding a position where I have more to do with the discipline of a *Division* than perhaps any other man in it. No, I am a *baby*—yes, a *baby*, and feel that if I was with you and Gibbie again I would not leave. Lillie—if I know myself, it is not the fear of bullets, for somehow I feel that your prayers, your love, and that of our darling or something else connected with you will carry me safely through all the bullets and shells the Confederacy can mould, nor is it yet the hardships of the service which I fear or of which I become weary.

No, it is rather that one is separated from everything one loves and cherishes, from every joy and attraction attendant upon a civilized state of society,—from almost every source of intellectual improvement. No, it is on the other hand that one is associated with that which is coarse, bestial, and unfeeling. You must have discipline if you have to chop the offending head off. You must drive up stragglers [even] if they die in their tracks. You must make yourself congenial and agreeable to the companions by whom the fortunes of war surround you, even though it be at the sacrifice of everything that is agreeable to yourself. Such is war. It is a giant evil, and all its outgrowths are evil. Armies are made up from men of all classes of society. You are forced to defer and conciliate and bow to the mandates of superior rank, even though represented in men with whom you would not walk the street in private life.

You find men who always act right *when it is possible*, and others who will do anything that is wrong when not controlled by the fear of punishment. In Loudoun County [Va.], while we were marching on the Leesburg Pike, a lady who resided on the road sent for me and requested a guard on her house, for her own protection. A scamp of a cavalryman, about an hour before, entered her house, put a pistol to her head, forced her into a private chamber, and outraged her person most shamefully, tearing almost all her clothes from her body. I can never recover from the mortification of such an act, and could I have seen the hound at the time, I would have shot him as a Christian duty. I could mention other cases of the grossest violation of every principle of common decency, but this is sufficient.

You may conclude that I have all of a sudden become terribly home-loving and service-sick. Allow me to caution you against such a conclusion. I do not know that I am now any more anxious to see this war concluded that at any other time since its commencement. Nor must you conclude that my associations are of an unpleasant character. Quite the reverse. Still, I must admit that it arises more from my good fortune than from any necessity in the cause [*sic*]. I only insist that a man who wishes to enjoy himself in the army ought not to love a sweet wife.

I was yesterday through Frederick City. Made a few purchases, such as socks, buckskin gloves, shaving utensils, stationery, etc. This city, you know, was forced on the morning of the 9th of July to pay to the rebels

$200,000 tribute money to save the town from destruction. The money was paid by the banks, and the loyal citizens refuse to contribute any portion of it. I trust they will be borne out in this determination, and that the whole draft will be thrown on the shoulders of rebel sympathizers. General Hunter, since we have arrived here, is forcing all disloyal people to leave the place and go South. The move creates quite a sensation in this town. Frederick City contains many loyal citizens and is noted for its pretty girls. To ride through this city and witness youth and beauty display itself in the shape of fascinating and voluptuous females is enough to make me [unclear] from ladies' society [unclear].

I did not tell you that Capt. Burnham's wife came to Washington to see him. She arrived there just before we left, and he had only time to hire a carriage and drive with her out to our camp beyond Georgetown. I met her there. She had not seen me since she left me in so great a hurry, sick at Mrs. Shepard's in Berryville, June 13th, 1863 [the day he was captured]. She thought that I had changed in appearance very much, and she would not have known me. Indeed, she said she never expected to see me again. The absence of my whiskers no doubt had much to do with the change she observed. Her own health is not very good at present, having recently been much troubled with hemorrhage,— I *presume* of the *lungs* though she did not say so. She looks quite well.[28]

You never saw her, I think, though she was at Harpers Ferry when you were there. Quite pretty. She and the Captain formerly have not lived on very good terms. For some time before he joined the army they did not live together. I think the fault was mainly his. She was an only daughter, and perhaps a little spoiled. They have one child—a very fine little boy. She was quite attentive and seemed solicitous for my welfare while I was sick at Berryville.

On Wednesday (this) morning the 6th Corps, with no great alacrity I assure you, struck tents, shouldered their muskets, fell into column and took up a line of march towards the Monocacy, leaving Frederick City on its left flank. We reached the Monocacy at Buckeystown, forded and encamped on the opposite bank. This is a pretty country. We have a nice place for the troops to encamp in the fields and woods on the bank of the stream. The troops, I guess, are generally pretty well pleased that they have made their seven mile march from their old camp near Frederick City. Water and plenty of it is a great consideration for a camp, both for the comfort and convenience of man and beast. Did you ever see 15,000 men bathing in a river at once? Of course not. What a foolish question! Well, my Dear, the Monocacy furnishes the water and the 6th Corps the men. The scene presents a beautiful as well as ludicrous aspect, particularly so, I should judge, to ladies who reside on commanding eminences in the vicinity of Buckeystown.

Well, here we are in our new Hd. Qrs. in another orchard, about one mile from Buckeystown and two and a half from Monocacy Junction. We are not all fixed for company yet, but I had my clerk put up my desk that I might write this letter. A rambling affair, isn't it? There is some prospect of rain, and the pioneers are trenching our tents as fast as possible. Gen'l. Ricketts has just received a letter from his wife. A woman, by the way, on whom he dotes. He is now commenting voluminously on the letter. I never saw a man in his position who seemed to enjoy his domestic correspondence so much.

What has become of Sallie? I hear nothing of her and she sends me no word or message. Say to her that I can't think it necessary that she should consecrate her pen to the Paymaster's Department.

Tell Gibbie papa sends him much love and will come home and see him bye & bye. Show him my picture and don't let him forget me. Tell him papa has "wings" again, and would like to have Gibbie open them as he used to.

My regards to Tommy & family and love to all.

Very Fondly Your Own—

Robert

August 4, 1864 (Diary)
Near Monocacy Junction, Md.

Mrs. Ricketts arrived from Washington. She and the General were called [upon] in the evening by Gen'ls. Wright and Upton.[29] Orders at midnight to be ready to move by daylight.

Aug 4/64
[Written over a period of four days ending August 7.—TMB.]
Hd. Qrs. 3rd Div. 6th A. Corps
Near Monocacy Junction, Md.
MY VERY DEAR ONE:—

Circumstances are propitious for a little scribble and perhaps I can not do better than indulge in one. Heigh Ho! What is this? General Ricketts and his wife have just arrived from the railroad station at Monocacy Junction in a carriage. The General telegraphed to Washington for her yesterday afternoon while we were on the way here. I never saw her before. She is a fine-looking lady, tall and graceful and seems very lively. She is dressed in black silk, with any amount of beadwork on the sleeves and body—wears a magnificent pair of gold bracelets, narrow white collar and gold chain. The General has had a large arbor erected before his tent, which adds to the comfort as well as the seclusion of the place. They are now discussing the propriety of putting the Quartermaster's tent in the rear of the General's, to add to its commodiousness. Qr. Master Morford offers to resign his tent and quarter with one of the other officers, but Mrs. R. Positively refuses to have any such thing done. She says she would feel absolutely disagreeable to think that nay officer had been deprived of his tent, or even discommoded on her account. Finally, they have concluded to put the wall tent which the clerks occupy in the rear of the General's, and let the clerks occupy a carpenter shop standing near at hand. It is done, and that subject is dismissed.

My tent is directly opposite the General's. Mrs. Ricketts is sitting under the arbor and the various members of the staff who are acquainted with her are coming forward to greet her. I cannot help overhearing every word. Mrs. R. evidently possesses rare conversational powers and entertains all hands delightfully. She is evidently educated and accomplished. I don't wonder the General feels proud of her. She is now taking lunch of toast and coffee.

4 o'clock P.M. General Ricketts has conferred upon me the honor of an introduction to his wife. I have been over in that arbor, and had quite a long conversation with her. General R. was not present all the time, either. She informs me that camp life is nothing new to her. She is from New Jersey, near Elizabethtown—is General R.'s second wife, has been married about ten years, was with the General in Mexico. She and the General have now gone over to Frederick City. Capt. Smith and myself are now going over to the Monocacy to take a swim and wash. We will be back in about an hour.

6 o'clock P.M. —Capt. Smith and I have just returned from a most delightful swim. Capt. S., you must know, is a staff officer (Assistant Commissary of Musters) now, since Capt. King has been wounded (Actg. [Acting] Ass't. Adj't. General). We put our clean clothes in my traveling bag (I have a new one, of a common kind, that I found it necessary to buy to put dirty clothes in), put in soap, towels, glass, comb & brush, mounted our horses, took along a mounted orderly who carried our valises, and rode over to the stream. We found a nice place where the water was deep and the bank clean. We spread a gum blanket down to undress and dress on—took splendid swim and wash, dressed in clean *duds* and ride back rejuvenated, with the clothes that had "the clean rubbed off of them" in the bag. General R. and his wife have returned from Frederick City. Major Gen'l. Wright is here to call on Mrs. R. I wish you could see what a happy manner she has

in all her conversation with him, understands herself perfectly. I am called to supper. We sup under the apple trees. Material for apple sauce very convenient.

10 o'clock P.M. After Gen'l. Wright left, Gen'l. Upton called to pay his respects to Mrs. Ricketts. We are having a lively evening. Rows of candles are burning along the ground between our rows of tents, and an accomplished band is discoursing most elegant music for our entertainment, more particularly for that of Mrs. R. Whisky Toddy is plenty—and our distinguished female guest takes her glass with the rest. Gen'l. Upton is still here and numerous other staff officers from other Head Quarters. The small hours of the morning will probably find many of them still up and hilarious. Good night, dear one. A sweet good night.

Aug. 5th, 10 A.M. Last night, orders came about midnight to be ready to march by daylight. We got ready but no orders to move have yet come. Mrs. Ricketts is sitting in the arbor opposite me, *mending the Gen'l.'s shirt. Good for her.* She is conversing with Capt. Burnham. By the way, I had perhaps make you acquainted with our Gen'l. & Staff. Here is the list.

Brig. Gen'l. J. B. Ricketts, U. S. A.

Capt. King, A. A. G. [Assistant Adjutant General], wounded, in Baltimore

Maj. Vredenburgh, A. I. G. [Acting Inspector General]

Capt. Smith, A. P. M. & A. A. A. G. [Assistant Provost Marshal & Acting Assistant Adjutant General]

Capt. R. T. Cornwell, Provost Marshal

Capt. Burnham, Ordnance Officer

Capt. Morford, Div. Qr. Master [Division Quarter master]

Capt. Buchanan, D. A. C. S. [Deputy Acting Commissary]

Capt. Damon, A. D. C. [Aide de Camp]

Capt. Prentiss, Capt. of Pioneers

Dr. Barr, Surgeon, Chief of Division

Capt. Richards, A. D. C. [Aide de Camp]

I have just received your fine long letter—two full sheets of *note.* Glad to hear that the pictures have arrived from Elmira and that you like them. I think you are mistaken about its being Gen'l. Wright's colored troops that fled in confusion in front of Petersburg. Gen'l. Wright commands our Corps and is here [and has not] been at Petersburg since the 5th of July. Gen'l. Wright has no colored troops. I think Gen'l. Hicks had command of the colored troops you referred to. You are right in your denunciations of such failures as that. They are sickening.[30]

I am sorry to hear that Mary is not well this Summer. When we were there this Spring she did not look like the sister I used to call Mary at all. Tell Gibbie my horse is a *dark bay*. You can show him a bay horse and he will understand what that color is. I am glad to know he is so natural to children of his age, and so conducive to good health. I just revert again to what you say of the 6th Corps in front of Petersburg. You say—"I see from the news from the front that the 6th Corps was ordered up late on Friday evening. Last night when I first saw the news of the picture of Wright's Colored troops making such a break and causing such a very sad change in the aspect of affairs among you, etc." Why my dear, the 6th Corps wasn't near the fight. It was in Maryland during the whole time. Whatever mistakes may have been made, Gen'l. Wright and the 6th Corps are in no manner responsible for them.

The adjutant is still with his regt. and I do not know that he has made any further effort to get out of the service. Capt. Carpenter is no longer at Annapolis. He appeared before a medical board and was pronounced unfit for field service. He has since been sent to Elmira, N. Y. and placed in charge of rebel prisoners.[31] He has, as we say in the army, a "soft thing" of it. Col. Staunton is sick at Georgetown. The Regt. Is now commanded by Capt. Barry of Co. "D," the only Capt. now with the Regt. Sergeant, or rather Lieutenant, Gay of my Company and Lieut. Clark of Company "F" have deserted. They left while the Division was on the railroad between Baltimore and Washington. This leaves my Company in command of Sergeant Brower. Col. Staunton is likely to get in more trouble. He is in very bad order with Gen'l. Ricketts.[32] Mr. & Mrs. Gen'l. Ricketts have rode [*sic*] over to pay respects to Gen'l. Wright.

Sunday, Aug. 7th/64 at Halltown, Va. Another change has come over the spirit of our dream. About 8 o'clock on the morning of the 5th, orders came to march. The 2nd Div. went first, then the 3rd, then the 1st. We marched to Monocacy Junction. Mrs. Ricketts rode down to Mr. Thomases' on the Monocacy battleground in an ambulance, where she stayed all night. Lt. Gen'l. U. S. Grant[33] was there, having come up from Washington to Gen'l. Hunter's Head Qrs. on that afternoon. He stayed all night at Mr. Thomases.' After arriving at Monocacy Junction, the 2nd and 3rd Divisions took cars from Harpers Ferry. The wagon train, ambulances & artillery took the pike, and the 1st Div. marched with them as a guard. The 2nd Div., which took the cars first, was all night embarking, so that we did not commence loading our Division before morning. Mrs. Ricketts took Gen'l. Grant's special train to Washington on yesterday morning. I had the pleasure of listening to Gen'l. Grant in conversation for some time. We arrived at Harpers Ferry

about noon and marched to this place [Halltown], where we encamped.
There are now more Maj. Generals at Harpers Ferry than you can shake
a stick at. I saw Maj. Genls. Hunter, Sheridan, Wright, Stahl [*sic*],[34]
Crook & Emery, and Brigadiers too numerous to name. There seems to
be preparations [in the] making for a vigorous campaign up the
Shenandoah. I shall not wonder if the memory of Chambersburg would
make it a pretty destructive affair. A Paymaster is here today, paying the
67th. I am very glad of it for the poor boys have been out of money a
long time. I now have a chance to send this letter by the carrier. My
love to all.

Very Fondly Yours,
Robert

7

Third Winchester, Fisher's Hill, and Cedar Creek
August 5–October 20, 1864

Cornwell's letters and diary begin this period by describing the Union army's hectic pursuit of Early after the Confederate general abandoned Washington and crossed the Potomac River on July 14. He was heading toward the Shenandoah Valley to regroup. Notably, the August 6 diary entry refers to Grant's statement that "Sheridan was on his way to join us." In fact, Cornwell was about to witness the coalescing of the Middle Military Division, popularly known as the Army of the Shenandoah.

It was a strong and well-equipped army, composed of Wright's VI Corps, Crook's VIII Corps, and the XIX Corps under Emory. On August 7, Maj. Gen. Philip H. Sheridan (1831–1888) took command of this army of 48,000 men. By contrast, Early's forces, including 3,500 men of Kershaw's division who were temporarily assigned, numbered only about 19,000 of all arms. Early was quite aware of the huge odds against him, and that in this campaign he was "leading a forlorn hope all the time."[1]

Even though Early was moving away from Washington back toward Berryville, the capitol remained in a state of shock from his raid. As well, he presented a continuing hostile threat to Maryland. The mission of the Army of the Shenandoah was therefore quite clear: close the back door on Washington by defeating Early, and secure the Valley. Federal control of the Valley would protect the capitol and the states of Maryland and Pennsylvania, from further raids, and also deprive the South of one of its most important sources of food.

Sheridan was cautious at first, waiting until his forces were fully joined. As Cornwell notes, only minor skirmishes occurred during the first days of August as Early moved toward Berryville, a town about ten miles east of Winchester. It was clear, however, that once he was ready Sheridan planned to wreak havoc on the Valley. His famous instruction (incorrectly quoted in Cornwell's August 8 letter) to General Hunter made that fact plain. Hunter's men were to "eat up Virginia clear and clean as far as they can go, so that crows flying over it for the balance of this season will have to carry their provender with them."[2]

Cornwell and the rest of the VI Corps struck tents on August 3 and marched to Monocacy Junction. They camped there for two days, then moved to Halltown for a week of much-needed rest. From Halltown the VI Corps marched to Winchester, where on the 21st they repulsed an attack by Early.

The pages for Cornwell's diary no longer exist for dates after August 8. That may be due to the almost constant activity of the VI Corps after that date. Fortunately, on August 8 Cornwell began a series of long letters to Lillie, each of which included a great amount of detail about events occurring over a number of days. Considering the fact that his previous letters often reflected events noted in his diary, it would seem that he maintained the diary after August 8 and that the pages were subsequently lost.

The battle of Winchester is described in Cornwell's August 24 letter, and he attributes part of the successful Union defense to the lines of fortifications they put up hastily when the Confederate charge began. One of the attacking Confederates later wrote an admiring description of them: "[They were] the best hurredly thrown up works I saw during the war. When we reached them, we found it a heavy task to remove them for the division to pass through."[3] Union forces left Winchester after the battle and returned to Halltown.

Cornwell did not write between August 27 and September 9, probably because of the constant activities of the Army of the Shenandoah. During that period Sheridan and Early both began moving back toward the Berryville-Winchester area, each trying to catch the other off balance. On the 16th, Early's relatively small force was further weakened by the loss of Kershaw's division, which was detached and returned to Petersburg.

Cornwell's September 23 letter describes "a terrific fight" near Winchester. This was "The Third Battle of Winchester." It was a stunning victory for Sheridan, due in part to the work of a local woman. Several days before the battle, a Confederate officer in Winchester told a Quaker girl named Rebecca Wright that Kershaw's division of infantry and a battalion of artillery were going to be detached and sent back to Lee at Petersburg.

Wright, who lost a teaching position because of her outspoken Union sympathies, promptly conveyed that piece of vital information to Sheridan. On the 19th, his army of some 40,000 men smashed into Early's small force. Despite some tactical errors, Early fought well but was overwhelmed. Union losses were about 5,000, but Early lost 3,900 irreplaceable men. Maj. Gen. Robert E. Rodes, considered one of the best division commanders in the Confederate army, was killed in the battle, as was Col. W. T. Patton. Maj. Gen. Fitzhugh Lee was seriously wounded. Four years later, through the aid of a grateful Sheridan, Rebecca Wright received a clerkship in the U.S. Treasury Department as a reward for her information.[4]

After the battle, the remnants of Early's army retreated to Fisher's Hill, south of Strasburg. It was a strong position, but Early did not have enough men to fill its nearly four miles of defensive lines. He mispositioned what men he had, leaving his left flank thinly defended by dismounted cavalry. Sheridan attacked on the morning of September 22, exploited the defenders' weaknesses, and by afternoon had badly defeated Early. A Confederate staff officer described the scene at the end of the fighting: "The rout of wagons, caissons, limbers, artillery, and flying men was fearful as the stream swept down the pike toward Woodstock."[5]

Early lost 1,235 men and twelve artillery pieces. Col. Alexander "Sandie" Pendleton, one of the ablest Confederate artillery officers, was killed while trying to stem the Union advance. Union losses were modest; just 582 men, of whom only fifty-two were killed.

Cornwell's September 23 letter vividly describes the battle, but as in his description of other battles, he omits any mention of his direct role in the events. His comment that "Early and his whole command...have...deserted the Valley" was wildly optimistic, but even Sheridan thought the Valley campaign was finished. With the apparent lack of a Confederate army to fight, Sheridan changed the Union army's campaign to one of terror and mass destruction against the civilian population of the Valley. As Cornwell says in his October 8 letter, the Union army was "cleaning nearly everything out of the Valley....Barns are all burned, together with grain and mills."

Much to Sheridan's great annoyance, Early's battered army received some reinforcements during the several weeks following Fisher's Hill. As he regrouped, scattered fighting and skirmishing on a relatively low level began anew, then increased and continued during this period.

Cornwell's October 2 letter mentions that Gen. Ricketts sent his name up for promotion because of gallantry on the field at Winchester and Fisher's Hill. Ricketts had indeed done so in his lengthy official report of September 27 that described the two battles. He concluded it by mentioning officers of his command "who have particularly distinguished themselves in the late engagements, and who are worthy and deserving of promotion." Among them was "Capt. Robert T. Cornwell, Sixty-seventh Pennsylvania Volunteers, provost-marshal."[6]

Sheridan took position on both sides of Cedar Creek on October 10, giving no thought to the possibility that Early's weakened and much smaller army would dare attack. However, Early had returned to Fisher's Hill, just a few miles away, and was scouting the situation at Cedar Creek. He had reports that Sheridan was going to detach elements of his command and send them to Grant at Petersburg within days. Although outnumbered more than two-to-one, Early decided that a daring, quick attack could prevent those reinforcements from being sent. Moreover, in the process he might recover the Valley for the Confederacy.

His staff officers on Massanutten Mountain had been carefully observing the Union lines for several days. They recommended attacking the thinly guarded Union left flank, believing it could be surprised and rolled up easily. Sheridan, unaware of any danger, left Cedar Creek on the 16th to attend a conference in Washington for several days.

Early on the foggy morning of October 19 Confederate troops stripped of cups, canteens, and any other noisy equipment that might give them away, smashed into the Union left flank. There was little resistance to the charge. The VIII Corps quickly stampeded away from the fighting, while Confederates turned around artillery they had captured and began firing upon the VI and XIX Corps.

Resistance crumbled throughout the morning. In a reverse of the scene at Fisher's Hill, panic-stricken Union troops flooded the roads and fields as they fled back to Winchester. A surgeon in the VI Corps observed:

> …stragglers filling the fields, taking rapid strides toward the rear,…scarce any two of them going together, some without hats, others destitute of coats or boots, a few guns, many wearing shoulder straps of officers, all bent on getting a good way to the rear.[7]

By noon, only the VI Corps still offered resistance, but it, too, was weakening. The turning point came when pursuing Confederate soldiers entered the abandoned Union camps. As far as the eye could see were shoes and clothing left behind by the retreating enemy. Food in abundance lay scattered all about, and entire meals still cooked over many hastily abandoned fires.

The temptation was too great for the starving, and in many cases barefoot, Confederates. The advance slowed as many of Early's men paused in the Union camps to acquire what they needed. The advance of other Confederate units also slowed as they became separated during the attack and tried to reform. Early, needing time to consolidate the large amount of prisoners and equipment in his hands and thinking he had already won a considerable victory, decided to halt the attack.

One of his division commanders pointed out that the VI Corps was still in the field and needed to be dealt with before the army could rest. Early, however, believed the VI Corps would soon be on its way back to Winchester with the rest of the Union army. In one of the critical missteps of the war, Early forbade an attack upon the VI Corps' position.

Meanwhile, Sheridan had returned from Washington and was at Winchester, where the sound of gunfire from Cedar Creek was clearly audible. He raced back toward the sound of battle, and by midmorning began to come across waves of his still-retreating soldiers. According to some accounts, Sheridan began exhorting all the men he saw to turn around and return with him to Cedar Creek. The sight of their general revitalized the soldiers, and they began streaming back to the battle.

As he arrived at the scene of the fighting, Sheridan rode along the lines of the VI Corps, to the great cheers of the men. During the next several hours large amounts of Union stragglers began arriving back in their lines, and by late afternoon Sheridan's force was strong enough to launch a counterattack. They rolled up the Confederate left flank, and soon it was Early's men who were in full retreat back to Fisher's Hill.[8]

"Sheridan's Ride" became one of the epic events of the war, immortalized in a poem of that name written by Thomas Buchanan Read of West Chester, Pennsylvania. Fanciful and somewhat inaccurate, the poem became a great favorite in the North. Cornwell, an eyewitness to the event, later said that while Sheridan's return to the scene did much to restore the confidence of his men, the situation at Cedar Creek was not nearly as dramatic as depicted in Read's poem.[9]

Early lost 2,910 out of 18,410 men engaged, while Sheridan's losses were 5,665 out of 30,829. Cedar Creek broke Early's little army and effectively gave the Union army full control over the Valley. One of Early's staff officers wrote in his diary "Thus was one of the most brilliant victories of the war turned into one of the most disgraceful defeats, and all owing to the delay in pressing the enemy after we got to Middletown."[10] Early simply said, "The Yankees got whipped and we got scared." Later he wrote about it in more detail:

> It may be asked why with so small a force I made the attack [at Cedar Creek]. I can only say we had been fighting large odds during the war, and I knew there was no chance of lessening them. It was of the utmost consequence that Sheridan should be prevented from sending troops to Grant, and General Lee, in a letter received a day or two before, had expressed an earnest desire that a victory should be gained in the Valley if possible, and it could not be gained without fighting for it.[11]

Early commanded Stonewall Jackson's old corps, but failed to heed his predecessor's advice given during a successful campaign in the Valley two years previously:

> Always mystify, mislead, and surprise the enemy if possible; and when you strike and overcome him, never let up in the pursuit so long as your men have strength to follow; for an army routed, if hotly pursued, becomes panic-stricken, and can be destroyed by half their number.[12]

August 5, 1864 (Diary)
Moving Toward Harpers Ferry

At 4 o'clock A.M. were all ready to march but nor orders came and we pitched our tents again. Mr. & Mrs. Gen'l. Ricketts rode to Corps Hd. Qrs. to pay their respects to Gen'l. Wright. Orders at 8 A.M. to move to Monocacy Junction immediately. Order of march, 2nd Div., 3rd, 1st. were to take cars at Junction for Harpers Ferry. Trains [of artillery and baggage] to go by pike. 1st Div. to guard them. Mrs. Ricketts took ambulance to Mr. Thomases' house, where she remained all night. Gen'l. U. S. Grant stayed at the same house.

August 6, 1864 (Diary)
Halltown, Va.

The 2nd Div. was all night embarking by rail. Our Div. commenced loading this morning. Saw Gen'l. Grant and listened to him in conversation. He said Sheridan was on his way to join us, and I understand is to take command of all the forces. The indications are that a vigorous campaign will be prosecuted in the Shenandoah Valley. Mrs. Ricketts went to Washington with Gen'l. Grant in special train. Reached Harpers Ferry about 12 P.M. and marched to Halltown. Wagon trains arrived about dark. All in camp [of] 4 lines [company streets], with trains parked by 10 o'clock P.M.

August 7, 1864 (Diary)
Halltown, Va.
    Laid in camp at Halltown. Wrote a letter to Lillie.

August 8, 1864 (Diary)
Halltown, Va.
    Laid in camp at Halltown. Received orders in the evening to march in the morning at 5 o'clock A.M.

August 8, 1864
Hd. Qrs. 3rd Div. 6th A. Corps
Halltown, Va.
MY DEAREST LOVE,
    We have laid [sic] here since night before last, awaiting the developments of each hour. In other words, we are hourly expecting an order to move. Vigorous preparations are making for an active campaign. Transportation is being reduced to the lowest possible limit, the most stringent orders to promote the efficiency of the command have been issued. And all superfluities and excrescences and every other thing calculated to embarrass the movements of a large army are sloughed off. Gen'l. Hunter, I believe, has command of the Dept. and Sheridan of the troops.
    I was mainly employed yesterday in straightening up affairs connected with my department. Last evening, I visited Gen'l. Wheaton and staff. We had a very nice time singing, etc. Sang "Come Where My Love Lies Dreaming," a quartet, and other very fine pieces. Gen'l. Wheaton commands the 1st brigade of [the] 2nd Division and is a very fine gentleman.[13] Robert Sutton, brother of Maj. White's wife, was just up here to see me. I did not know that he was in the service. He enlisted seven months ago in the Signal Service, and is attached to the 19th Corps. He says that he has not heard from home for two or three weeks. At that time, his friends had not heard from Maj. White for more than four months. When last heard from, he was still at Saulsbury [sic], N.C. The enemy show themselves once in awhile in

our front, but in small force. Night before last some of Imboden's[14] men gobbled a "safe guard" that the Second Division had placed on a house just in front of our line.[15] A citizen by the name of Lynch has been seized as a hostage for the man captured. I think the commanding officers intend making this campaign up the valley a pretty rough one, not leaving enough in it to subsist a crow, if they can help it.

Aug. 9th 10 o'clock A.M. [Continued in the same letter.—TMB].

The morning is very pleasant, but the prospect of unpleasant warmth at the thermal meridian of the day. Last night, or rather this morning, one of our cavalry pickets [a mounted sentry] was brought in badly wounded. I have not heard the particulars. Think I will ride down to Harpers Ferry today to see my lady friends there, and perhaps purchase a little gold lace to stitch down my pant legs as staff insignia. I have had the infantry buttons on my coat and blouse [military coat] changed for staff buttons, and this is the only staff designation I have heretofore worn.[16] I wear my dark blue uniform pants habitually and my blouse. Keep my coat for special occasions.[17] My vest lies at rest in my valise. During the hot weather, I have discarded this article of wearing apparel entirely. I like the boots I had made in West Chester very much, they are very serviceable.

I am frequently interrupted in my writing whenever I sit down. Just now, I have had over 100 men sent to me from the Corps Prov. Mas. [provost marshal]. The men are convalescent stragglers and others who I have sent to their respective Brigades and Regiments. It was ten o'clock when I first sat down and now it is about dinner time. Our mess consists of six officers—viz. Capt. Truesdell—Capt. Oaks, the two Lieuts of my guard, the [New York] *Herald* correspondent and myself. Our cooks forage [take from the countryside or from farmers] green corn, chickens, etc. And we buy bread, butter pickles, ham, coffee, sugar, and etc. We forage green apples for sauce. We live pretty well. Gen'l. Ricketts, Capt. Smith and Capt. Richards mess together, and Maj. Vredenburgh and Capt. Damon constitute another mess. Each mess has its "Mess Kit," which consists of a box containing our knives, forks, spoons, plates, cups and saucers, etc. Please excuse me while I eat some dinner.

We had an excellent dinner [of] green corn, tomatoes, cucumbers, cabbage, potatoes, ham, soft and fresh bread & butter. And coffee with milk and white sugar. I ate heartily and do not know, in consideration of the heat of the day, but I am commencing to write too soon after dinner. The attempt is an experiment, however, and if I get sleepy I suppose I will gratify my desires. I am becoming a little doubtful about my going to Harpers Ferry today. The weather is excessively warm and the distance [is] 3 1/2 miles. I am doubtful whether the sight of Miss Nellie Row and Miss Mattie

Fossett would pay me for the vital energy expended in riding there and back. They would probably give me some supper, but not probably any better, if so good, as I will get here. Now, I have no particular interest in going and having a formal talk with some lady who has no more interest in me than she has in mankind in general. Whose heart has no responsive throb for every joy and sorrow known to my own. In short and in plain, there is a dear lady I know who would put her arms around my neck and caress and kiss me, and who at all times is mine as I am hers. —She I would go to see now—at all times—in rain or shine, as far as a leave of absence would carry me. I have just stopped to read this page over. It sounds *flat*, don't [*sic*] it? Well, I can't help it. I didn't stop to think how it would sound, I only know I didn't feel flat about it when I wrote it, and can't say that I do now.

The soldiers of the Corps are becoming quite rested and refreshed. The whistling, the shouting and laughing, the sport and hilarious mirth are all indicative the Soldier is rested and is himself again. You would laugh immediately if you were to walk around among them and hear the jokes some of them get off. Many of them the best I have ever heard. Calling the 6th Corps *Harper's Weekly* is a joke that originated with a private in our Division.[18] When Gen'l. Wright first heard it he laughed violently. It was gotten off day before yesterday, and was all over the Corps before night.

I was up to the Reg't. yesterday and had a talk with Adjt. Young and Frank. They were full of business, making out returns, etc. Frank was very much out of humor about the affairs of his own company, because his returns were back and he couldn't get something, or *this* was lost and *that* was somewhere else, and he couldn't make them out. Indeed, and without any joking, a line officer's life in an active campaign like this Summer's has been the life of a dog. They have not a solitary comfort or privilege beyond those of the privates they command. They have for nights in succession to sleep in the rifle pits and go for weeks without a change of clothing, and must carry all their immediate comforts on their backs. The 67th Reg't. was paid off a few days ago, and the boys have been running to Harpers Ferry expressing their money home.

Who do you correspond with now? I write to no one but you. Do you write to Mother or sisters frequently? Do you write to Ada or Mrs. Brooks? I have not heard from Westlake since I saw him at Washington. How does Sallie like her new dress? Miss Nellie Row wants you to send her your picture and mine and Gibbie's. She asked me for it when I was there some two weeks ago. Can you do so? What recreations do you take? Do you avail yourself of all the pleasures within your reach? This life cannot be made one of melancholy without serious detriment to one's physical appearance and constitution. Forgive me if I do you any injustice by implication when I express the hope that you will not allow yourself to give room to glowing forebodings. Let us be joyful that we live and love and in the anticipation of earthly and heavenly joys in years to come, when this cruel war is a creature only of history and memory.

Remember, Lillie, it is every one's duty *to be happy*. We were intended to be so.

Dear Little Gibbie! How does he do? And what is he doing? The possession of such a child is joy and happiness itself.

Tell Sister Sallie that when you and I and Gibbie get to *keeping house* and Mr. And Mrs. M—h[19] come to see us—won't that be nice?

Remember me kindly to Grandfather, mother and all.

Ever fondly Yours,

Robert

Aug. 14th/64
Hd. Qrs. 3rd Div. 6th A. Corps
Near Middletown, Va.
MY OWN DEAR.

Your lovely letter reached me this morning. I can't tell you how much I was pleased to hear that you had all been to a fine social "Pic-nic" on the picturesque and historic banks of the Brandywine.[20] But it is not mainly that the ground was beautiful and historic that I delight in your description, it is rather that you all enjoyed yourselves except, if I must except, Sallie, who was sick. Though I presume she enjoyed herself more than she would have done at home. Dear me, I am very sorry on her account, for I have every reason to rejoice in her joy and grieve with her sorrow.

Lillie, you can't think how I am scratching this off. The fact is, the mail boy is to leave in twenty minutes for Washington and this must go with him. We left Halltown, where I wrote my last on the morning of the 10th, and have been on the continuous motion since from early morn till late at night. First night put up about 4 miles from Berryville. Next day, 12th, marched to Middletown on the Sharpsburg Pike. I passed through here once a *prisoner of war* —I recollect.

13th, marched to Sharpsburg, where we came up to the rebels in force. They were in a very strong position. The strongest in the Valley. They were on what is called "Fishers Hill" and "Round Top" and the high mountains on either side prevented a flank movement. We laid in front of them and looked at them all day, and they looked at us. We came, we saw, but we haven't yet conquered. We have seen the enemy, but they are not yet ours. At night, we fell back about two miles to our trains. Today, 4 days rations are being issued, and what we will do next I suppose lies with circumstances and Gen'l. Sheridan. By the way, Gen'l. Sheridan is the smartest-looking general I have yet seen. This morning, I have shaved, clothed, washed and feel elegant. This neat epistle I must close immediately, but will write soon again.

I send herewith two rare pictures that I know you will be pleased with and value highly—Gen'l. Ricketts and his wife, Fanny. The letter I received this morning. She sent it from Washington in a letter to the Gen'l.

Lillie, I will tell you what I want you to do for me. Go to Philadelphia to the best artist there and get a good Vignette of yourself. Try and keep trying till you are satisfied. Then get lots of copies. I would value a good picture of you, very, very highly. Have it taken—do.

Give Gibbie Pappa's love.

Fondly Your Own,

Robert

Aug. 14th 1864

Hd. Qrs. 3rd Div. 6th A. Corps

In The Field

MY OWN LOVE:—

My letter containing the pictures has just started. No orders have yet come to move, and I embrace the opportunity to commence another letter to be completed as opportunity offers. I can only write when we halt for the night and pitch tents. Then the Hd. Qr. wagons come up and I get my valise which contains all my writing utensils except a little paper and pencil that I carry in my pocket for emergencies.

I carry in my saddle bag some soap, a towel, looking glass, comb and brush. My gum blanket is rolled up and strapped to my saddle, these are all I carry on my horse. My woolen blankets are rolled up and put in the wagons. My mess kit is carried in the wagons, but I have a pack mule which my cook rides and carries a basket of lunch and such things as he can forage on the road. So it goes. I do not always get my dinner from the basket, however. I often have an opportunity to do better.

When I get hungry on the march, I ride ahead aways and when I see a fine-looking residence, ride up to it. The people always want a guard to protect their house and surroundings from the soldiers. If there be no good reason for refusing it, I furnish the guard and they invite me into the house and treat me to the best it affords. Thus do I secure many a good dinner while the column is passing, the price of which is accredited to the profit and loss account.

Just as we were entering Middletown the other day, and while passing a very fine residence, a soldier came up to me and said a young lady at that house wished to see me, that she said she was acquainted with me. Of course, I was immediately filled with speculations more or less pleasant as to who she could be, and rode straightaway back to the house. The fair damsel met me at the gate, gave me a very scrutinizing look, and modestly and easily apologized for being mistaken in the person. She immediately changed the subject and begged me to come into the house and drive [away] the soldiers who she said were taking all they had to eat and treating Ma very rudely.

I rode into the yard, a Negress held my horse. The soldiers ran from the house as soon as they saw me, to escape arrest. Ma was a very fine-looking woman, and she and her daughter tried to express how grateful they were. Wanted me to stay and take something to eat, for the best they had was at my service. I very respectfully declined, on the ground I was not hungry. They then gave me a very pressing invitation, in case we encamped any where near the town, to come and stay with them all night. I of course told her I would be very happy to do so. Placed a guard on the house and went on.

These are incidents of daily, often times hourly, occurrence. Sometimes these people claim to be Union in their sentiments—others openly acknowledge that they are rebels, and some go so far as to confess that they can't blame our soldiers for taking all they have, when, they think how *their* soldiers acted while they were in Penna. and Maryland.

The other day I searched a house in Newtown from top to bottom. The owner of the house was a violent rebel and had fled, leaving his wife, a few daughters & a young son at home. I received the information that goods taken from Maryland during the late raid were secreted in the house. I took a Sargent [*sic*] and two men from my guard and attempted to find them. I found some tents, government blankets, overcoats, guns and ammunition, all of which I took away. The daughters protested very indignantly when I came to their trunks, but they had to come open; some interesting revelations are made during such searches.

The day is intensely warm. This morning we had a little shower. Since about 9 o'clock the air has been very close and the sun pours down his hottest rays. It is so very close and hot as to portend rain before night. Fortunate this is for us that we are not marching. How is Col. George Smith getting on? Do you know whether he expects to rejoin his command soon or not? His regiment is in the second Division of this Corps, I believe. Dinner is ready and I am hungry. The inner man must be replenished. We have active picket firing in our front continually.

August 15, 1864 [continued in the same letter.—TMB].

Did not get your letter again yesterday. Picket firing was very continuous during the whole day.[21] I commenced reading a book—*Very Hard Cash*. 9 o'clock P.M., picket firing very active. We drove in their skirmishers this afternoon and advanced our lines nearly a mile. They opened with artillery firing shell and grape & canister.

This evening we had a *raffle* at these Hd. Qrs. for a fine brown horse belonging to Capt. King, who is now at Baltimore, wounded. To sell him we put him (the horse) up at $300—in 30 chances of $10 each. Col. Kent at Corps Hd. Qrs. won him. You ask, my dear, isn't this gambling? And do you approve of it? Perhaps it is, but I am not quite clear but that in this case it was right. King is a great favorite with all his acquaintances. He has been unfortunate and needs money. It would be wounding to his pride, almost cruel, to make it a downright donation. So, we put up his horse, which we knew he wished to sell, at $300, $100 more than it was worth, and 30 of his friends put in ten dollars each and lo! his horse is sold and he has his $300 and we our fun. I took a share and I am sure I was not prompted to do so by any hope of winning the horse.

August 16, 1864 [continued in the same letter.—TMB].

The morning has been quite pleasant & cloudy. In the night at intervals while I was awake I heard sprinkles of rain on my canvas house. Since transportation has been reduced, we have reduced our Hd. Qrs. tents to *four*. Three of us—Capt. Damon, Capt. Prentiss and myself occupy one. We have a thick coating of straw spread on the ground and our blankets spread thereon. I sleep very well, but I thought I felt flies several times last night. We are not far from a large barn. I think we ought to move from this before long because food is getting scarce.

Green corn is a great staff of life during this season, and it is becoming very scarce for miles around. I can almost live on it. Eat about 12 ears per diem. Yesterday, our boys got some honey. Near here there was a farmer [who] had from 75 to 100 hives. They have all been turned over and the honey taken out. I am fond of honey and corn and lamb and vegetables, but this foraging is a rough business. Who knows how many people suffer for the want of what we take from them. An army like this cleans the country for miles around. The boys are now obliged to make 3 days rations last *four*, but if they had their full allowance of government rations it would be scarcely any better, for they want [lack] vegetables, and vegetables they will have if they can get their hands on them.

Foraging is reduced to a sort of system. Every mess sends out its foragers with instructions not to come back till they get all they are sent for. With officers it becomes a necessity, for though we are allowed to purchase of the commissaries, yet very often the trains are not up and we must get food any way we can. Living in the army is at times quite precarious.

My health is very good and my appetite very vigorous. I have just sent a commissioned officer and 20 men from my guard with a wagon after hay. All the hay in this vicinity has been consumed, so that we have to send several miles for it, making a guard necessary to protect the party from guerrillas (I am writing this on my knee, and the wind dashes my paper from side to side, making frequent blots and unintelligible scrawls).

Lillie, I hope you will not forget the Vignettes I spoke to you about in my last, send me some and some of Gibbie's that we had taken at Woodward's. If his have all been disposed of, get some more taken, or rather struck off from the same negative, for I don't think we can do better. My dearest, you alone can perhaps appreciate the pride I take in my little family at home. You will not doubt that my love for it elevates the tone of my mind above the coarse and sensual modes of enjoyment so much indulged in army life. Ah, Lillie, what sacrifice is too great for your love. I am sure I take no delight or permanent interest in any thing in which you are not concerned. Ah, it is exquisite to live for those who live for me.

Give my love to our dear friends.

Ever Fondly Your Own,

Robert

<hr>

[There are no writings for August 17–20.—TMB].

<hr>

Aug. 21 [1864]
Hd. Qrs 3rd Div. 6th A. Corps
Near Charleston, Va.
MY OWN FOND LILLIE:—

My last letter was written form the vicinity of Strasburg, about 32 miles from here. Yesterday, I received two delightfully long and interesting letters from you, full of interest and happiness for me. I suppose I must account for briefly for being in our present position, but really I cannot tell why we came unless it was to prevent being cut off by Longstreet's force, which had come down the Valley and with the advance guard of which our country under Gen'l. [unclear, probably Torbert][22] had an engagement at

Front Royal where we captured 260 prisoners, including 25 officers, with very slight loss to ourselves.

We left Strasburg at 8 o'clock P.M. and reached Winchester (18 miles) by daylight the next morning, where we halted for breakfast. While at Winchester I visited the family that befriended me so much while I was a prisoner over a year ago at that place. They are a fine family and still staunch Unionists. I took breakfast with them. We then took up the march again, and upon reaching the heights on the South side of the Opequon Creek encamped for the night. From these heights we could see and hear a brisk fight going on near Winchester, the nature of which we did not then understand but afterward learned it was between Longstreet's forces and one brigade of the first division of our Corps, commanded by Col. Penrose.[23]

The brigade had been temporarily detached to support Gen'l. Torbert's cavalry. The brigade was of course overpowered, for it had to deploy its whole force as skirmishers to cover the front of the enemy, which consisted of two heavy lines of battle. We met with considerable loss, the extent of which has not yet been accurately ascertained. The next morning we proceeded to Berryville, where I visited my old friend Mrs. Sheppard. They were all well and apparently very glad to see me. Mrs. Sheppard informs me that it is with the greatest difficulty now that she obtains enough to keep her family. The Corps did not halt at Berryville, but kept up its march and at night arrived at this place.

August 24th/64 [continued in the same letter.—TMB].

Well, my dear, I was called away from my letter commenced the 21st and have just returned to it. In the meantime, we have had a fight of one day's duration. Last Sunday morning [August 21] the rebel force made a vigorous charge upon us. We were lying in camp, not in line of battle, but you would have been astonished to see how soon we were in line of battle. The men behind our line of skirmishers threw up two lines of breast works along our whole line in *no* time. Well, we pitched into one another all day long. The air was filled with screaming shells, solid shot, musket balls and all sorts of missiles, making one feel when not excited just the *least* bit uneasy. When it grew dark we stopped, and they had signally failed to budge us from our line. But, our position was very unfavorable for using our artillery, and under cover of darkness and a heavy picket line we withdrew about five miles, to Halltown, and [now] hold a position from which the combined armies could not drive us. Early and Longstreet[24] in our front with their fifty or sixty thousand[25] men *let us alone* with the exception of engaging our skirmishers *"semi-occassionally."*

Aug. 25/64 [continued in the same letter.—TMB].

I was interrupted again, and another night passes before I can resume the thread of my ramble. We have our Hd. Qrs. here in previously the same place we were in before. Yesterday, a reconnaissance was made by [generals] Crook & Emory to their front, but the force soon found the enemy and could learn nothing of it except that its picket line was very heavy.

Tell Gibbie I have something nice for him if I can only succeed in getting it home. It is a beautiful roan colt, about 3 yrs. old, kind and gentle. I have had it shod. The colt had never been shod before but he stood it like an old horse. I have a surcingle and watering bridle on him. He looks very pretty. I had two [colts] and let Gen'l. Ricketts have one. He thinks a great deal of his. I received yesterday another fine letter from you. I have not yet met Major Hickman in the army. I will make an effort to do so. I will write to Grandmother Jackson. Her address is Mrs. Sarah L. Jackson, Avondale, Chester Co., Pa., is it not? Oh! What a dream. Tell mother I think she must have been eating something indigestible for supper, and that I prescribe for a similar case in future that she awake without delay, take a bumper of that venerable grape wine and lie down on the other side. It will afford speedy relief. In the absence of wine, take a *good look* at Gibbie.

Give my love to Sallie, Mother & Grandfather. Kiss Gibbie for his Papa and love him.

Fondly,
Robert

Aug. 26th, 1864
Hd. Qrs. 3rd Div. 6th A. C.
MY OWN DEAR LILLIE:—

Still lying at camp from which I completed my last letter. Health good, troops in good spirits. Weather fine. Yesterday afternoon I was down at Bolivar. Saw Mrs. Mattie Fossett & Nellie Row. Mrs. Row has at length grown as tired of the annoyances and depredation of soldiers that she is going to move to the western part of Virginia where her son lives. She is going as soon as the railroad from here to Martinsburg is repaired and rendered passable.

She went out there about the middle of July, after which the R.R. [railroad] was destroyed and she had to come back by way of Wheeling, Pittsburgh, Harrisburg & Baltimore. I am really sorry for Mrs. Fossett's people. They are subject to every kind of annoyance, and I do not see how they managed to live. Besides, when Mrs. Row leaves they will be bereft of all society, to which they have any affinity.

I have no news for you. The rebs (I think wisely for them) let us alone, with the exception of engaging our skirmishers now and then.
August 27, 1864 [continued in the same letter.—TMB].

We have a new Inspector General—Adjutant Tracy. He is a fine young fellow, unaddicted to any habits of dissipation, and seems quite a conscientious, modest fellow. Our old Inspector's time is out and he leaves the last of this month. Col. Staunton's trial is over. I have not yet heard the action of the court in his case, but the general impression is that it will be heavily against him.

I was over to see the Adjt. yesterday, and had a fine talk with him. He is one of nature's noblemen. I heard from Carpenter through the Adjt. He simply writes sending the Adjt. a copy of the order assigning him to duty at Elmira, and asking why he does not write.

William McCutcheon, our regimental sutler,[26] is here and has set up his stand. He says his family is all well.

The General sent for his wife by telegraph. Expects her here today. While he risks sending for his wife, I am almost afraid to send for mine. I do not think we can remain here long, and am under apprehensions that the railroad at Point of Rocks or that vicinity will be destroyed by a raiding party from the enemy down Loudoun Valley. (Dr. Barr says, "tell Mrs. C. I am alive). If the R.R. at that point should be interfered with, your *retreat* would be cut off. Oh! how much I should like to have you come. I do think, however, that my precautions are wise. If I can consider it safe I will telegraph you without delay. My love to all. If Mr. Westlake has sent you any of my pictures, please send me four or five.

Fondly Yours,
Robert

Sept. 10th 1864
Hd. Qrs. 3rd Div. 6th A.C.
Near Berryville, Va.
MY DEAR LILLIE:—

I have not written you in so long that I deem it a duty to drop a mere line in the absence of writing facilities for a more extended communication. Have received your nice letter and the "cards." Gave them away in about five minutes after they arrived. Don't know what you think, but I don't like either of my Washington pictures so well as the one taken by Woodward.[27] Everybody wants Gibbie's. All fall in love with it, and it is not strange.

Have not yet seen either Col. Smith or Maj. Hickman. Have not heard of Hickman's arrest. Will take a ride over to 2nd Div. And try to find them one of these days. Health is good. Troops in fine spirits. Expect to move. Some firing on our right this morning. Presume it is a cavalry reconnaissance.

Love and kisses to Gibbie, Sallie[28] & Mother.

Fondly Yours,

Robert

Sept. 23rd 1864

Hd. Qrs. 3rd Div., 6th A. C.

Woodstock, Va.

DEAREST LILLIE:—

We are having the most exciting and successful experience of the war. Last Monday [September 19] we had a terrific fight throughout the day within about 3 miles of Winchester. Never were more gallant and grand charges made. The line of battle was about four miles in length. The artillery display was terribly sublime. Early and his rebel band fought with desperation but we fought harder. Gallant Sheridan rode along the lines cheering the men, and after a succession of brilliant charges (in each of which we drove them back and then held our new line) we broke them and the most perfect rout ensued that was ever seen.

Citizens of Winchester say there never was anything in the Valley like it. They [Confederate soldiers] went over the country and through Winchester pell-mell. That night we quartered beyond, and at daylight next morning were in hot pursuit. We knew very well where they would stop, viz. at Fisher's Hill near Strasburg. It is the strongest position in the Valley. And they have strong earthworks up entirely across this natural fortress. It took us one day to fight ourselves into advantageous position.

I cannot describe the place to you nor the fight that came off yesterday. It was the sublimest affair imaginable. I cannot describe. It was the one scene of a lifetime. And when I saw our men fight and press on over dead and dying, never faltering, never despairing, but with a shout of triumph constantly bursting from their lips. I was proud of my countrymen.

But it was reserved for our own 3rd Div. to do the greatest thing of the day. We first broke their line in a desperate charge in the face of bullets, grape, and canister, and up a steep hill. Their irresistible determination to take the point upon which their attack was ordered alone carried them through. They were successful, and forced their way over into the works. Then followed a scene before which even the battle of Winchester wanes. Their whole line rolled up and back against the irresistible tide. The rout was even greater than at Winchester. Our Division captured four cannon.

The cavalry charged them, the infantry pressed them with whizzing bullets, and the artillery poured in shell & case shot. We captured a large number and pressed them all night. We have just arrived here this morning. I am well, but since the excitement has subsided I am very sleepy. I have any amount of prisoners in charge, and turn them over this morning. The roads are strewn with wagons, guns, equipment, etc., etc.

Fondly Yours &c.

Robert

P. S. Kiss for Gibbie. You will see better accounts in the paper.

Sept. 27th, 1864
Hd. Qrs. 3rd Div. 6th A.C.
Near Harrisonburg, Va.
MY OWN DEAR LILLIE:—

We arrived here on the evening of the 25th—twenty five miles from Staunton. After our second glorious victory, which took place at Fisher's Hill near Strasburg, we pushed on after them to Woodstock the same night, where I wrote you last. The next day we arrived at Edenburg, and the following day overtook the rebs at Mt. Jackson. Here a number of their wounded that they were obliged to abandon fell into our hands. They, the rebels, were formed on a hill beyond Mount Jackson, and we brought artillery to bear on them when they soon broke and fled again. We pursued, constantly firing on them and harassing their rear until we arrived about five miles this side of New Market, where we encamped for the night. We took numerous prisoners all the way. Their army is in total rout. Thousands have thrown away their arms and fled to the mountains. They confess a most inglorious thrashing. The next day we arrived here. Early and his whole command except the stragglers have escaped through one of the gaps in the mountain, and deserted the Valley. When the supply train arrives, we will probably push on for Staunton. I remember this whole country as it looked when I went through here as a prisoner.

Yesterday, as Provost Marshal, I seized about four thousand pounds worth of chewing and smoking tobacco and issued it to the troops. There are great quantities of very fine tobacco here. Citizens have for some time been investing their money (Confederate) in tobacco, as presuming at some future time they will be able to realize good money on it.

We have our Hd. Qrs. at the house of a Mr. Gray, who claims to be a Union man. He is wealthy and has a splendid property.

Everybody here seems very anxious to see peace restored. The young ladies are the most deficient. Young men there are none. I am entirely well, and for the past week, like everyone else in Sheridan's army, have been excited and jubilant beyond measure. Adjutant Young has come off safely through all the bullets of the 19th and 22nd. So has Frank. Major Vredenburgh, our former Inspector General, was killed with a number of other valuable officers.[29] General Russell, commanding [the] 1st Division, 6th Corps was killed. The rebs had two general officers killed and three wounded.[30] At the battle of Winchester we captured five pieces of artillery, which we thought was a *big thing*, but at Fisher's Hill we captured twenty-one pieces,[31] making twenty-six in all, and any amount of small arms. Give Sallie and Mother and Gibbie kisses and love. Say I hope to be home the last of next month.[32]

Fondly Your Own,

Robert

[There are no letters for September 28–October 1.—TMB].

Oct. 2nd, 1864
Hd. Qrs. 3rd Div. 6th A. Corps
Harrisonburg, Va.
DEAREST LILLIE:—

Your letters of the 18th and 19th of Sept. came to hand early this morning. You of course had then heard nothing of our bloody fights and triumphant victories. You did not know that while you were writing on Monday the 19th we were having a terrible fight. You have probably read the whole account of the fight there [Winchester] and at Fisher's Hill before this. I have seen only the papers of the 21st and 27th. The account of the fight at Fisher's Hill in the newspapers falls far short of the reality. Every general officer there says that nothing in his experience ever equaled it.

Day before yesterday we went to Mount Crawford, about 8 miles further up the Valley. Here we seized all the mills, took millers from the command and ground grain enough for one issue to the army of flour, then retired to this place, burning all the mills and grain in that part of the Valley. Last night the supply train arrived with papers and five days mail. It was with it that your letter of the 18th arrived.

News has reached us of the success of Birney and Ord on the North side of the James and of the fall of Mobile.[33] I am entirely well. I will not say much of myself at present. You will be gratified to know that the Gen'l. has sent my name up for promotion for gallantry on the fields of Winchester and Fisher's Hill

Tell Gibbie I love to read his messages and love him because he is a good boy. Tell him that his colt grows and is as fat as a mule. He [unclear] and trots beautifully. It made a narrow escape of being killed on Monday the 19th. A cannon ball during the charge passed under its neck and between its head and body, just grazing its throat.

My Love To All,

Fondly Yours,

Robert

P.S. Do not blame me for being so brief. The Supply Train goes back immediately, and this must go with it.

R.

Oct. 8th/64

Hd. Qrs. 3rd Div. 6th A. Corps.

Fisher's Hill [, Va.]

DEAR LILLIE:—

Your letter of the 27th came to hand this evening. We arrived at this point on our way back this evening, where we met the Supply Train with mail, papers, &c. &c. The train leaves this place to return in the morning. I have no conveniences and am writing this on my knee by the light of a large fire. We have cleaned nearly everything out of the Valley as far back as Staunton. Barns are all burned, together with grain and mills. I cannot tell how people are to live here this winter. Large numbers of blacks and whites are with us, on their way to the North. Am quite well, with the exception of some cold.

Fondly Yours,

Robert

October 20th, 1864

Hd. Qrs. Third Division Sixth Corps

Cedar Creek, Va.

MY DEAREST,

Your letter of the 10th has just come to hand. We have just ended another terrible fight and glorious victory. Rather, the fighting ended last night, but the numerous dead are not all buried yet. Nor are all the wounded yet cared for. It was a terrible day but it ended gloriously. General Ricketts was wounded but a short distance from me. He was struck by a ball in the left breast near the shoulder. It is thought that he will recover.[34] Gen'l. Bidwell of the 2nd Div. 6th Corps, commanding a brigade, was killed.[35] Very many valuable officers and men are among the killed and wounded.

Now for a brief outline of the affair. The rebels, about 25,000 [approximately 18,000.—TMB] strong, have been lying in our front at Fisher's Hill for several days. Night before last, under cover of fog and darkness, their whole force was moved over against side of the mountain and passed single file along a mountain path around our left flank. Our force laid in the following order: Eighth Corps on the left, Nineteenth Corps in the middle, and the Sixth Corps on the extreme right. At dawn of day [October 19] the rebs attacked us in full force on the [left] flank. It was a complete surprise. Many men in [the] Eighth Corps had not even time to dress. The whole Corps fled in the wildest confusion, and the 19th Corps with them.

Our Corps sprang to their feet and into line. Wagons were packed and sent off in a trice. Artillery was wheeled into position, and by the time the rebs had moved up our line as far as our position, we had a stubborn front to present. We showered them with bullets and grape & canister, slaying them by hundreds and wounding by thousands. In the meantime, every effort was made to men of the 8th and 19th Corps, and many splendid Staff Officers lost their lives in trying to rally the men. But the effort was almost futile. Many did not stop till they reached Winchester.

The enemy could not drive our Corps from the front, but as their line was much longer than ours they occasionally flanked us, obliging us to fall back, which we did in line. Thus, we fought until we had fallen back about three miles. Here a good position enabled us to make a protracted stand. Remnants of the other two Corps were brought up and put in line and cavalry held our flanks.

Just at this crisis, Gen'l. Sheridan arrived. He had been absent several days—I do not know where, but presume at Washington. He was provoked beyond measure but set to work at once to retrieve the fortunes of the day. The rebels had already captured 18 or 20 pieces of artillery from the 19th and 8th Corps, a number of wagons and ambulances and considerable camp equippage. Sheridan rode along the lines, and the boys cheered him vociferously. Soldiers never had more confidence in a Comd'g. General.

He told them we would "flank Hell out of them before night." About noon they made a terrific charge on us. I never heard such musketry. It was roll upon roll, and one long incessant roll. Our men stood firm and the rebs were obliged to fall back. Arrangements were then made to assume the offensive. About four o'clock everything was in readiness and the whole line charged them. They fought us with stubborn resistance for about an hour. Then they broke and fled in the *wildest confusion.*

Our boys cheered and shouted and pressed them so closely that they were unable to make a stand. Cavalry pressed their flanks, they went back over and through Cedar Creek Hill pell-mell, capturing between two and three thousand prisoners, fifty two pieces of artillery—among which were our own recaptured—over one hundred wagons, lots of ambulances. Among the prisoners was Gen'l. Ramseur—Maj. Gen'l.[36] We encamped at night in the same ground we left the morning, but the cavalry held Fisher's Hill and the rebel army is scattered everywhere. Our dead and wounded the rebs had stripped of their clothing. My Dear, it is a terrible scene to travel the battlefield. I cannot attempt to describe it. Give my love to Gibbie, Mother and Sallie.

Fondly Yours,

Robert

That was the last letter. On October 27, Capt. Robert T. Cornwell's term of service was fulfilled and he was discharged from the army. Early remained in the Valley for another five months, but his devastated Second Corps posed no further threat to Sheridan. Lee transferred all but a thousand of Early's men to Petersburg, and the victorious Sheridan transferred most of his own army to Grant.

Early fought a desperate last battle at Waynesboro on March 2, 1865. He was overwhelmed, and most of his men were captured by Union cavalry. Later in the month, Lee ordered Early to turn over his command to another officer and to go home and await further orders. The orders never arrived. Early was still at home when the surrender took place at Appomattox.

Epilogue

Robert Thompson Cornwell returned to West Chester. However, rather than resuming his prewar teaching career, he decided to become a lawyer. Perhaps his experiences as a provost marshal had some bearing upon his choice of a new profession. Possibly, it may have been that West Chester, his new home, was the governmental and legal seat of a growing and prosperous county. The courthouse dominated the center of town, and the surrounding streets were filled with the offices of lawyers.

In any event, Cornwell began reading law in the office of William B. Waddell, a prominent West Chester attorney who later became president judge of the Chester County courts. The former army officer was a diligent student and easily passed the bar examination. He was admitted to practice on December 10, 1866, and was immediately hired by William Darlington, another well-known local attorney with an extensive practice. Cornwell soon became a partner in the firm, which was renamed Darlington & Cornwell. He practiced there for about ten years, then left to open his own office. Upon his departure, Darlington published an enthusiastic recommendation of his former partner.[1]

Robert T. Cornwell practiced law for fifty-six years. He became an eminent member of the Chester County bar and enjoyed a prosperous career. He also maintained a deep involvement in the affairs of his community, including a life-long interest in local education. In 1869 some West Chester citizens decided to open a "Normal School," or teachers' college. At that time in Pennsylvania such schools were privately funded ventures owned by shareholders, and the school's sponsors asked Cornwell to address members of the public about contributing to the construction of the new school.

He was by then an influential member of the community, and also had prewar experience in opening and developing new schools. His fundraising efforts were successful. All the shares, priced at $50.00 each, were subscribed, including two shares Cornwell purchased for himself. The school, now known as West Chester University, was successful, and Cornwell served on its board of trustees for many years. He was secretary of the board from 1871 to 1875, then president from 1894 to 1896 and again from 1912 to 1914. He also served for twenty-five years on the board of directors of the West Chester School Board, much of the time as its president.

Commercial activities were of no less interest to him. He was a director of the Dime Savings Bank and the National Bank of Chester County, and served for a number of years as president of the board of managers of the Chester County Hospital. He continued actively working with those organizations until just a few weeks before his death. Cornwell also maintained his interest in military affairs. From 1873 to 1878 he was an officer in the National Guard of Pennsylvania, commanding Company "I," the "Wayne Fencibles," of the 11th Regiment. During the railroad riots of 1877 his unit protected the special train that carried the governor of the state.

He was an active member for many years in the McCall Post #31 Grand Army of the Republic, the Union army veterans' association, as well as the Loyal Legion, an organization of former Union army officers. He seems to have particularly enjoyed attending a reunion of the 67th Regiment on July 9, 1889, at the site of the battle at Monocacy. There, he and the other members of the regiment raised half of the $10,000 needed to place a monument to their service at the site. Cornwell noted that the weather on the anniversary day was as hot and dry as it had been twenty-five years earlier, on the day of the battle.

Robert and Lillie had four more children, three daughters and another son. His law practice permitted them to live in considerable comfort, and the couple enjoyed a long life together. It was said of Lillie that she was a woman of unusual vigor, devoted to her family and close friends. Her health was somewhat impaired during the last three or four years of her life. She died at home on February 1, 1907.[2]

Robert continued to practice law until his eighty-sixth year. After retirement, he devoted much of his time to his varied business and community interests in West Chester. Martha Jackson Cornwell, one of his daughters and a sculptress of some renown, returned from New York to stay with her father at his house during the last two years of his life. On his ninety-second birthday, three months before his death, Cornwell was asked by a newspaper reporter for the secret of living a long life. His reply, given with a twinkle of his eyes according to the reporter, was, "I have never had any desire to stop living, and for that reason I believe there is no mystery in the number of years I have lived."[3] Robert T. Cornwell died peacefully at his house on April 26, 1927.

Gibbons Gray "Gibbie" Cornwell. The boy mentioned so lovingly in Robert's letters graduated from Yale University in 1886. He read law in his father's office, was admitted to the Chester County Bar on June 10, 1889, and went into partnership with his father in the firm of Cornwell & Cornwell. On January 18, 1899, he married Ella Eberman, a popular schoolteacher from neighboring Lancaster County. The couple had four children.

He was a member of the 6th Regiment of the Pennsylvania National Guard for many years, including the six months it was mustered into the U.S. Army during the Spanish-American war. Gibbons was well liked by his men, who regarded him as one of the best officers in the National Guard, and he eventually became colonel of the regiment. He served as vice president of the school board, and belonged to a number of social and fraternal organizations in West Chester. According to contemporary accounts, Gibbie was a respected and immensely popular figure in West Chester business and social circles, and his death shocked the community. On October 7, 1912, concerned about financial irregularities in several of his clients' accounts, Gibbons Gray Cornwell committed suicide.

Maj. Gen. Benjamin F. Butler. In late 1864, Butler commanded a force of some 6,500 soldiers and sixty ships in an attempt to capture Wilmington, N.C., the last major blockade running port in the South. On December 23 he launched an amphibious assault against Fort Fisher, the "Gibraltar of the Confederacy," located twenty miles from Wilmington. Although vastly outnumbered, the fort's five hundred defenders forced Butler into an ignominious retreat back to his ships. Because of this and his suspected political machinations during the 1864 presidential election, Butler was relieved from duty on January 7, 1865.

He returned to Massachusetts, and in 1866 won a seat in the U.S. House of Representatives, which he held except for one term until 1879. In 1867 he sat on the board selected to prosecute President Andrew Johnson during impeachment hearings. He was defeated for reelection in 1879 and returned to his law practice. Butler was elected governor of Massachusetts in 1882, and two years later he ran unsuccessfully for president as the "People's Party" candidate.

He later purchased the racing yacht *America*, for which the "America's Cup" was named. Fitted out in considerable opulence, the yacht became his home and entertainment center during the summer months. He died in 1893.

Major General Jubal A. Early. For four years after Appomattox Early lived in Texas, Nassau, Havana, Canada, and Mexico. While in Canada in 1866 he published a book about the Valley Campaign. He returned to Virginia in 1868 when President Johnson issued a blanket amnesty to all ex-Confederates. Early resumed his law practice in Lynchburg, and an 1877 appointment as a commissioner of the Louisiana lottery assured his financial well-being.

An unreconstructed rebel who always wore grey, Early became a prolific and influential speaker and writer on matters regarding the war. He was one of the foremost proponents of the Lost Cause cult, served as president of the Southern Historical Society, and was a co-founder of the Association of the Army of Northern Virginia. He died in Lynchburg on March 2, 1894. The notes for his autobiography were edited and published posthumously by his niece under the title *Narrative of the War Between the States.*

Libby Prison. After Richmond was occupied, the Union army for a short time used Libby as a prison for captured Confederates. Among them was Richard Turner, the former registrar. The building returned to private ownership several years later. A fertilizer company used part of the premises until 1887, when the building was sold to a group of Chicago businessmen.

They had it completely dismantled, and sent the carefully numbered pieces to Chicago, where they were reassembled as the "Libby Prison War Museum." It was a popular attraction for about five years, but subsequently became insolvent when tourist revenues slackened and was torn down in 1899. Many of the bricks were used by local contractors in the construction of new buildings, and the Chicago Historical Society acquired enough Libby bricks to construct one wall of its Civil War Room.

Charles Danielson, a state senator from Indiana, bought many of the beams and timbers, and some of the bricks, which he used to construct a barn on his property. The barn was razed in 1960, but the Libby materials were saved and are still in storage. Construction of the Richmond flood wall in the 1990s eliminated most of the physical site of Libby Prison. The small remaining section is a park, dedicated to the memory of those who were imprisoned there.

Col. Robert C. Ould. The Confederate agent for the exchange of prisoners was detained for a while after the war, during an investigation into the treatment of Union prisoners. Ould was absolved of any wrongdoing and returned to the practice of law. He died in 1881.

Maj. Gen. James Brewerton Ricketts. Battlefield surgeons at Cedar Creek removed bullets from devastating wounds in Ricketts' chest and right shoulder, then put him on a train for Washington. He spent the next six months there under Fanny's care, recovering somewhat from his injuries. On April 7, 1865, two days before Lee's surrender, Ricketts resumed command of the Third Division, VI Corps.

He continued in the greatly reduced peacetime army, but reverted to his Regular Army rank of major. However, because of his distinguished service he was promoted to major general in the Regular Army, to rank from March 13, 1865. The effects of his wounds received at Cedar Creek were so severe that he was forced to retire in 1867, although he was able to serve on courts-martial boards until 1869. He spent the rest of his life in considerable pain. General Ricketts died in 1887 and is buried in Arlington National Cemetery.

Erasmus Ross. The clerk of Libby Prison died in a hotel fire in 1870.

Sixty-seventh Regiment Pennsylvania Volunteer Infantry: After Cedar Creek, Cornwell's old regiment served at Petersburg until the city fell in April 1865. They fought at Saylor's Creek and were present at Appomattox when the Army of Northern Virginia surrendered. The regiment then marched to Danville, Virginia, serving there and in Richmond until the end of May. The 67th took part in the Corps Review in Washington on June 8 and was mustered out of service on July 17, 1865.

Maj. Thomas Turner. When the war ended, the commandant of Libby Prison fled out of the country, eventually settling in Canada. He returned to the United

States ten years later and lived in Tennessee, where he practiced dentistry. Turner died in greatly reduced circumstances in 1901.

Richard Turner. After the fall of Richmond, Union authorities put the former Libby adjutant into one of the prison's dungeons, where he was harshly treated. He escaped but was recaptured a month later when he returned to Richmond to see his family. Turner was returned to Libby, but this time to one of the large upstairs rooms. He was paroled in June 1866 and subsequently became a successful businessman. He died in 1901.

Appendix A

Union Army Clothing and Equipment Receipt

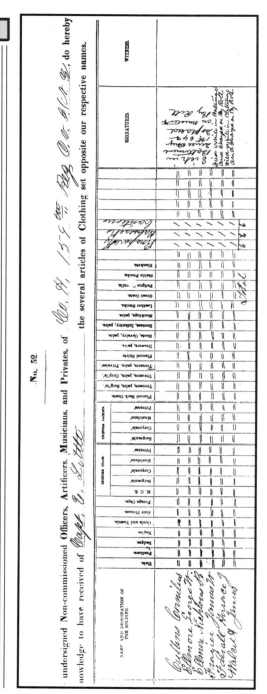

Greatly reduced in size from the original, this was just one of many such detailed forms Cornwell complained about when he was a company officer. The columns contain entries for items such as hat feathers, uniform coats and jackets, trousers, shirts, bootees, and fatigue overalls. In this case, each man named received a knapsack, haversack, and canteen.

Courtesy of Robert Sullivan

190

Appendix B

Contents of the Dahlgren Papers

The papers reportedly found upon Dahlgren's body gave detailed instructions to the raiding party as to what was to be done once they arrived in Richmond. The orders were lengthy, and are abbreviated here to include only the salient points. The full text can be found in a number of published works, including Varina Davis, *Jefferson Davis: A Memoir By His Wife Varina Davis*, vol. 2 (New York: Belford & Co., 1890), pp. 467–470.

> All mills must be burned, and the canal destroyed….We will try and secure the bridge to the city (one mile below Belle Isle) and release the prisoners at the same time….The bridges once secured and the prisoners loose and over the river, the bridges will be secured and the city destroyed….and once in the city, it must be destroyed, and Jeff Davis and the cabinet killed. Prisoners will go along with combustible material….Horses and cattle which we do not need immediately must be shot rather than left. Everything on the canal and elsewhere of service to the rebels must be destroyed….The pioneers [engineers]…must have plenty of oakum and turpentine for burning, which will be rolled into soaked balls, and given to the men to burn when we get into the city. Torpedoes will only be used by the pioneers for destroying the main bridges, etc. They must be prepared to destroy railroads…Men will stop at Bellona arsenal and totally destroy it, and anything else but hospitals;….

Notes

Introduction

1. From an untitled newspaper biography of Robert T. Cornwell. *Daily Local News* (West Chester, Pa.), July 1, 1912.

2. "Census History of Robert T. Cornwell." Family genealogical data extracted from the 1850 Census of the United States for Sullivan County, New York. This and all subsequent documents relating to the Cornwell genealogy are in the possession of Richard Cornwell unless otherwise noted.

3. "Robert T. Cornwell," *Biographical and Portrait Cyclopedia of Chester County, Pennsylvania* (Richmond, Ind.: Gresham Publishing Co., 1893), pp. 614–16.

4. It is now called Millersville State University.

5. *Daily Local News*, July 1, 1912.

6. Extract taken from the 1860 U.S. Census for Westtown Township, Chester County, Pa.

7. *Cyclopedia of Chester County*, p. 614.

Chapter 1

1. The size of the Regular Army was only 16,367 men. E. B. Long with Barbara Long, *The Civil War Day By Day* (New York: Doubleday & Co., 1971), p. 707.

2. Samuel P. Bates, *History of the Pennsylvania Volunteers 1861–5* (Harrisburg, Pa., 1869), 2: 634.

3. Richard A. Sauers, *Advance the Colors! Pennsylvania Civil War Battle Flags*, vol. 1 (Harrisburg, Pa.: 1987, The Capitol Preservation Committee), p. 184.

4. "Death's Work," West Chester (Pennsylvania) *Daily Local News*, April 26, 1927.

5. Individual Muster-in Roll, Co. B, 67th Reg. Pa. Infantry. Compiled Military Service Records. Robert T. Cornwell. National Archives, Washington, D.C. Hereinafter, "Service Record."

6. James I. Robertson, Jr., *Soldiers Blue and Gray* (New York: Warner Books, Inc., 1988), pp. 49–50, quoting George F. Eggleston, *A Rebel's Recollections* (New York: 1875), p. 20; S. Millett Thompson, *Thirteenth Regiment of New Hampshire Volunteer Infantry in the War of Rebellion, 1861–1865* (Boston: Houghton Mifflin Co., 1885), p. 3; and Francis H. Buffum, *A Memorial of the Great Rebellion: Being a History of the Fourteenth Regiment, New Hampshire Volunteers* (Boston: Rand, Avery & Co., 1882), p. 45.

7. Capt. August V. Kautz, *The Company Clerk: Showing How and When To Make All The Returns, Reports, Rolls, And Other Papers, And What To Do With Them* (Philadelphia: J. B. Lippincott & Co., 1863), pp. 12–16, 105.

8. Ezra J. Warner, *Generals in Blue* (Baton Rouge: Louisiana State University Press, 1964), pp. 257–58.

9. Possibly the wife of John F. Young, the regimental adjutant. Bates, p. 634.

10. Gibbons Gray Cornwell, Robert and Lillie's infant son, born August 18, 1861.

11. Lillie's sister, Sarah Jackson, born November 11, 1838. Extracts from the 1850 and 1860 U.S. Censuses for Chester County, Pa., Gibbons Gray head of family, contained in "Census History of Mary Gray."

12. Harry White was also the 67th regiment's recruiting officer.

13. Bates, p. 634, Mark Miller, "67th Pennsylvania Infantry Regiment," 1996 (?), p. 1, the author, Escondito, Ca.

14. Bates, pp. 634, 649.

15. At Camp Curtin, a "camp of instruction" located on the grounds of the Dauphin County Agricultural Society near Harrisburg. It opened on April 18, 1861, and was named in honor of Andrew Gregg Curtin, the governor of Pennsylvania at the time. Camp Curtin was one of the largest basic training camps for Union army recruits.

16. Federal, state, and even local governments often paid cash bounties to encourage men to join the army. These bounties could amount to two or three times a soldier's annual military pay.

17. School of the soldier: The basic elements of drill and learning to handle and fire a musket.

18. The Westlakes were friends of Robert and Lillie's from Indiana County. He owned a part interest in the local newspaper. See letter dated December 2, 1863.

19. Unsigned and not actually mailed until September 8, 1862, when it was enclosed with another letter of that date.

20. Railroad passenger cars.

21. Ft. Ellsworth was part of Washington's ring of defensive fortifications. It was located above Cameron Creek, in Alexandria, Virginia. A map of Washington's defenses is included among the illustrations.

22. Major General George Brinton McClellan (1826–1885). On September 2, 1862, McClellan replaced Pope and assumed command of the combined Army of Virginia and the Army of the Potomac.

23. Apparently because he was awaiting a commission, Cornwell was allowed to store his own clothing in a trunk. At the Round House his trunk and that of a senior officer of another regiment were loaded into a military baggage wagon that was to accompany the marching troops. The trunk was lost in the confusion of the march.

24. Col. John F. Staunton, commanding the 67th Regiment. Bates, p. 634.

25. These may have been Sibley tents. They were large, conical tents, common to the Union army early in the war. Each tent had its own stove and could shelter twenty men.

26. The fighting at Second Manassas (Bull Run) began on Friday, August 29, 1862, and concluded on Monday, September 1.

27. Lt. Col. Horace B. Burnham, 67th P.V.I. Bates, p. 634.

28. Lieutenant Carpenter is not identified in Bates, but the March 14, 1864, entry in Cornwell's diary mentions a Captain Carpenter of the 67th Regiment. Robert Barr was the regimental surgeon. Bates, p. 634.

29. The Pennsylvania state capitol.

30. Maj. Harry White, 67th P.V.I. Bates, p. 634.

31. Volunteer commissions were issued by the governors of the various states. Cornwell was trying to secure his commission in the 67th Pennsylvania. Union army regulations then in force for volunteer regiments allowed each such infantry company to have one captain, one first lieutenant, and one second lieutenant. Philip Katcher, *The Civil War Source Book* (New York: Facts on File, 1992), p. 151.

32. On September 17, 1862. Service Record, *Individual Muster-in Roll.*

33. "Aunt Massey" was Lillie's aunt, Mary Jackson, born in 1812 or 1813. Extract from the 1900 Census of the United States, Chester County, Pa., Sheet 12, Enumeration District # 126, Dwelling # 257. The relationship of the "Cheyney's" is not certain.

34. Soldiers typically carried homemade sewing kits such as these, which they called "housewives."

35. Officers' fatigue suits were custom-tailored versions of the enlisted men's four-button fatigue blouse or "sack coat" and a pair of durable trousers. These suits were extremely popular for field use.

36. Lillie was preparing to move to her parents' house in West Chester.

37. The Union prisoners had been captured during the battles at South Mountain, September 14; Harpers Ferry, September 15; Antietam, September 17; and Blackford's Ford, September 19.

38. Dixon S. Miles commanded Federal defenses at Harpers Ferry.

39. In 1862, there were 549 students and 13 instructions at Millersville Normal School. *The National Almanac and Annual Record for the Year 1864* (Philadelphia, 1864), p. 338.

40. William Hemsley Emory (1811–1887).

41. "Marquee" was a term not much in use since the eighteenth century. Cornwell was probably referring to a wall tent. These rectangular canvas tents were roughly 14 feet square, with 4½ foot walls rising to a peak of about 11 feet in the center. Wall tents were used by officers and for field hospitals.

42. These may have been the only occasions when Cornwell wore his sash. As a badge of this particular duty, Officers of the Day wore their sashes over their right shoulders, knotted under the left arm.

43. Paroles and countersigns were the challenges and passwords that allowed one to enter or leave a camp. The words or phrases were usually changed daily.

44. The average monthly salary of a female high school teacher in Pennsylvania at that time was $18.55. Male teachers received $23.81. *National Almanac 1864*, p. 337.

45. James Greer.

46. William E. Tucker.

47. Military police.

48. The deception was carried on in Tucker's official service records: "Died Nov. 2, 1862, of wounds received in action." Bates, p. 652.

49. Cornwell's comment about his pay is in accordance with the maximum official army pay tables. The base pay of an infantry captain was $60 per month. Depending upon circumstances, he could also receive another $36 for commuted rations and $22.50 for the commuted service of one servant. Commanding officers of companies received an additional $10. By contrast, a private was paid $13 per month. *National Almanac*, pp. 147–48.

50. George W. Simpson.

51. Probably the wife of Capt. John F. Young, regimental adjutant.

52. Horace B. Burnham.

Chapter 2

1. Bates, p. 634.

2. Wristers were knitted wrist coverings.

3. 1st Lieut. Lyman Borchers of Co. "C."

4. Edward George Earle Lytton Bulwer (1803–1873), also known as Edward Bulwer-Lytton, was a prolific and popular writer and poet of the era.

5. Cornwell may have meant 1st Lieut. Dallas *Sutton*.

6. Possibly the man who tailored Cornwell's uniforms.

7. Unidentified.

8. Brigadier General Benjamin F. *Kelley* (1807–1891), commanding the Federal Department of West Virginia.

9. The man is unidentified.

10. Adams Express was a major delivery company, and offered a popular method of forwarding money in special envelopes. The company survives today, not as a delivery service but as a closed-end mutual fund.

11. Pennsylvania's nickname is the "Keystone State."

12. Cornwell was raised in Orange County; Young was probably a friend or relative.

13. Fort Sumter was fired upon on April 12, 1861, an event that inflamed the political passions in the still-uncommitted state of Maryland. On April 19, the 6th Massachusetts Regiment was passing through Baltimore en route to reinforce Washington, D.C. when it was attacked by a large crowd. A riot ensued, shots were exchanged, and four soldiers and nine civilians were killed. The security of the Federal capitol required the neutralization of Maryland as a potential state for the Confederacy. By the end of April so many Union troops were in the state that Maryland's legislators were unable to act upon the secession question. On May 13, Brigadier General Benjamin F. Butler and his troops occupied the city and fortified it against its own residents.

14. A town in the vicinity of Harpers Ferry.

15. Two or three guns.

16. About 25 men.

17. Aligned his men facing the expected direction of the enemy.

18. Francis A. Hubble.

19. Burnham.

20. Jacob H. Arndt.

21. Probably Capt. Lynford Trock of Co. "H," killed at Winchester on June 15, 1863. Bates, p. 639.

22. The reports were correct. During the preceding nine days, as Lee's army began entering Maryland, there was fighting there and in Virginia. Harrisburg, the capital of Pennsylvania, was in a state of alarm.

Chapter 3

1. William B. Hesseltine, ed., *Civil War Prisons* (Kent, Ohio: Kent State University Press, 1995), p. 96; J. Michael Horigan, "Elmira Prison Camp—A Second Opinion," The Chemung Historical Journal (March 1985), p. 3451.

2. Ibid., p. 3455.

3. *The War of the Rebellion: A Compilation of the Official Records of the Union and Confederate Armies* (Washington, D.C.: Government Printing Office, 1880–1901), ser. 2, 8: 340–1. Hereinafter, "*O.R.*"

4. Hesseltine, p. 7.

5. Long, pp. 710, 712.

6. Miller, p. 2.

7. Bell Irvin Wiley, *The Life of Johnnie Reb* (Baton Rouge: Louisiana State University Press, 1992), pp. 244–69.

8. One authority states that only three Confederate prisoner of war books were printed in the South. Richard B. Harwell. *The Confederate Reader: How the South Saw the War* (New York: Dover Publications, Inc., 1989), p. 321.

9. *O.R.*, ser. 2, 1:166–67.

10. Warner, p. 61.

11. Long, pp. 378–79, 381.

12. Sandra V. Parker, *Richmond's Civil War Prisons* (Lynchburg, Va.: H. E. Howard, Inc., 1990), pp. 2–3.

13. Libby was the only Civil War prison to feature enclosed washrooms and toilets.

14. *O.R.*, ser. 2, 6: 544–45.

15. F. F. Cavada, *Libby Life: Experiences Of A Prisoner Of War In Richmond, Va., 1863–64* (Philadelphia: 1864), pp. 24–25.

16. Parker, 23.

17. John Beauchamp Jones, *A Rebel War Clerk's Diary*, ed. Earl Schenk Miers (New York: 1958), p. 243.

18. An important Union fortress and depot located in Virginia at the southern tip of the Peninsula.

19. Sullivan A. Meredith, of Philadelphia. After recovering from a severe wound at Second Manassas, he became the commissioner for the exchange of prisoners.

20. William Levis James, captain and assistant quartermaster. Promoted to brigadier general of volunteers on March 1, 1866.

21. Robert Ould was the Confederate exchange agent.

22. Provost marshal of Richmond and in overall command of the city's military prisons.

23. The son of General Winder.

24. LaTouche was the adjutant of Libby Prison.

25. Cavada, pp. 23, 29. Those prices were 30 to 50 percent more than civilians paid for the same items. Cf. Jones, various pp.

26. "The Prisons at Richmond," *Harper's Weekly*, October 17, 1863.

27. Cavada, pp. 33–34.

28. The Civil War Library and Museum in Philadelphia owns an original printed handbill announcing one such play at Libby. Evidently, the prisoners were able to have the handbills printed in Richmond.

29. Parker, p. 42.

30. Cavada, pp. 68–69.

31. Thomas Turner, commandant of the prison.

32. The first draft in the North occurred in July 1863. Three more took place by the end of 1864. In total, 249,259 men were drafted, 35 percent of whom bought substitutes to take their places. Long, p. 707.

33. There were eight officers named White in Libby at this time. Cavada, pp. 99, 206, 210, 215, 217, 220.

34. Approximately 175,000 German-born soldiers served in the Union army. Long, p. 707.

35. Prisoners were permitted to burn candles until midnight on New Year's Eve. To celebrate, one group shared a carefully-horded flask of Drake's Plantation Bitters. After the stroke of midnight they also sang "The Star Spangled Banner" and "Auld Lang Syne." The "ball" mentioned by Cornwell took place in the prison kitchen. It led off with two officers dressed outrageously as a Negro woman and her beau. Several hundred other prisoners danced to the music of the prison orchestra. Cavada, pp. 103, 125–26.

36. Brig. Gen. John Hunt Morgan was famous for his dashing cavalry operations in Kentucky and Tennessee. He was captured during a raid into Indiana and Ohio in July 1863, and imprisoned in the Ohio State Penitentiary. Morgan escaped from the prison by tunneling out of it on November 27 and returning to Confederate lines. Mark M. Boatner, III, *The Civil War Dictionary* (New York: Random House, 1991), p. 566; Parker, pp. 44–46.

37. The exchange of prisoners.

38. In mid-April 1863, 1,700 men under command of Col. Abel D. Streight, 51st Indiana, commenced a series of raids intended to disrupt Confederate rail service in Georgia and Alabama. On May 3, he and his men were captured in Alabama by Nathan Bedford Forrest. Once at Libby, Streight wrote an endless stream of letters to Confederate and Union authorities, complaining about the lack of food in prison. Late in 1863 Streight and his adjutant, possibly the Reed mentioned above, attempted to escape from the prison. Both were recaptured and placed in the dungeon for a while.

39. A prisoner of war camp was established in late 1861 at an abandoned cotton factory in Salisbury, North Carolina. Conditions were good there for the first 1,500 prisoners, but deteriorated rapidly in late 1864 when more than 10,000 men were held in the camp.

40. In Libby at about this time there began to develop "a frightful epidemic of that alarming malady known as 'Exchange on the brain.'" Cavada, p. 128.

41. Except for a symbolic exchange of about six hundred men by each side at Christmas 1863, the exchange of prisoners had ceased while negotiators attempted to work out the question of captured Negro soldiers.

42. Carpenter was an officer in the 67th Pa. See diary entry for March 14, 1864.

43. Between March and April 1864, three hundred fifty veterans of the 67th regiment were also granted a one-month furlough. Leaving two hundred newer men behind at Brandy Station, the veterans, with their weapons, departed for Philadelphia. They met at Philadelphia thirty days later and rejoined the regiment in Washington, D.C. Bates, pp. 637–38.

44. Lieut. John LaTouche.

45. Belle Isle was an eighty-acre island in the James River. For a number of years before the war it was home to an ironworks and village for the workers. When converted to a prison camp, the island was designed to accommodate 3,000 prisoners in relative comfort, but by early 1864 more than 8,000 crowded the facility. The threadbare prisoners suffered greatly during the winter of 1863–1864. The only shelter for many of them were shallow pits scratched into the soil. The fortunate ones covered their pits with a torn blanket. So little food was available that on one occasion the men killed and ate the commandant's dog.

46. Guerrilla.

47. "Fresh fish" was a common Civil War expression applied by veterans to newly arrived soldiers. Whether on the battlefield or in prison, fresh fish were a prime source of news about events in the outside world. "Suckers" were relatively new prisoners, "dry cods" had been imprisoned for longer periods, and "pickled sardines" were long-term prisoners. Parker, p. 40.

48. Sixty-year-old Brigadier General Neal Dow of Maine was an abolitionist, temperance fanatic and ex-Quaker. He wrote the "Maine Law" that prohibited the sale of liquor in that state. Dow entered Libby in June 1863 and kept an interesting, if somewhat biased and bitter, diary of his experiences there.

49. Possibly Major John Henry, 5th Ohio Cavalry.

50. The Richmond *Examiner*, one of the local newspapers prisoners could buy from vendors.

51. Possibly one of the Negro employees of the prison.

52. Beginning in late 1863, a wave of self-instruction swept the prison population at Libby. "There have been at different times in the prison classes of French, German, Spanish, Italian, Latin and Greek, English Grammar, Phonography, Fencing, Dancing, Military Tactics and a Bible Class. Of course this educational enthusiasm is very ephemeral; these studies are taken up with avidity, to be dropped in disgust at an early day. What the prisoner seeks, in most cases, is not so much information as amusement." Cavada, p. 158.

53. Possibly Capt. H. W. Sawyer, 12th New Jersey Cavalry, and Lt. N. L. Wood, Jr., 12th U.S. Infantry. Cavada, pp. 203, 210.

54. Ould, a Virginian, was the senior Confederate agent for the exchange of prisoners. Before the war he was an influential district attorney in Washington and served as brigadier general of the capitol's volunteer National Guard troops. He resigned those positions when Virginia seceded. Robert Underwood Johnson and Clarence Clough Buel, eds., *Battles and Leaders of the Civil War*, vol. 1 (New York: Thomas Yoseloff, Inc., 1956), pp. 6, 12, 20. Hereinafter "*B&L.*"

55. The Confederate House of Representatives sent a committee to visit and investigate the conditions in the military prisons. It concluded that although the rations for Union prisoners often lacked meat, the prisoners were as well fed as the Confederate garrison in Richmond. Hesseltine, p. 67.

56. Possibly Col. W. H. Powell. Cavada, p. 208.

57. Maj. E. N. Bates, 80th Illinois Regiment, and Capt. John F. Porter, Jr., 14th New York Cavalry. Cavada, pp. 140, 214, 219.

58. Carothers and King were in the 3rd Ohio; Cupp was in the 176th Pennsylvania. Of the five, Porter reached Union lines and the other four were recaptured.

59. Erasmus Ross, prison registrar.

Chapter 4

1.   Parker, p. 45; Robert B. Thomas, pub., *The Old Farmer's Almanac 1863* (Boston, Brewer & Tileson, 1863), p. 41.

2.   James A. Gindlesperger, *Escape From Libby Prison* (Shippensburg, Pa.: Burd Street Press, 1996), various; Parker, pp. 61–62; Cavada, pp. 167–73.

3.   *O.R.*, ser. 2, 6: 1, 127; Parker, pp. 37–38.

4.   Letters and reports concerning the Kellogg situation are found on various pages in *O.R.*, ser. 2: 4, 6. A description of Kellogg and a copy of his letter to his family are in Cavada, pp. 64–68.

5.   This poem was popular among Union troops. It refers to the fact that the Confederate government encouraged its people to save urine. That by-product was then added to other ingredients to produce artificial niter, or saltpeter, the key ingredient in gunpowder. Although it was successful as a patriotic effort, the vast majority of Confederate niter was mined in its natural form in caves. "F. F. V.s" were the First Families of Virginia.

6.   "Two more of our number have been sent to Saulsbury [*sic*], North Carolina,…They are Captain Ives, 10th Massachusetts, and Captain J. E. B. Reed, 51st Indiana." Cavada, p. 141.

7.   Jackass guns were small-calibre artillery.

8.   "The tocsin is sounding at 9 A. M. It appears that Gen. Butler is marching up the Peninsula….the local defense men must be relied on to defend Richmond." Jones, p. 334.

9.   Cornwell's request for virus may have related to an earlier situation at Libby. In September, 1863 John Wilkins, the surgeon of Libby Prison, wrote to General Winder: "Contrary to my advice, an assistant surgeon of the Federal Army vaccinated a number of the officers with pus (not lymph) taken from the arm of another assistant surgeon (also a prisoner), producing a spurious form of vaccination from which a number are now suffering. This virus had probably passed through a system affected with secondary syphilis." *O.R.,* ser. 2, 6: 262.

10. An officer ranking as major or above.

11. Forty-five-year-old Lt. Col. John P. Spofford, 97th New York Volunteers, was one of the oldest escapees.

12. Returned escapees were put into jail cells located in the basement of the prison.

13. "Among them [the escapees] we regret to have to class the notorious Col. Streight." Richmond *Examiner*, Feb. 11, 1864, quoted in Gindlesperger, p. 221.

14. Double quick is a rapid marching pace, i.e., walking briskly.

15. "This was the coldest morning of the winter. There was ice in the wash-basins in our bed chambers, the first we have seen there." Jones, p. 338.

16. City Point was located at the junction of the James and Appomattox Rivers, about 30 miles southeast of Richmond.

17. Louis T. Wigfall, prewar lawyer, U.S. senator from Texas, and Southern "fire-eater." He became a general in the Confederate army, but resigned to serve in the Confederate Congress.

18. Johnston's Island was a prison camp for Confederate officers. The island was in Lake Erie, about three miles offshore from Sandusky, Ohio. Conditions there were every bit as wretched as those at Libby.

19. Carving rings and other trinkets from old meat bones was a popular pastime among the prisoners.

20. "Old Ben" was a Negro worker at the prison. He awakened the prisoners in the mornings by yelling out the news headlines of the day. Cavada, p. 47.

21. The battle of Olustee, west of Jacksonville. On February 20, Confederate troops under Gen. Joseph Finnegan routed Gen. Truman A. Seymour's Federal forces. As a result, Florida continued in its role as a main supplier of beef and other foodstuffs to the Confederate armies.

22. Brig. Gen. Eliakim Parker Scammon (1816–1894).

23. An Indiana County, Pa. newspaper.

24. The prison escape sent Major Turner and his staff into a frenzy of activity. Every two hours the guards thoroughly searched the building, and then began "roll-calls without number." During the time the prisoners were in the kitchen, mentioned in Cornwell's account, the guards removed all the pocket knives, files, and little tools used by the prisoners to cut bone or make bone trinkets. Cavada, pp. 191–92.

25. Lillie's grandmother.

26. Cornwell had a younger sister named Mary. Census History of Robert T. Cornwell.

27. This was either Cornwell's sister or a relative of Lillie's, probably an aunt, named Mary Jackson who resided with her parents. One-page "Census History of Mary Gray," n.d., n.p. In the possession of Richard Cornwell.

Chapter 5

1. Cavada, p. 196.

2. Cavada, pp. 195–96; Jones, p. 344.

3. Richard N. Current, ed. *Encyclopedia of the Confederacy* (New York: Simon & Schuster, 1993), vol. 2; S. V. "Dahlgren Papers," by Michael J. Andrus; Boatner, p. 218.

4. Parker, pp. 62–63.

5. Cavada, pp. 34–35.

6. *O.R.*, ser. 2, 6: 1110–11.

7. Butler is quoted in *O.R.*, ser. 2, 6: 1122; Jones's diary entry is on p. 357.

8. Butler is quoted in *O.R.*, ser. 2, 7: 31; Grant in *O.R.*, ser. 2, 1: 62–63.

9. At many Civil War prisons there was a "deadline," a real or imaginary point beyond which a prisoner could not advance without the risk of being fired upon by the guards without warning.

10. The officer's story was incorrect and fanciful.

11. The officer is identified as "Lieut. Hammond, a cavalry officer." Cavada, p. 198. During Dahlgren's raid several days earlier, Major Turner warned that any prisoners who approached the windows or touched the window bars would be shot without warning.

12. Maj. Gen. Arnold Elzey (1816–1871), commander of the Dept. of Richmond.

13. Cornwell's description of the body was copied from an article in the March 10 issue of the Richmond *Dispatch*. It is also included in Jones, p. 348.

14. Took turns cooking.

15. It was not uncommon for civilians, including ladies, to visit prisoner of war camps. At Elmira, citizens did not even have to bother entering the camp: two three-story public observation platforms were constructed across from the prison. Admission to the towers cost ten cents; viewers who were hungry or thirsty could purchase "lemon pop, ginger cakes, beer and hard liquor" from vendors. Thomas E. Byrne, "Elmira's Civil War Prison Camp: 1864–65," The Chemung Historical Journal (September 1964), p. 1282.

16. Possibly Col. W. T. Wilson, 123rd Ohio Volunteers. Cavada, p. 218. Lt. Col. W. S. Northcott. Cavada, p. 211.

17. Confederate exchange agent.

18. Forty Union officers, seventy-seven noncommissioned officers, and 332 privates were received for exchange at City Point on March 15. *O.R.*, ser. 2, 7: 37.

19. They were going to Camp Sumter, which gained infamy under the more familiar name of "Andersonville."

20. Richmond civilians endured the same shortages. On March 9, J. B. Jones wrote in his diary, "This is the famine month. Prices of every commodity in the market—up, up, up." Jones, p. 348.

21. On March 12, Lee's commissary officer reported that the army was out of meat. Gen. Braxton Bragg then took steps to transport quantities of meat and other military food supplies. Four

days later "Much food for Lee's army has arrived [in Richmond] during the last two days." Jones, pp. 349–50.

22. Fifty imprisoned Confederate officers and six hundred enlisted men were exchanged at City Point on March 15. *O.R.*, ser. 2, 7: 38.

23. Possibly Lieut. Fred J. Brownell. Cavada, p. 214.

24. Sixty-two Union officers and 1,109 enlisted men were received for exchange at City Point on March 21. *O.R.*, ser. 2, 7: 37.

25. Col. Louis de Cesnola, 4th New York Cavalry. Cavada, p. 205.

26. The pay of Union soldiers accrued while they were imprisoned. General Order No. 9, 1862: "The Secretary of War directs that officers and soldiers of the United States who are or may be prisoners of war shall during their imprisonmnent be considered entitled to and receive the same pay as if they were doing active duty." *O.R.*, ser. 2, 5: 259.

27. There was no glass in any of the windows at Libby.

28. A Capt. J. C. Hagenbush of the 67th Pa. Vols. was in Libby. Cavada, p. 218.

29. Lt. Col. H. B. Hunter and Lt. F. L. Schyler were in the 123rd Ohio Volunteers. Cavada, p. 219.

30. Capt. Solomon G. Hamlin, 134th New York Volunteers, and Capt. Samuel McKee, 14th Kentucky Cavalry. Cavada, pp. 215, 221.

31. Maj. John E. Clark. Cavada, p. 208.

32. Lt. William Blanchard, 2nd United States Cavalry. Cavada, p. 209.

33. "Buck and ball" musket loads had been used by American infantrymen since at least the Revolutionary War. The load consisted of a musket ball and some buckshot. When fired, the charge produced a spray of projectiles.

34. Many Civil War soldiers were freemasons, and whenever possible practiced the tenets of the fraternity throughout the war. A "Masonic Prison Association" was established by Confederate officers imprisoned at Johnson's Island, Ohio. It is likely that similar groups were found in most of the prisons. *O.R.*, ser. 2, 1: 625.

35. Capt. E. E. Chase, 1st Rhode Island Cavalry, together with Capt. J. B. Litchfield, 4th Maine Infantry, and Capt. J. L. Kendall, 1st Massachusetts Infantry, were sent from Libby in December 1863 to the Salisbury, North Carolina prison camp. They were sentenced to hard labor there in retaliation for the same sentence allegedly given to some Confederate prisoners. Cavada, p. 99.

36. "The famine [among the civilian population in Richmond] is becoming more terrible daily." Jones, p. 361.

37. Ft. Pillow was a small earthwork fortification on the eastern bank of the Mississippi River above Memphis. On the morning of April 12, 1,500 cavalrymen under Maj. Gen. Nathan Bedford Forrest (1821–1877) attacked the fort, which was defended by some 258 Negro and 295 white soldiers. The defenders were backed by six pieces of artillery and the gunboat *New Era*. Forrest's offer of a surrender on honorable terms was, after much delay, refused by the fort's commander. During the delay, movements within the fort indicated not surrender but a renewal of hostilities. As well, according to Confederate reports, Negro soldiers on the walls hurled insults and made rude gestures to Forrest's men. Forrest attacked and quickly overwhelmed the fort. Accounts of what took place within are still controversial. Of the Union defenders, about 231 were killed, 100 were seriously wounded, and 226 taken prisoner. Forrest lost only fourteen killed and eighty-six wounded. Negro soldiers in particular suffered grievously at the hands of the Confederates. The Northern press called the affair a "massacre," while Southern accounts said that the disproportionate losses were the result of drunkenness among the defenders and their failure to surrender even at point-blank range.

38. The occupation of Baltimore by Union troops.

39. Late on April 17, Confederate forces under Brig. Gen. Robert F. Hoke (1837–1912) began an attack upon the Union garrison at Plymouth, a town on the Roanoke River in North Carolina. Fighting continued the next day. The newly-built ironclad, CSS *Albemarle*, a warship literally constructed in a cornfield, arrived on the 19th. She sank one Union warship, damaged another, and drove off the remaining enemy ships. The garrison surrendered on April 20. Hoke was

promoted to major general the same day, a reward for his skill and winning a significant victory in an area where the Confederacy had little recent success. Union losses including prisoners were more than 2,800 men; among them was Brig. Gen. Henry W. Wessels (1809–1889).

40. Mary E. Walker, captured at Tunnel Hill, Georgia, on May 7, was the first female assistant surgeon in the U.S. army. She received special treatment as a prisoner, and was often allowed to stroll around Richmond, where her "Bloomer costume, blouse, trowsers and boots secured her a following of astonished and admiring boys. She was quite chatty and seemed rather to enjoy the notoriety of her position." Walker later became a women's rights activist and wore male clothing for the rest of her life. Parker, p. 26; Boatner, p. 885.

41. In early 1864 some of Richmond's excess Union prisoners were sent to Danville, a town in Pittsylvania County, Va., on the Virginia-North Carolina border.

42. During the Civil War, the term "ambulance" also referred to a wagon rather than a conveyance for the injured.

43. Major Mulford was apparently assigned to the *New York*, along with Dorothea Dix, to see to the well-being of released officers. Cavada, p. 200.

44. As an exchanged prisoner, Cornwell was a "parolee" in the same camp he guarded more than eighteen months earlier.

Chapter 6

1. "Paroled prisoner granted leave of absence for 20 days per S.O. No. 168 W. D. as of May 5/64." Service Record.

2. The expiration date used by the doctor is two days later than indicated in Cornwell's service record.

3. Service Record.

4. Miller, p. 1.

5. Ibid.

6. Service Record. Return for the months of June–August 1864.

7. Ibid., Return dated August 26, 1864, cites provost marshal assignment contained in General Order 18, Third Division, June 29, 1864.

8. *O.R.,* ser. 2, 4: 363–64.

9. Philip Katcher, "James Brewerton Ricketts: Major General of Volunteers, U.S. Army," (unpublished biographical sketch, 1995, Devon, Pa.), p. 9, quoting David S. Sparks, *Inside Lincoln's Army* (New York, 1964), p. 157.

10. Katcher, various.

11. Due to atmospheric conditions the mountain tops often appear to be tinged with blue, hence the name "Blue Ridge."

12. Britain was officially neutral but privately sympathetic to the Confederacy. Southern agents obtained vast amounts of military supplies from British sources in exchange for cotton. Had the South won a decisive victory, such as the capture of Washington, Britain might have openly declared its support for the Confederacy. That would have resulted in immense political and military pressure on the Federal government to negotiate a settlement to the war. Lincoln's reelection might never have occurred. See Thomas Boaz, *Guns For Cotton: England Arms The Confederacy* (Shippensburg, Pa.: White Mane Publishing Co., 1996).

13. John Esten Cooke, *Wearing of the Grey* (Gaithersburg, Maryland: Olde Soldier Books, Inc., 1988), p. 99.

14. G. Moxley Sorrell, *Recollections of a Confederate Staff Officer* (New York: Bantam Books, 1992), pp. 33–34.

15. Gen. Jubal A. Early, *Autobiographical Sketch and Narrative of the War Between the States* (Philadelphia, Lippincott & Co., 1912; reprint, New York: Da Capo Press, 1989), p. iv (page reference is to the reprint edition).

16. Early, p. 380.

17. "Captain R. T. Cornwell's Return," West Chester, Pa. *Daily Local News*, July 11, 1889.

18. Early, p. 390.

19. Ibid., p. 404.

20. Possibly referring to those captured among the 1,700 Union soldiers lost in fighting on the Jerusalem Plank Road on June 22.

21. Brig. Gen. George Crook (1828–1890).

22. Elements of the Union army were beginning to coalesce in the area of Berryville in an attempt to engage Early, who was moving back up the Valley.

23. Carpenter is identified in the diary entry for March 14, 1864. Capt. John F. Young, the regimental adjutant, appears to have taken command of the 67th Regiment in early September 1864, after Col. J. F. Staunton "was out of the service" and Lt. Col. H. B. Burnham was discharged. Bates, p. 639.

24. Presumably, influential local citizens or politicians.

25. Brig. Gens. George Washington Getty (1819–1901), Frank Wheaton (1833–1903), and David Allen Russell (1820–1864).

26. None of these people have been identified. They would appear to be related to Lillie's family.

27. Maj. Gen. Horatio Gouverneur Wright (1820–1899). "Wright was a steady and dependable subordinate, but when an opportunity for greatness was thrust upon him at Cedar Creek…there was something lacking." After the war Wright served as a lieutenant colonel of engineers, and completed the building of the Washington Monument. Warner, pp. 575–76.

28. It was commonly believed at that time that hemorrhaging from the lungs while otherwise giving the appearance of robust health was symptomatic of tuberculosis.

29. Brig. Gen. Emory Upton (1839–1881) graduated from West Point in May 1861. He was an exceptional officer who had a meteoric career; in May 1864 he was promoted to brigadier general.

30. Probably a reference to the July 30 detonation of the mine under the Confederate lines at Petersburg. A Union officer and former mining engineer persuaded Burnside to have a huge mine dug under the Confederate lines, claiming that its detonation would allow Union soldiers to attack the demoralized and shocked Confederate survivors and breach their defenses. The idea appealed to Burnside, and Grant, though not enthusiastic, gave his approval. Tunneling began June 25, and when finished the mine contained eight tons of gunpowder. The plan was simple: immediately following the explosion, troops would pour through the breach in the line and assault the demoralized Confederates before they could reform their defenses. Burnside intended to have a division of U.S. Colored Troops lead the assault, but they were ill-trained and for political reasons it was decided that white soldiers would lead with the colored following. Command for the assault was decided by drawing straws. Brig. Gen. James H. Ledlie (1832–1882), one of the most inept officers in the Union army, drew the short straw. He failed to follow Burnside's instructions, or even to make any basic preparations necessary for launching his troops from their positions after the explosion. Moreover, rather than leading his men after the mine was detonated, Ledlie hid in a bombproof behind his own lines. He was joined there by Brig. Gen. Edward Ferrero (1831–1899), the white officer in command of the Negro division. The first Union troops to attack after the explosion were white soldiers, who moved into the crater, rather than around it. Ferrero's Negro troops followed several hours later. The result was a disaster. The Confederates quickly rallied, reestablished their lines, and slaughtered the Union soldiers trapped within and near the crater. During the fighting, Negro troops attacked with considerable bravery, but were met with withering Confederate fire. Disorganized, they attempted to reform, but unsupported and under heavy fire, their attack dissolved into a rout that carried many of them back into the crater and others back into the Union lines. When it was over, 4,500 Union soldiers were lost. The Negro troops in particular suffered grievously. Confederate losses were about 1,500. Grant said, "It was the saddest affair I have ever witnessed in the war." Burnside was removed from command and Ledlie resigned his commission. See *B&L*, vol. 4, pp. 545–67.

31. Elmira Prison Camp received its first Confederate prisoners on July 6, 1864. Up to one-third of the prisoners there died, making Elmira's death rate far worse than Andersonville's. Heseltine, p. 80.

32. Staunton commanded the 6th Maryland, 67th Pennsylvania, and part of the 122nd Ohio at Monocacy. There is no record of the cause of his "trouble" with Ricketts. However, in a report dated November 6, 1864 Col. J. Warren Keifer, commanding the 2nd brigade at Monocacy, wrote that Staunton and his command "did not, in consequence of unnecessary delays caused by him [Staunton], arrive at Monocacy, but joined the brigade after the battle…" *O.R.*, ser. 1, 37 pt. 1: 206. Staunton defended himself by claiming that his command was "delayed by the slowness of the transports." Ibid., 274. This incident may have been the basis for his problems with Ricketts and others. Whether due to resignation of his commission or the expiration of his term of enlistment, Staunton is listed as being "out of the service" in early September 1864. Capt. and Adjutant John F. Young then assumed command of the 67th Regiment. Bates, p. 639.

33. Grant's (1822–1885) name was Hiram Ulysses, but the congressman who appointed him reported his name to the West Point admissions office as Ulysses Simpson, Simpson being his mother's maiden name. Warner, pp. 183–84.

34. Philip H. Sheridan (1831–1888) and Julius *Stahel* (Hungary, 1825–1912).

Chapter 7

1. Cooke, p. 97.
2. *O.R.*, ser. 1, 37 pt. 2: 301.
3. John H. Worsham, *One of Jackson's Foot Cavalry* (Wilmington, N.C., 1987), p. 163.
4. Ibid., pp. 173–74.
5. Jedediah Hotchkiss, *Make Me a Map of the Valley*, ed. Archie P. McDonald (Dallas: Southern Methodist University Press, 1973), p. 231.
6. *O.R.*, ser. 1, 43 pt. 1: 224.
7. George T. Stevens, *Three Years in the Sixth Corps* (Albany, New York, 1866), p. 416, quoted in Philip Katcher, *Lethal Glory: Dramatic Defeats of the Civil War* (London: Arms and Armour Press, 1995), p. 199.
8. Ibid., pp. 194–206; also, Dupuy, pp. 348–50; Worsham, pp. 176–79.
9. *Daily Local News* (West Chester, Pennsylvania), September 19, 1894.
10. Hotchkiss, pp. 237–40.
11. Early, p. 453.
12. *B&L*, vol. 2, p. 297.
13. General Wheaton was thirty-one years old. He was born in Rhode Island, attended Brown University briefly, and received a commission in the 1st U.S. Cavalry in 1855. At the outbreak of war he became lieutenant-colonel of the 2nd Rhode Island Infantry. His father-in-law, Samuel Cooper, although a native of New York, was adjutant-general of the Confederate army. His mother-in-law was the sister of James Mason, the Confederate commissioner to England.
14. Brig. Gen. John D. Imboden, C.S.A. Warner, p. 553.
15. Safe guards were soldiers assigned by the provost marshal to protect civilian houses and property located in the area. Often, the properties were owned by civilians sympathetic to the invading army.
16. The "gold lace" for his trousers was actually a woven gold cord one-eighth-inch wide. A "staff [officer's] button" had an eagle with the national shield on its breast, and stars in a semi-circle underneath. The regulation infantry buttons he replaced had an eagle with the letter "I" in a shield on its breast, and oak leaves in a semi-circle underneath. The differences, though subtle, were important to staff officers. As a staff officer, Cornwell was also entitled to wear a different model sword and a buff-colored sash. Katcher, *Civil War Source* Book, pp. 135–36. The sword is shown in the illustrations.
17. His "blouse" was the sack coat popular among Union officers and soldiers. Cornwell's first sack coat was custom tailored; this one may have been an issue version. "My coat" refers to the more expensive, and less comfortable, officer's frock coat.

18. *Harper's Weekly* was one of the leading illustrated newspapers in the North. The joke may refer to the fact that the VI Corps was marching to and from Harpers Ferry almost weekly during this period.

19. Possibly the surname of Sallie's beau. See "Major Hickman" in the August 25 letter.

20. The Brandywine Creek was the scene of a major battle during the Revolutionary War. The site was not far from the Jackson's residence in Westtown Township.

21. Sheridan at this time was beginning to withdraw from the Cedar Creek area back toward Winchester. The fighting was desultory, consisting of skirmishes and firing between pickets.

22. Brig. Gen. Alfred T. A. Torbert (1833–1880) was a well-regarded infantry and cavalry officer. He commanded one of Sheridan's cavalry divisions during the Valley campaign. Warner, p. 508.

23. At this time, Col. William H. Penrose (1832–1903) commanded the 1st brigade, First Division, VI Corps. Warner, p. 366; Boatner, p. 640.

24. Longstreet's Corps was led by Lt. Gen. Richard H. Anderson (1821–1879) while Longstreet himself recovered from wounds received at the Wilderness. As Cornwell noted, the Army of the Shenandoah was in a secure location, but it was no longer in the Valley.

25. Confederate strength was approximately 19,000 men.

26. Sutlers were civilian merchants attached to a regiment. They were the forerunner of the post exchange store, selling newspapers, tobacco, food, clothing, and a wide variety of personal items needed by soldiers.

27. The "cards" were cartes-de-visite, or photographic visiting cards, so-called because their 2" by 4" size was approximately the same as calling cards of that time. A multiple-lens camera produced several images on a single glass plate. "CDVs" were immensely popular because copies could be made easily and cheaply. Friends often exchanged photographs of themselves and their families as keepsakes.

28. Sallie Jackson (b. November 19, 1838) is listed as one of Lillie's sisters. "Descendants of Isaac and Ann Jackson," n.d., n.p. One page genealogical worksheet in the possession of Richard Cornwell.

29. Maj. Peter Vredenburgh was struck and killed by a shell on September 19 while leading the 14th New Jersey at Third Winchester. His final words were, "Guide on me boys; I will do the best I can." *O.R.,* ser. 1, 43 pt. 1: 222.

30. Brig. Gen. Archibald C. Godwin, Maj. Gen. Robert E. Rodes, and Col. George E. Patton were killed at Winchester; Maj. Gen. Fitzhugh Lee and Brig. Gen. Zebulon York were seriously wounded.

31. The Confederate loss in artillery at Fisher's Hill was twelve guns. Boatner, p. 281.

32. Cornwell's enlistment was due to expire on October 27, 1864. Service Record.

33. On September 29 Grant sent two corps under the command of Maj. Generals David B. Birney (1825–1864) and Edward O. C. Ord (1818–1883) to attack Forts Harrison and Gilmer, near Richmond, in order to prevent reinforcements from that area being sent to Early. Fort Harrison was captured, but Fort Gilmer remained in Confederate hands. After a fierce battle against Confederate ships and forts, a Union naval force of eighteen warships under the command of Rear Adm. David G. Farragut (1801–1870) took control of Mobile Bay on August 5. This action eliminated Mobile as a port for blockade runners although the city itself did not fall until April 12, 1865.

34. See Epilogue.

35. Brig. Gen. Daniel D. Bidwell (1819–1864) was killed in action while commanding the 3rd brigade, Third Division, VI Corps. Warner, pp. 32–33.

36. Twenty-seven-year-old Maj. Gen. Stephen Dodson Ramseur had been married for a year and was the father of an infant daughter he had never seen. Just before the battle he said to another officer, "Douglas, I want to win this battle, for I must see my wife and baby." Ramseur was a prisoner because of a severe wound received in the battle. He died the next day at Sheridan's

headquarters in Winchester. Henry Kydd Douglas, *I Rode With Stonewall* (Chapel Hill: University of North Carolina Press, 1940), p. 317.

Epilogue

1. "Captain Cornwell Is 92 To-Day," West Chester, Pa. *Daily Local News*, January 29, 1927; "Death's Work," Ibid., April 26, 1927.
2. Lydia Jackson Cornwell Obituaries, West Chester, Pa. *Daily Local News*, February 12–15, 1907.
3. Ibid.

Bibliography

Books

Altman, James David. *Three Hundred Important Dates Of The War Between The States*. Charleston: Privately Printed, n.d.

Bates, Samuel P. *History of the Pennsylvania Volunteers 1861–5*. Vol. 2. Harrisburg, Pa.: B. Singerly, State Printer, 1869.

Biographical and Portrait Cyclopedia of Chester County, Pennsylvania. Richmond, Ind.: Gresham Publishing Co., 1893.

Boatner, Mark M., III. *The Civil War Dictionary*. New York: Random House, Inc., 1991.

Cavada, Lt. Col. F. F. *Libby Life: Experiences of a Prisoner of War in Richmond, Va., 1863–1864*. Philadelphia, 1864.

Cooke, John Esten. *Wearing of the Gray*. Richmond, 1865.

Current, Richard N., ed. *Encyclopedia of the Confederacy*. 4 vols. New York: Simon & Schuster, 1993.

Davis, Varina. *Jefferson Davis: A Memoir By His Wife*. Vol. 2. New York: Belford Co., 1890.

Douglas, Henry Kydd. *I Rode With Stonewall*. Chapel Hill: University of North Carolina Press, 1940.

Dupuy, R. Ernest, and Trevor N. *The Compact History of the Civil War*. New York: Collier Books, 1962.

Early, Lt. Gen. Jubal Anderson. *Autobiographical Sketch and Narrative of the War Between The States*. Philadelphia: Lippincott & Co., 1912; reprint, New York: Da Capo Press, 1989.

Escott, Paul D., Lawrence N. Powell, James I. Robertson, Emory M. Thomas, eds. *Encyclopedia of the Confederacy*. New York: Simon & Schuster, Inc., 1993. S. v. "Libby Prison," by Frank L. Byrne.

Gindlesperger, James. *Escape From Libby Prison.* Shippensburg, Pa.: White Mane Publishing Co./Burd Street Press, 1996.

Gragg, Rod. *The Illustrated Confederate Reader.* New York: Harper Perennial, 1989.

————. *The Civil War Quiz & Fact Book.* New York: Promontory Press, 1993.

Hardee, Brevet Lieutenant W. J. *Hardee's Rifle and Light Infantry Tactics.* New York: J. O. Kane, Publisher, 1862.

Harwell, Richard B., ed. *The Confederate Reader: How the South Saw the War.* New York: Dover Publications, Inc., 1989.

Hesseltine, William B. *Civil War Prisons.* Kent, Ohio: Kent State University Press, 1995.

Hotchkiss, Jedediah. *Make Me A Map Of The Valley.* Edited by Archie P. McDonald. Dallas: Southern Methodist University Press, 1973.

Johnson, Robert U., and Clarence C. Buel. *Battles and Leaders of the Civil War.* 4 vols. New York: Thomas Yoseloff, 1956.

Johnston, Capt. I. N. *Four Months in Libby, and the Campaign Against Atlanta.* Cincinnati: Methodist Book Concern, 1864.

Katcher, Philip. *The Civil War Source Book.* New York: Facts on File, Inc., 1992.

————. *Lethal Glory: Dramatic Defeats of the Civil War.* London: Arms and Armour Press, 1995.

Kautz, Capt. August V. *The Company Clerk: Showing How To Make Out All The Returns, Reports, Rolls, And Other Papers, And What To Do With Them.* Philadelphia: J. B. Lippincott & Co., 1863. Reprint, West Chester, Pa.: Sullivan Press, 1997.

Long, E. B., with Barbara Long. *The Civil War Day By Day.* New York: Doubleday & Co., 1971.

Lytle, Andrew Nelson. *Bedford Forrest and His Critter Company.* Nashville: J. S. Saunders & Company, 1992.

McKean, Wm. V., ed. *The National Almanac and Annual Record for the Year 1864.* Philadelphia: George W. Childs, 1864.

Miller, Francis T., ed. *The Photographic History of the Civil War.* Secaucus, N.J., 1987.

The Oxford English Dictionary. Vol. 12. Oxford: Oxford University Press, 1933.

Parker, Sandra V. *Richmond's Civil War Prisons.* Lynchburg, Va.: H. E. Howard, Inc., 1990.

Roberts, Allen E. *House Undivided.* Richmond: Macoy Publishing and Masonic Supply Co., 1990.

Robertson, James I., Jr. *Soldiers Blue and Gray.* New York: Warner Books, Inc., 1988.

Sauers, Richard A. *Advance the Colors! Pennsylvania Civil War Battle Flags.* Vol. 1. Harrisburg, Pa.: The Capitol Preservation Committee, 1987.

Sorrell, G. Moxley. *Recollections of a Confederate Staff Officer.* New York: Bantam Books, 1992.

Sturzebecker, Dr. Russell L. *Centennial History of West Chester State College.* West Chester, Pa.: By the author, 1971.

Tucker, Edward, ed. *Moulton's Library of Literary Criticism of English and American Authors.* Vol. 3. New York: Frederick Ungar Publishing Co., 1966.

Vandiver, Frank E. *Jubal's Raid.* New York: McGraw-Hill Book Company, 1960.

Warner, Ezra J. *Generals In Blue.* Baton Rouge: Louisiana State University Press, 1964.

Wiley, Bell Irvin. *The Life of Johnny Reb.* Baton Rouge: Louisiana State University Press, 1992.

Worsham, John H. *One of Jackson's Foot Cavalry.* Wilmington, N.C.: Broadfoot Publishing Co., 1987.

Unpublished Materials

"Census History of Robert T. Cornwell," extracted from the 1850 Census of the United States for Sullivan County, New York. In the possession of Dick Cornwell, Escondito, Ca.

"Census History of Mary Gray," extracted from the 1850 Census of the United States for Westtown, Chester County, Pa. In the possession of Dick Cornwell, Escondito, Ca.

Cornwell, Gibbons Gray, Jr., "Sheridan's Ride," unpublished family memoir n.d., West Chester, Pa.: Original in the possession of Daniel Cornwell, West Chester, Pa.

Cornwell, G. Thomas, letter to Dick Cornwell dated November 2, 1993. In the possession of Dick Cornwell, Escondito, Ca.

"Descendants of Isaac and Ann Jackson," n.d., n.p. In the possession of Dick Cornwell.

Extracts from the 1870 Census of the United States for Chester County, Pa., pp. 15–16. In the possession of Dick Cornwell, Escondito, Ca.

Katcher, Philip. "James Brewerton Ricketts, Major General of Volunteers, U. S. Army," unpublished magazine article 1995, Devon, Pa.

Miller, Mark. "67th Pennsylvania Infantry Regiment," 1996, Escondito, Ca.

Government Documents

Compiled Service Record, Capt. Robert T. Cornwell, Co. B, I, 67 Pennsylvania Inf. Washington, D.C., National Archives.

Confederate States of America War Department. *Regulations for the Army of the Confederate States, 1863.* Richmond: J. W. Randolph, 1863.

The War of the Rebellion: A Compilation of the Official Records of the Union and Confederate Armies (O.R.). 130 vols. Washington, D.C.: Government Printing Office, 1880–1901.

Periodicals

Bennett, Joseph E., FPS. "The Two Faces of Ben Butler." *The Philalethes Magazine* (February 1997): 5–9.

Byre, Thomas E. "Elmira's Civil War Prison Camp: 1864–65." *The Chemung Historical Journal* (September 1964): 1279–1300.

Horigan, J. Michael. "Elmira Prison Camp—A Second Opinion." *The Chemung Historical Journal* (March 1985): 3449–3457.

Newspapers

"Captain R. T. Cornwell's Return." West Chester (Pa.) *Daily Local News*, July 11, 1889, n.p.

"Captain Cornwell Is 92 To-Day," West Chester (Pa.) *Daily Local News*, January 29, 1927, n.p.

"Death's Work." West Chester (Pa.) *Daily Local News*, April 12, 1927, n.p.

Brice, George. "Civil War Recalled in Diary, Letters of Robert Cornwell." West Chester (Pa.) *Daily Local News*, April 12, 1961, n.p.

"The Prisons at Richmond." *Harper's Weekly*, October 17, 1863.

West Chester (Pa.) *Daily Local News*, December 15, 1866; February 9, 1869; August 14, 1878; September 19, October 27, 1894; June 12, 1908; July 1, 7, 1912; January 29, 1915; April 30, 1921; n.p.

Index